Media Studies 2.0

Media Studies 2.0 offers an exploration of the digital revolution and its consequences for media and communication studies, arguing that the new era requires an upgraded discipline: a media studies 2.0.

The book traces the history of mass media and computing, exploring their merger at the end of the 20th century and the material, ecological, cultural and personal elements of this digital transformation. It considers the history of media and communication studies, arguing that the academic discipline was a product of the analogue, broadcast era, emerging in the early 20th century as a response to the success of newspapers, radio and cinema and reflecting that era back in its organisation, themes and concepts.

Digitalisation, however, takes us beyond this analogue era (media studies 1.0) into a new, post-broadcast era. Merrin argues that the digital era demands an upgraded academic discipline: one reflecting the real media life of its students and teaching the key skills needed by the 21st-century user. Media 2.0 demand a media studies 2.0

This original and critical overview of contemporary developments within media studies is ideal for general students of media and communication, as well as those specifically studying new and digital media.

William Merrin is an Associate Professor in Media Studies at Swansea University, with research interests in media theory, digital media and culture and media history. He is the author of *Baudrillard and the Media* (2005) and co-editor of *Jean Baudrillard: Fatal Theories* (Routledge, 2008).

Media Studies 2.0

William Merrin

Routledge
Taylor & Francis Group

LONDON AND NEW YORK

First published 2014
by Routledge
2 Park Square, Milton Park, Abingdon, Oxon OX14 4RN

and by Routledge
711 Third Avenue, New York, NY 10017

Routledge is an imprint of the Taylor & Francis Group, an informa business

British Library Cataloguing in Publication Data
A catalogue record for this book is available from the British Library

Library of Congress Cataloging in Publication Data
Merrin, William.
Media studies 2.0 / William Merrin.
pages cm
Includes bibliographical references and index.
1. Mass media. 2. Digital media. I. Title.
P90.M455 2014
302.23–dc23
2013040863

ISBN: 978-0-415-63862-3 (hbk)
ISBN: 978-0-415-63863-0 (pbk)
ISBN: 978-0-203-08358-1 (ebk)

Typeset in Sabon
by Taylor & Francis Books

Contents

Introduction
Media studies gone wrong

This book begins with an apology to my then 10-year-old son, Henry, for my complete hypocrisy. Moments after I sat down to write this introduction I was disturbed by him asking if he 'could have a YouTube channel'. All his friends had them, he said, and he only wanted it to message them. I immediately explained why this wasn't going to happen. After half an hour of tantrums (mine as well as his) and several uninspired attempts to find a way to open the book I gave up and said I'd look into it: we'd see if it was legal and if it could be set up with the appropriate controls. It was then that I discovered there was already a YouTube account registered with the email address I used for him. I asked if he already had an account and he denied it, several times, before admitting that, yes, actually, he did have one and he'd just forgotten about it. I asked if that was really true and he said it was, several times, before admitting that he hadn't forgotten it, only the password, hence he wanted a new account. After further grilling I discovered that a couple of nights before, during a sleepover, he and a friend had got bored of watching videos, had decided to create their own channels and had spent the evening accruing a number of friends and followers and 'favouriting' a variety of inappropriate videos. More importantly he'd also created and posted his first video.

I hadn't thought that was possible: he didn't have a camera and I didn't think he'd know how to post anything to the site. In fact he and his friend had simply Googled 'How do you make a YouTube video?' and discovered a video-creation app that allowed them to create animations and the soundtrack for them. For reasons that remain unclear, they'd created a video entitled 'Love Gone Wrong', comprising an argument between a fizzy drink and a hamburger. When I first watched it I was confused as I thought it was in Spanish but when I listened closely I realised the content was explicit, mostly involving the drink and burger telling each other where to go and what they could do. The reason it was difficult to follow was because the dialogue had to be typed in and, thanks to the deficiencies of their local primary school and its helpful policy of not correcting errors in case it upsets the children, their spelling was frankly appalling. Then they'd posted it to a global audience.

The difference between my media world and my son's is a difference of *kind*, not degree. Compare that to my relationship to my parents' childhood experiences.

The only real difference between the world I grew up within and my parents' was two more TV channels and commercial radio, whilst my better-off friends had colour TV and, by the early 1980s, VCRs too. This was a world of separate and limited forms: the telephone, that you didn't own, was screwed to the wall as a family resource and couldn't take photographs or videos; you couldn't get radio on the television; films didn't have special features, commentaries or alternative endings; and no one tried to break into your television to steal your money or identity. It was also a world of scarcity. Information was hard to come by, with its acquisition often being physically laborious, involving trips to shops or libraries.

Most importantly this was a world of powerlessness. As a consumer one had little control: you followed the schedules of the broadcasters or producers, with favourite shows available once a week and anything you missed was as good as gone forever. As a producer the situation was even worse. I as a 10-year-old, like most of the population, had little or no capacity to produce and share information. Our only means of feedback were tightly controlled and very little slipped through the media gatekeepers. Hence my delight one morning in 1984 watching the children's show *Saturday Superstore* when during a live, audience phone-in to a pop band one caller managed to shout down the phone, 'Matt Bianco? You're a bunch of wankers'. This was an oasis of real participation in a world that prevented it. But even if we'd been able to produce our own output there was little interest in non-professional production. Had I written down my thoughts in the morning and presented these 'updates' to my school friends before assembly they'd have laughed at me. We expected information and entertainment to come from particular, official, high-quality, culturally acceptable sources.

Whilst my childhood media world and my parents' were recognisably similar, there is a chasm between my childhood world and my son's. Though one might easily dismiss his YouTube video when compared with the output, audience and impact of major broadcasters such as the BBC, from another perspective the comparison is more revealing. When I was 10 neither the BBC, nor any other UK broadcaster or producer, could publish instantly and globally. UK broadcasters could reach the nation but beyond that boundary publication was more complex and out of their control. My son, however, was under no such constraints. Clicking 'upload' immediately made his video available to anyone, anywhere, and in that moment he accrued more productive and distributive power than the entire BBC had when I was his age.

But this isn't what I find most remarkable. What amazes me most is what my son was thinking. I'd been using YouTube for years but for me it was mainly a source of entertainment: I just watched videos. My son, within two months of discovering YouTube, had decided to make one. Having explored *WWE*, *Halo* and 'Fail' videos, he and his friend had decided to add their own. And why not? The videos had all been put there by someone so why couldn't they do it? It's what YouTube *was*. It wasn't just something to watch, it was something to do.

And they'd been having fun. Henry had given himself the name 'The-HardCoreAssassin1' (a moniker whose threat level was undercut by the profile picture he'd chosen of a cartoon cow in sunglasses with the tag line 'hello sexy'), whilst his friend, 'OfficialSniperPS3', had chosen something slightly more outré. In fact in the days since, his friend had been especially busy. Listing himself as aged 19 he'd already created six videos and gained a number of followers and views from the school with his magnum opus to date being a slide show of old people, babies and assorted others all giving 'the bird', sound-tracked to a popular song of the moment, with opening and end credits professionally faded in.

Hence this belated apology to my son, who, as I write this now, is above me, barking orders to someone in Utah as part of a joint Welsh–American initiative battling their way through *Halo* under his command. Because whilst my outrage at discovering him setting up profiles and posting material online was justified from a parental perspective, I knew, even as the words were coming out of my mouth, that *this was his world*. He was being punished for what was, for him, a normal, natural, everyday mode of behaviour among his peers. Considering how controversial some media lecturers find digital media, I wondered how they'd cope with what they had coming in eight years' time. I also wondered what media lecturers would have left to teach these students other than personal morality, an acceptable vocabulary, the use of a spell-checker and the importance of remembering passwords. Luckily my son won't read this apology. Given his preference for online games and videos above homework and the likely cost of university education by the time he reaches 18, he's unlikely to see this book.

My son's world is also our students' world. I noticed it a while ago when I started teaching modules on digital media: students *knew stuff*. They varied considerably in their individual familiarity with specific technologies, their personalised range of media experiences, and their ability to subject these to critical analysis, but they had their own knowledge and use of a range of technologies, services, platforms and content, much of which was new to me. I realised then that media lecturers didn't know enough about their students' media worlds: entire ecologies of use and content were passing them by and the proliferation of these ecologies and the speed of change made them almost impossible to follow. It was also apparent that many media lecturers weren't even trying. Many had their eyes firmly on the traditional broadcast forms and in particular on highly specialised and limited debates carried out within a tiny circle of academics. Media lecturers often paid more attention to the discipline, and to each new book by their disciplinary colleagues, than to the real world of media and the new developments happening there.

Lecturers, of course, could point to their disciplinary knowledge to justify their expert position, but I wondered about the value of that knowledge if it didn't relate to the actual media worlds our students lived within. Today we were having to play catch-up with our students, waiting for our children or broadsheet-of-choice to bring new developments to our attention. Whereas in the broadcast era few things happened in radio, film and TV that you wouldn't hear about or be able to understand, in today's fragmented digital landscape that was no longer the case. Academic specialisation was now a hindrance:

where once watching a film was sufficient, now you needed to be able to roam across issues of digital production, software, new modes of distribution and consumption, post-PC experiences, copyright, DRM, security, privacy, peer-to-peer sharing, remixing and remaking before you even began to understand what was happening in cinema. And Professors, once the apex of their subject, were looking especially vulnerable, with reputations built on publications about a vanishing media world and practical skills that were being rapidly left behind by new developments.

The key problem we face is that students applying to media courses don't realise they aren't coming to study media, they're coming to study 'media studies'. They are coming to study what the academic discipline says about media – media, that is, as mediated by the discipline. This wasn't a problem in the broadcast era when the two were in accord; when the student's experience of mass media was accurately reflected in the disciplinary focus on radio, television, print and cinema. But when the two diverged – when the student's digital experiences fragmented and proliferated whilst the discipline retained a focus on broadcast forms, concepts and categories – then this became an issue. Our students come to study the media worlds they live, to find out about the technologies and platforms that excite them, and they discover a discipline desperate to teach them 'the hypodermic syringe' model, 'the two-step flow' model, 'the active audience' and semiology. That sound? That's our students' heads hitting the desks in our introductory modules.

Our introductory modules and textbooks only explain what media studies thinks: its approaches, theories, methods, tools and conclusions. Ironically, an academic discipline that is so interested in getting students to understand constructed representations and meanings and the ideological functioning of texts rarely invites them to reflect upon how their own modules and textbooks do the same: how they naturalise its knowledge; how they tell the story of media studies and its contributions; how their selection of material and truth-claims remain contestable; how they evade the issue of the discipline's complicit relationship with the media; and how historically-situated their insights are. Our introductory media modules and textbooks explain what media studies argues, *but not what it is*. They offer little information about its origins and history, its development, its relationship to other disciplines and its strengths and limitations. They don't reveal its lacunae, its failings, its illogic, its historical complicity with government and the industries it studies, its biases, its misrepresentation of media, its hostility to certain positions or authors, or the underlying philosophical assumptions that frame its approaches and claims.

So our students have to accept that what they're given *is* what media is about and how it should be studied. Faced with modules and texts that don't have much to do with their own lives and struggling to adapt to the knowledge about media they're given, they have to learn to separate their own use and practice out from their courses, waiting for a module that tells them, with the air of revelation, that something called 'social media' now exist, or for the final-year dissertation when they might, finally, be able to address their own experiences.

Though this book has many points of origin, one of these is a discontent with these failings. I'd been teaching media since the early 1990s, first in college then in university, and over time I'd become aware of disciplinary quirks – ideas, topics, thinkers, arguments, histories, media, technologies, etc. that the subject and its texts seemed to ignore. As my teaching and research came to focus more on digital media and the rapid changes that were transforming every established industry this awareness of the discipline's limitations became more acute and I increasingly came to understand that it couldn't do the work required. I realised that because of the digital revolution, media studies required a systematic updating, upgrading and rethinking: the ideas, assumptions, knowledge and classifications formed in one era and honed over decades of debate were no longer adequate for a different era.

In November 2006 I coined the term 'media studies 2.0' to describe the upgraded discipline that was needed. I was lucky enough to have Professor David Gauntlett independently arrive at a similar set of ideas and the same term and together we sparked a debate in the discipline. Unsurprisingly, the claims proved controversial. Academics who've built their careers upon specialised research into one aspect of one medium and who've accumulated boxes of lecture notes to be reused each year were never going to like the idea that their knowledge had to change by the day. But that's the reality today and it's also the future of the discipline. Because when my son's generation arrive at university to study media, any introduction that doesn't begin from *their world* and that doesn't tell them something they don't already know isn't going to cut it.

We don't have time to solve this problem. We're already failing our current students. Marshall McLuhan said we live in the 'rear-view mirror' – travelling forwards whilst looking backwards; refusing to see what's happening now in favour of the comfortable and familiar; in favour of what's already passed. And this is what our courses do. Our theoretical modules explain an already-passing world, training students to understand the broadcast skills of media consumption, whilst the practical modules train students for declining broadcast era roles such as TV presenters, weather people or even journalists. Our students don't need this. They need theoretical modules that begin from their own lives and give them the skills to navigate the digital ecology as a producer and distributor and they need practical modules that teach them how to produce digital objects and protect their online activities.

Given that lecturers don't have all the knowledge today the only way this can work is through an *open-source* media studies: a discipline that not only invites students in to discuss its content but one that invites them to discuss the discipline itself. Just as open-source software opens its underlying code for anyone to understand and improve, so media studies should open up its own code – its origins, history, assumptions, philosophical bases and biases – for anyone to evaluate, rewrite and improve. In a rapidly evolving ecology what media studies is and what it could be should be open to debate and re-direction. As 'big media' have learnt, we're moving from an age of one-way lectures to an age of conversations, and media studies needs to follow this, to invite its students into its discussion.

Academia's broadcast organisation resists this, allowing debate only around the content it provides. In the post-broadcast era, however, knowledge is more diffused and it becomes possible to accept broader contributions about media use and effects and to open up discussion of the discipline's own basis, its role and its future. Instead of an encyclopaedia, run by experts with carefully selected content, we need to think of media studies as a wiki: as a tool open for us all to add to and update; one orientated towards daily, or even near real-time, developments.

We have to realise two things: that the media are changing and that our students are changing them. That last point is crucial. Our students are living through a transition to digital media that is transforming every aspect of media production, distribution and consumption. Their experience of this has brought them to university but the important point is that they are not simply watching the media ecology form and reform around them but it is forming and reforming *with them, through them* and *by them*. They are not spectators of this transformation but active participants in this process. Hence the students who are today producing our media environment should help produce the discipline that studies it.

This helps to explain what this book isn't. Most importantly it isn't another textbook. We don't need another top-down, expert summary of the approved ideas of the discipline to be uncritically absorbed and copied back in essays and exams. We don't need another book that explains the world the lecturers grew up within, privileging broadcast forms and concepts and adding brief references to YouTube and mobile-phones to simulate contemporary relevance. What we need is a book that confronts the world the students are living in; that explains the present to them, and that opens up the discipline for their understanding, evaluation and improvement. What we need is not a final statement but an opening move in a conversation, helping students to respond to the form as well as the content of their study. Such a book can't pretend to neutrality – to the aloof voice-of-the-expert looking down objectively on the field – but this is its strength. In the spirit of an open-source discipline, and unlike the textbooks, this book makes its own approaches, biases and selections clear. Its position is simple: it argues that a new digital ecology is emerging; that a broadcast era media studies has to be upgraded to reflect and understand this, and that our students have a part to play in producing that new discipline. I've called that new discipline 'media studies 2.0', a term, I've noted, that was co-developed with David Gauntlett. I explain in Chapter 8 the relationship between our two uses but I should point out here that this book primarily focuses on my own understanding of this idea. This is partly due to my desire to set out my own ideas in a book-length form, but it is also to ensure that Professor Gauntlett isn't held responsible for any of the more controversial opinions here and that any criticism the book receives is directed at the proper person.

The first five chapters attempt to explain the elements of the digital revolution. Chapter 1 traces the development of mass media and the rise of computing whilst Chapter 2 explores the first element of the digital revolution: the material transformation of analogue forms into digital forms. It considers how mass media became absorbed by computing and the significance of this material shift. Chapter 3 explains the transformation in the dominant media ecology caused by the rise of digital media and Chapter 4 traces the attendant cultural revolution with the passage from a broadcast to a post-broadcast model of media production, distribution and consumption. Chapter 5 completes this analysis by looking at the new centrality of the individual in the digital ecology and the rise of what I call 'me-dia'.

The rest of the book considers the implications of this revolution for the academic discipline. Chapter 6 explores the history and development of media studies; Chapter 7 explains the problems with its approaches to media and the illogic of its positions; whilst Chapter 8 builds on this, making an argument for upgrading the discipline. Chapter 9 argues that the revolution in productive and distributive capacity should be central to this upgraded discipline, offering a survey of the key issues for a 21st-century media studies and Chapter 10 considers the consequences of these changes for education itself and its relationship with its students and the broader public.

It's customary to acknowledge one's intellectual and personal debts in a book's introduction. Professionally I'd like to single out David Gauntlett, whose generosity in linking to my original discussion of 'media studies 2.0' was greatly appreciated and Jon Dovey and Martin Lister at UWE (University of the West of England) for their kind invitation to speak at their December 2008 symposium on 'the challenge of new media'. I'd also like to thank the staff who invited me to and attended seminars on MS2.0 at London Metropolitan University, Coventry University, the University of Winchester, Nottingham University, Lincoln University, Warwick University and Birmingham City University and the Higher Education Academy: Art, Design, Media Subject Centre for their kind invitation to work with them. Most of my acknowledgements, however, are personal. The last few years have been very difficult and only the friendship and support of good friends has enabled me to finally complete this project. I'm especially grateful to Rob Long, Andrew Hoskins, Adrian Ayres, Marcus Leaning, David Berry, Paul Blackledge, Paul Taylor, Nicola Cooper, Ben O'Loughlin, Alexia Bowler, Matthew Allen, Mostyn Jones, Leighton Evans, Huey Tan, Phil Banyard and John Armitage. I'd also like to apologise to anyone whose emails I failed to reply to over the last few years and confirm that one day I'll work my way back through them. This book is dedicated to Henry Merrin, Alice Merrin and Hector Merrin, who are everything.

1 Two trajectories
The rise of mass media and computing

The aim of this book is to offer a reflection on the contemporary discipline of media studies. Its central argument is that media studies emerged as a response to and reflection of the broadcast era and that, therefore, the digital transformation of older media forms and our passage to a post-broadcast era requires a new, upgraded discipline to reflect contemporary changes and understand the new media reality.

Very simply we can say that the broadcast era was marked by the dominance of a small number of analogue forms with large-scale companies and institutions employing a 'broadcast model' to mass produce content for mass distribution and mass consumption. It was this era, these media and this model that media studies developed to study. 'Communication studies' emerged in the early–mid-20th century as a response to the growing social power of newspapers, radio and cinema, researching the effects of these and the mass audience's response. By the end of the century 'media studies' had developed as a distinct and successful disciplinary branch, focusing upon mass media production, content and reception. In the last decades of that century, however, an important development was becoming clear. Digital technologies were absorbing these older media, transforming the entire system of media production, distribution and consumption and creating what could be called a 'post-broadcast' era. This new era requires, I argue, a different media studies: media 2.0 demand a media studies 2.0.

This suggests, of course, that we are dealing with a revolutionary rather than an evolutionary process: a transformation of such scale that it requires a similarly radical revision of the discipline. Academics, however, dislike the term 'revolution'. Naturally cautious, for them this term smacks of historical sloppiness and over-generalisation. Re-immersed in the quotidian complexity of everyday life, and the continuities this implies, nothing is ever revolutionary, merely repeating and extending what already exists. Except the problem of this approach is that revolutionary changes do occur and the passage to digitality, I argue, constitutes one of them. In order to make the case for a new discipline, therefore, I first need to establish the existence and significance of this digital revolution. One way to begin this is to think about the passage from the analogue to the digital and the transformation of older media into digital media.

A good place to approach this is through J. C. R. Licklider and Robert W. Taylor's 1968 paper 'The Computer as Communication Device'. At a time when the computer was primarily thought of as a calculating device, Licklider asserts that it is not only 'a medium' but one whose potential impact is greater than both print and television:

> Creative, interactive communication requires a plastic or moldable medium that can be modeled, a dynamic medium in which premises will flow into consequences, and above all a common medium that can be contributed to and experimented with by all. Such a medium is at hand – the programmed digital computer. Its presence can change the nature and value of communication even more profoundly than did the printing press and the picture tube, for, as we shall show, a well-programmed computer can provide direct access both to informational resources and to the processes for making use of the resources.

Licklider was right about this. Whilst the printing press impacted upon the mechanics of production and upon the process of distribution and consumption, it had only a limited effect on who could actually produce and distribute. The computer, however, had the potential to democratise production and empower the user to create: 'a well-programmed computer can provide direct access both to informational resources and to the *processes* for making use of the resources'.

This was an astute position, but for it to become a reality the computer had to become culturally successful: it had to become an everyday technology; it had to eclipse and absorb other media; it had to become the dominant model of informational storage and manipulation, and its cultural adoption had to exploit this capacity. As Lev Manovich explains, this is exactly what has happened. In *The Language of New Media* (2001) he agrees that the computer is a more important force than the printing press, due, he says, to its absorption of all older media forms:

> [J]ust as the printing press in the fourteenth century and photography in the nineteenth century had a revolutionary impact on the development of modern society and culture, today we are in the middle of a new media revolution – the shift of all culture to computer-mediated forms of production, distribution, and communication. This new revolution is arguably more profound than the previous ones, and we are just beginning to register its initial effects. Indeed, the introduction of the printing press affected only one stage of cultural communication – the distribution of media. Similarly, the introduction of photography affected only one type of cultural communication – still images. In contrast, the computer media revolution affects all stages of communication, including acquisition, manipulation, storage and distribution; it also affects all types of media – texts, still images, moving images, sound and spatial constructions.

How then to map such a shift? Manovich asks. His answer is simple and effective. New media, he says, 'represents a convergence of two separate historical trajectories: computing and media technologies. Both begin in the 1830s with Babbage's Analytical Engine and Daguerre's daguerreotype'. For Manovich what we have witnessed since the early part of the 19th century is the rise of *two trajectories*, that of mass media and of computing technology, and the meeting and merger of these at the end of the 20th century. I take Manovich's analysis here as the basis for my own overview of the digital transformation. I want to follow his argument to trace in this chapter the historical rise of mass media broadcasting and networked computing. In the next chapter I will then explore their meeting and merger and the subsequent revolution in the material basis of our media.

The age of broadcasting

Although 'broadcasting' is often identified with electronic transmission, this is too narrow a definition. 'Broadcasting' was originally an agricultural term, referring to the hand-sowing of seeds by scattering them over a wide area to ensure their successful propagation. By the late 19th century the term was already in use to describe informational distribution, hence *Notes on the Writing of General Histories of Kansas* reports in 1883 how 'unscrupulous newspaper correspondents ... sent broadcast over the country, contradictory or false reports ... ', whilst the term also appeared in the title of the US paper, *Twin City Broadcaster*, published in Ardmore, Oklahoma, from 1894–1922. By broadcasting, therefore, we mean a historical mode of mass-reproduction and distribution of information for consumption by a mass audience. This model reached its height in the 20th century, with the success of newspapers, radio, cinema and television, but media studies usually traces its roots back to the birth of mass communication with the development of moveable-type printing and the passage from hand-written manuscripts to mass-produced books.

The invention of moveable-type printing by Johann Gutenberg in Mainz around 1450–55 was an epochal event, aiding the transformation of the oral and imagic medieval culture into the literate culture of the modern world. Printing wasn't new but it took advantage of new European developments such as the rise of a written culture in the 12th–13th centuries and new secular markets for books. Its success was built upon mass-reproduction – first of the individual letters, then of the pages, and, finally, of the books themselves. Gutenberg's most famous book, his '42 line' bible was a hybrid form, simulating illuminated manuscripts whilst showcasing the benefits of print in the precision and quality of the error-free pages but also in the speed of production and print run of about 180 copies.

Commercial printing spread through Europe. At a time when the population of Europe was under 100 million, and only a minority of these could read, an estimated 30,000 titles (15–20 million books) were printed before 1500 and another 150–200,000 titles (representing another 150–200 million books) were printed between 1500 and 1600. Printing expanded the reading public and material available. The profitability of vernacular publishing brought a broader audience whilst also helping to fix national languages and grammar, fostering national literatures and identity and aiding the rise of the nation state. Though at first reproducing older knowledge, printing helped spread new ideas, aiding the rise of secular humanist and scientific thought.

Its greatest effect was the democratisation of information, in allowing people to follow debates and develop their own opinions upon matters that had previously excluded them and in opening authorities up to scrutiny and criticism. In the Protestant Reformation, for example, print was used by all sides to advance their cause. As Man (2002) says, Martin Luther became 'a publishing phenomenon, unrivalled anywhere' as his sermons and tracts 'streamed from the presses by the hundreds and thousands across the lands'. Political authorities recognised the dangers of print. Tudor Britain developed an effective system of state control and censorship, limiting the numbers of printers, what could be published and the print runs. This lasted until the eve of the Civil War when the collapse of censorship led to a publishing explosion by both Monarchical and Parliamentary supporters. Though Cromwell and the restored monarchy re-imposed controls, the growth of publishing led to their final collapse in May 1695. The modern newspaper industry begins here with new titles appearing within days and the first daily newspaper, *The Daily Courant*, appearing in March 1702.

The 18th century saw the steady growth of the London and provincial press and of a broader print culture (including pamphlets, periodicals, journals and novels) distributed by courier or available in shops, coffee-houses, libraries and reading-rooms. Print's success was linked to the social and economic changes by the mid-18th century. A rising urban population, the development of commerce and the early industrial revolution saw the ascent of a new middle class, the 'bourgeoisie', who, excluded from power within the aristocratic system, used newspapers to debate political life, creating a 'public sphere' to promote reform. The state's response included a new Stamp tax introduced in 1712 and strict libel laws threatening publishers with prison leading to an interlinked fight for 'the liberty of the press' and political reform that would continue into the 19th century. By the 1820s press freedom had effectively been won but just as important was the victory of the idea that the press spoke for the public as the medium of a 'public opinion' that was now the real judge of government actions.

This 'public', of course, included the emerging industrial working class, the 'proletariat' whose own 'radical press' survived until mid-century when reductions in newspaper taxes (from 1853–61) allowed the 'respectable press' to lower cover-prices and attract its readership. Rapid developments in the second-half of the 19th century saw the industrialisation of the newspaper. Railways allowed national distribution, the rotary press (1868) and linotype (1876) increased print runs and lowered costs, and the electric telegraph, telephone, typewriter and half-tone photographic printing transformed journalism. So too did developments in style with the rise of a lighter reporting style more concerned with human-interest stories. By the century's end, therefore, newspaper publishing had moved out of the hands of individuals to become a major commercial enterprise requiring considerable investment in premises, staff, technology, printing, distribution, retail and marketing.

The early 20th century saw the rise of mass-circulation newspapers with *The Daily Mail*, launched in 1896 by Alfred Harmsworth (later Lord Northcliffe), selling around a million copies a day by the new century, prompting imitators such as *The Daily Express* (1900) and *The Daily Mirror* (1903). *The Daily Mail* also inaugurated the 'Northcliffe revolution' in Fleet Street where, in a circular process, the paper's lighter style and low cover price built a mass readership that attracted advertisers whose revenue was used to subsidise the low price. The success of this strategy would echo through the century, shifting the economics of the industry from the cover price to advertising whilst polarising the industry between downmarket, mass circulation tabloids and smaller-circulation, upmarket, elite broadsheets, each surviving by delivering specific socio-economic groups to the advertising industry.

By the early 20th century, therefore, newspapers had evolved into major commercial enterprises, mass-producing and distributing information and entertainment. The industry high point was between 1919–39 during which time total sales more than doubled, with more than half the total circulation figures being accounted for by the top three titles: *The Daily Mail*, *The Daily Express* and *The Daily Herald*. This was also the age of the 'Press Baron' – of ennobled businessmen like Lord Northcliffe, Lord Beaverbrook and Lord Rothermere who owned stables of newspapers, competing for mass readership whilst using their titles and position to promote their own opinions and political status. Claiming to speak for 'the people', they exploited their mass readership for personal advantage, building a power base lying not in political but in media representation: in the public they could mobilise.

Visual media followed the same path of commercial mass production. Woodcut prints appeared in Germany from the 14th century, but it was the 15th-century invention of printing from etched metal plates that laid the basis for a commercial print industry. By the late 18th century prints had moved from the preserve of wealthy collectors to become available through book illustrations. Satirical illustrated pamphlets were popular by the early 19th century and by the 1830s illustrated papers achieved a wide circulation in an increasingly imagic culture. After the invention of the 'wet collodion' process in 1851, allowing any number of card prints from a glass-plate image, photography also became a broadcast medium, with the success of mass-produced celebrity 'cartes-de-visite' from 1854 and of the 3D 'stereographs' produced in huge numbers for stereoscope viewers from the 1850s until the early 20th century. Glass-plate photography also revolutionised the magic lantern industry, with mass-produced photographic slides becoming available to buy or rent, bringing a new realism and educational purpose to the medium from the 1870s.

A commercial sheet-music industry had developed from the mid-19th century, closely aligned with the music hall whose stars produced 'hit' songs to be played on the family piano, but it took the development of sound recording (experimentally by Edouard-Leon Scott de Martinville's 'phonautograph' in 1860 and practically by Thomas Edison's 'phonograph' in 1877) for music itself to become a *thing* and thus a commodity for commercial exploitation. Chichester Bell and Charles Tainter's 1886 invention of the 'graphophone' and Emile Berliner's 1887 'gramophone' led Edison to revisit and improve his own phonograph in 1887. The commercial success of public jukeboxes and storefront parlours in the 1890s encouraged companies to produce machines and recordings for this emerging market, establishing the basis for the modern music industry. The limitations of the technology, the novelty of the medium and disdain of established stars ensured the most common recordings were music hall parlour songs, small orchestra, band or solo instrumentals and spoken word pieces, whilst the limited playback time and popular market benefitted simple songs with catchy hooks, all of which played a major role in the evolution of popular song.

It took until about 1900 for the problem of the mass reproduction of recordings to be solved, with the production of recordings from a master, but the industry still suffered from competing cylinder and disc formats, different recording and playback speeds and differences in cutting that led to incompatibility between machines. Nevertheless sales were good, rising from 500,000 records in 1897 to 2.9 million by 1899. The early 20th century saw the internationalisation of the industry as the big three US companies expanded abroad; ever-increasing sales; the development of a range of machines, including luxury cabinet models; and a new respectability for the medium with more high-brow recordings becoming profitable. Sales boomed after WWI, with 100 million records sold in the USA in 1920 and 140 million in 1921, and although over-competition led to problems in 1923 the introduction of electrical machines in 1925 helped sales to rise again from 100 million in 1925 to a high of 150 million by 1929.

Cinema, the final broadcast form of the 19th century, took its place, therefore, within a rich, existing, exhibitionary and broadcasting culture, exploiting the same urban mass audiences. Cinema evolved from international research into the science of perception, high-speed sequential photography, celluloid manufacture and camera and projector design. Its most important precursor was Edison's single-viewer machine the 'kinetoscope' which was available in storefront parlours from 1894. International demonstrations of projection in 1895 led to the first accepted commercial cinema screening by Auguste and Louis Lumiere's 'cinematographe' in the basement of the Grand Café, 14 Boulevard des Capucines in Paris on 28 December 1895.

The early years of cinema were a period of experimentation. The novelty of 'living photographs' attracted a large audience, exploited by new showmen. Early films were 'actualities', usually unrelated scenes of everyday life, events and spectacles comprising what Gunning famously called 'a cinema of attractions'. This dominance meant narrative cinema didn't emerge until the early 20th century in films such as George Melies' *A Trip to the Moon* (1902) and Edwin S. Porter's *The Great Train Robbery* (1903) and over the next decade film-makers like D. W. Griffith helped to develop modern film grammar. Film exhibition also developed with parlours giving way to Nickelodeons and later purpose-built cinema houses and the early emphasis on film company 'brands' changed after 1910 when public pressure led to actors being credited and the emergence of a 'star system' employing modern publicity and marketing. The opening of new studios in California brought better shooting conditions and a new scale and scenery to US film, enabling it to compete with the European 'feature films'. These films brought a more respectable middle-class audience, prompting another wave of cinema-building from 1913. By WWI cinema had become a global business and the most popular entertainment medium, shown in new, luxurious 'movie palaces'.

Pressure for the concentration of production, distribution and exhibition led to the development by 1928 of the 'Hollywood studio system' that, would dominate until the late 1940s. This was built upon a combination of oligarchical control by a small number of companies and vertical integration, with each company controlling their own production, distribution and exhibition. During this time the 'Big Five' conglomerates (Paramount, 20th Century Fox, Warner Bros., RKO and Loew's Inc, owners of MGM), together with the 'Little Three' (Universal, Columbia and United Artists) accounted for three-quarters of US film production. Cinema now matured as a broadcast medium. As hierarchical big businesses with a complex division of labour, the major studios became Fordist production lines, mass producing standardised products for mass consumption. Based in New York and integrated into the banking structure, these companies employed economies of scale to maximise profits, benefitting from centralised management, accounting and advertising and the control of exhibition. They colluded on spheres of influence whilst forcing a block-booking system on independent exhibitors to ensure all their films were bought. Through the 1930s and the following decades the products of the Hollywood factories achieved a global market and fame and cinema and its stars came to colonise the life and dreams of ordinary people.

One of the few competitors for cinema was radio. It wasn't the first electric medium, being preceded by the electric telegraph that had been commercially developed in 1837–38 by William Cook and Charles Wheatstone in the UK and Samuel Morse (using Alfred Vail's 'Morse code') in the USA; nor was it the first electrical broadcast medium, as telephone services developed in Europe after 1881 to broadcast live opera and theatre, news or entertainment to subscribers. Radio emerged from the work of Faraday, Maxwell and Hertz into electro-magnetism but, as Oliver Lodge's April 1894 demonstration showed, the scientific interest in radio waves didn't extend to a recognition of their communicative potential. Guglielmo Marconi is usually credited with this breakthrough. Experiments in 1895 led to an 1897 demonstration to the UK government and by 1899 his signals could cross the channel. Although his claim of transatlantic signalling on 12 December 1901 has been questioned, he achieved this feat in 1902, enabling him to establish a business based upon ship-to-ship and ship-to-shore communication.

Radio's success owed much to the invention of vacuum tubes or 'valves' (Ambrose Fleming's 1904 diode and Lee de Forest's 1906 triode) which amplified its signals. On 23 December 1900 Canadian Reginald Fessenden made the first audio transmission, transmitting speech over 1.6 kilometres and on 24 December 1906 he used triodes to broadcast a programme of music and speech from Massachusetts to ships along the Atlantic coast. Few people at the time, however, saw radio's future in broadcasting with its lack of privacy being seen as its greatest weakness rather than as the basis of an industry. Hence radio's broadcast potential was first developed by the amateur community. Charles Herrold's 'Herrold College of Wireless and Engineering' in San Jose, California, began transmission in 1909 and the farmer's son claimed to be the first to apply the agricultural term 'broadcasting' to radio. Amateur radio, however, was banned during WWI and broadcasting only developed in the post-war period with its take-up by big business.

The US government helped to create the Radio Corporation of America (RCA) in 1919 as a public company owned by General Electric to pool patents, avoid foreign control of the industry and market General Electric and Westinghouse equipment. The first licensed station was KDKA in Pittsburgh which had been broadcasting as 8XK in 1916 before Westinghouse began broadcasts on 22 November 1922. The introduction of commercial advertising on WEAF in New York would establish the economic basis of the new industry. Radio spread rapidly with 1922 sales of 100,000 sets, rising to 500,000 sales in 1923. Christmas 1924 became the 'radio Christmas' due to the receiver's success and by 1925 there were 5.5 million sets in the USA. Hundreds of stations created a 'chaos in the ether' until the emergence of 'network radio': a monopolistic system developing with the recognition that AT&T's phone lines could carry radio programmes from a central producer to local stations. Chains of local stations were now organised into a network with the owner producing and distributing programme content funded by advertising revenue.

The first network was the National Broadcasting Company (NBC), formed in November 1926 as a subsidiary of the newly independent RCA who soon added another network to its assets, renaming its two parts NBC-Red and NBC-Blue. The Columbia Broadcasting System (CBS) emerged in 1927, the Mutual Broadcasting System (MBS) in 1934 and the American Broadcasting System was created in 1943 (becoming ABC in 1945) when RCA was forced to sell its blue network by the Federal Communications Commission (FCC). With the regulation of amateur production, the entry of business, its mass production and distribution of content, its reliance on advertising and mass audiences, the emergence of monopolistic companies, its regulation by government and the evolution of its financial and competitive relationship with the music industry and cinema, radio became a central broadcasting industry through the 1920s–30s.

Radio in the UK took a different path, following mail, telephony and telegraphy in being taken under governmental control in 1904 when the Wireless Telegraphy Act nationalised the wireless stations under the control of the Post office and Postmaster General. Amateur licences were issued until WWI, when a ban was imposed that lasted until 1922 when licences were granted for experimental broadcasts. High demand led the Postmaster General to reconsider and, sensitive to the chaos and commercialism of the unregulated US system, he recommended a single, state-licensed broadcaster be formed. The British Broadcasting Company began broadcasting on 14 November 1922, receiving its first two-year licence on 18 January 1923, being funded by a licence fee on each receiver and royalties from set sales.

In December 1922 John Reith became the BBC's first manager, with his paternalistic vision providing the basis for 'public service broadcasting'. As he explained in *Broadcast Over Britain* (1924) this had four elements: a rejection of commercialism, with guaranteed public funding; a public service available to all and serving no particular interests; a monopolistic position so as not to have to compete for attention; and the maintenance of the highest-possible programming standards. With no pressure to attract advertisers or compete for audiences, the company could focus, therefore, on the core ideals of public service broadcast: the obligation to educate, inform and raise the listener and 'to carry into the greatest number of homes everything that was best in every department of human knowledge, endeavor and achievement; and to avoid whatever was or might be hurtful'.

Radio's position, however, wasn't secure and it had to negotiate its relationship with older media such as newspapers. Its broadly pro-government coverage of the General Strike in 1926 won it the authorities' trust and it was rewarded with the renewal of its licence and a Royal Charter, becoming the British Broadcasting Corporation on 1 January 1927. Radio's greatest period of success began in the 1930s. Improvements in set design and sound quality and reduced prices increased audiences and with the arrival of cheap 'utility sets' in 1944 radio was accessible to the poorest. By then it had become established as the primary domestic broadcast entertainment, bringing live stories, news, events and music into the home with an intimacy and urgency no other form could match and that politicians of all persuasions attempted to exploit.

By then the medium that would dominate broadcasting in the second half of the 20th century was already in existence. 'Television' (a term in use by 1900) originated in the idea of scanning an image by a beam of light, converting the signals into electrical impulses to be amplified and transmitted to be re-converted at the receiving end. Scanning could either be mechanical (as conceived by Paul Nipkow in 1894) or electronic (as suggested by Rosing in 1907 and Campbell Swinton in 1908). Despite numerous experiments it took until the 1920s to produce a working system. John Logie Baird pioneered television in the UK, beginning work on a mechanical system and achieving his first images in 1923 and publicly demonstrating his system in 1925–26. Having begun unofficial broadcasting using the BBC's aerials in 1926, on 30 September 1929 Baird got permission to launch an experimental television service through the BBC which ran from August 1932 to September 1935 to a small local population with DIY receivers. By then international experiments were proving successful, with demonstrations in Germany, Japan and Russia in the mid–late 1920s. In the USA, Charles Francis Jenkins demonstrated a mechanical system in 1925 leading to the first US broadcasting station, W3XK, which began transmissions on 2 July 1928 from Wheaton, Maryland.

The future of television, however, was electronic. Philo T. Farnsworth produced an electronic system in the USA in 1927 which he improved through the 1930s. Meanwhile Zworykin was working on a similar system for RCA whilst Tihanyi in Hungary was developing key elements of the camera tube that would become part of RCA's 'iconoscope' camera that would become the US standard until 1946. EMI in the UK were also developing an electronic system, demonstrating it to the BBC in 1934. With its committee tasked with considering 'the development of television' and advising the Postmaster General on the relative merits of the competing systems available, the January 1935 Selsdon Report recommended the BBC conduct a test of both Baird's mechanical and Marconi-EMI's electronic systems, with the aim of establishing a regular broadcasting service.

The UK television service was suspended with the outbreak of war in September 1939. It resumed on 7 June 1946, though it faced the problem of radio's strengthened position, institutional disinterest, the cost of sets and production and limited coverage. In 1948 only 49, 000 people out of a population of 50 million owned a television and the unimaginative content and restricted hours of service did little to improve the audience. It was the Queen's coronation on 2 June 1953 that spurred public interest with the day's events broadcast live to a population who rented sets or gathered in neighbours' homes. The coronation's success and rising wages led to a rise in TV ownership from 4 per cent in 1950 to 80 per cent by 1960 alongside a rise in transmission times. By then the BBC's broadcasting monopoly had ended. Discontent with the BBC, business pressure for advertising space, a campaign for commercial television and a sympathetic Conservative government led to the 1954 Television Act which established 'Independent Television' (ITV) around a regulated network of regional producers.

ITV began broadcasting on 22 September 1955 and proved so successful that the ITA chairman claimed it had captured 79 per cent of the audience by 1957. However, widespread criticism of its populist programming, commercialism and US imports and fears of cultural decline led to the Government setting up the Pilkington Committee in 1960 to consider the future of broadcasting in Britain. Its 1962 Report largely agreed with these criticisms and its conclusions praised the BBC for its quality and forced ITV to include more public service broadcasting. The BBC was rewarded for its efforts in the 1963 Television Act with a second channel, BBC2, launched on 21 April 1964. With ITV's improvements and with the modernisation of the BBC under Director General Hugh Greene, the period of 1964 to 1979 is now widely seen as 'the golden age of British television broadcasting'. Sympathetic programming mixing quality and populist output for a shared mass audience ensured television became the dominant broadcast medium.

Its largest audience was in America. Several corporations had run experimental broadcasts through the 1930s and in April 1939 NBC launched a regular broadcasting service that lasted until May 1940 when the FCC forced it to return to an experimental status and set up the National Television Standards Committee (NTSC) to decide the issue of technical standards. Following its recommendations, the FCC subsequently ruled a 525-line commercial service could begin on 1 July 1941 although the arrival of war in December 1941 meant that few stations or sets were available and commercial television didn't take off until after 1946.

Regular broadcasts began again on the DuMont Television network in 1946, joined by NBC in 1947 and CBS and ABC in 1948. Post-war television was an immediate success with television ownership rising from 350,000 sets in 1948 to 2 million by 1949, 8 million by October 1950, 20 million by the end of 1952 and 41 million by 1957. Like radio, US television followed the 'network model' with local stations carrying centrally produced product. By May 1953 there were 103 stations across 60 cities, rising by March 1954 to 370 stations. Television's success led advertisers to embrace the medium. By 1952 companies were spending US $288m a year on TV advertising, up 38.8 per cent on 1951, leading the three big networks, NBC, CBS and ABC, to shift their priorities away from radio. By 1964 television's dominance meant CBS could charge US$50,000 per prime-time minute for advertising. During the 1960s television established itself as the preeminent broadcast medium eclipsing other media as an economic and cultural force with a global audience of around 750 million viewers.

What we see here, therefore, is the historical development of a model of mass production and reproduction of information or entertainment products for mass distribution and mass consumption; a model increasingly requiring a significant mobilisation of technological resources, capital and people in order to organise sufficient capacity to attain an audience or market share. We see the development of large companies or institutions around separate media forms which, once stabilised and available for exploitation, enter into competition with other companies or institutions as well as with other broadcast media forms in a relatively simple ecology dominated by a small number of forms – print, visual, music, radio, cinema and television – available in standardised modes of presentation.

This was the broadcast world I grew up within. Between my parents watching the Queen's Coronation in 1953 and myself as a child watching the Jubilee in 1977, little changed. Commercial television and radio and developments within the BBC gave us two more channels and more radio stations, and colour television and VCRs were available to the wealthy, but it was recognisably the same media world. Limited production and availability meant a broadly similar media experience for the mass of the population. My son, born in 2000, is part of a different world. His is a fluid, connected, always-on digital ecology of hybrid intercommunicating forms, messages, content and activities – personalised and individually available; controlled, changed and manipulated at will and feeding-into, promoting or giving rise to personal production and content and meaning-creation. He exists at the centre of his media experiences rather than as the terminal of a broadcast network. The chasm between my childhood world and his is due to the development of computer technology, its subsumption of older media forms and the new possibilities it has enabled.

The origin of the PCs

One way to trace the origins of computing is through the history of computation. There is a long history of the use of technological aids in calculation. Leonardo Da Vinci is credited with the invention of the first mechanical calculator, based upon designs in his notebooks and through the 17th and 18th centuries a variety of devices were constructed (such as Pascal's 1642 'Pascaline' and Leibniz's 1673 'stepped reckoner'), though most were scientific curiosities with little practical take-up. Problems of calculation became important during the industrial revolution with the British empire, shipping, industry and engineering all requiring precise, error-free mathematical tables, hence Charles Babbage's 1821 idea to mechanise their production through a calculating machine.

Babbage began work on his government-funded 'difference engine' in 1822, though he had only completed a portion by 1832. From 1834–36 his attention turned to a broader project he called the 'analytical engine'. Though this was also uncompleted, its importance lies in its conception as a general-purpose computing machine whose designs embody most of the major principles of the modern digital computer. It would employ a 'mill' (like our central processing unit) to perform calculations, with a separate store (or memory) to hold numbers used in the calculations, receiving instructions (being programmed) by the punched cards Jacquard had developed for his programmable weaving loom in 1801 and using a printer for the results, or outputting on punched cards. Few at the time saw the radicality of the engine, though Ada Lovelace, who helped interpret and publicise Babbage's work, foresaw the engine's potential as a symbolic rather than merely numerical manipulator, bringing her vision closer to the modern idea of general-purpose computing.

In the USA Herman Hollerith had more success, producing a working mechanical data processor, the 'Hollerith Tabulator and Sorter', that proved its worth in the 1890 census. It processed over 62 million cards punched with individual data – twice the information that had been collected in the 1880 census – completing the calculations in two years: one third the time of the earlier human operators in 1880. After this success Hollerith set up a Tabulating Machines Company selling tabulators to railways, companies and industrial concerns. By the time his merged company merged again in 1924 to form International Business Machines (IBM), mechanical and electromechanical tabulating, sorting and calculating devices were in use throughout the accountancy, engineering, banking, manufacturing and insurance industries.

By the 1930s electromechanical computers were being built using telephone relays but machines of this era were still only improved calculators. The idea of modern computing was, however, emerging. British mathematician Alan Turing's 1936 paper 'On computable numbers with an application to the Entscheidungs problem' described a hypothetical, general-purpose symbol manipulating 'universal computing machine' whilst others were beginning to build modern computers. In Germany Konrad Zuse's 'Experimental Model 1' equation-solver was the first to use binary calculations and by 1943 he and Helmet Schreyer had built their

Z-3 programmable binary computer using relays. In the USA John Atanasoff created the Atanasoff-Berry computer (ABC), in use by 1942, which used binary arithmetic as well as electronic switching, though, like Zuse, his work was not widely known.

It was the exigencies of WWII and new government funding that provided the major spur to computing as anti-aircraft guns required complex calculations to hit fast-moving targets. The US Navy and IBM helped Howard H. Aiken build the Harvard Mark 1, in use at Harvard by February 1944, and the US Army funded John W. Mauchly and J. Presper Eckert's project the ENIAC (Electronic Numerical Integrator and Calculator) at the University of Pennsylvania, though it wasn't operational until July 1947. In the UK computing was developed for code-breaking purposes. At Bletchley Park, electromechanical devices called 'bombes' worked against the German Enigma coding machine but couldn't break the improved Geheimschrieber machine so a team headed by M. H. A. Newman and T. H. Flowers built a computer called Colossus, operational by December 1944, for that task.

Where the Harvard machine was an electromechanical, decimally based programmable machine, Colossus was a binary, electronic, programmable machine, using vacuum tubes (valves) as fast switching devices. Their use ushered in the era of electronic computing, replacing the electromechanical machines. ENIAC was also electronic and was manually programmable, but it used the decimal system rather than binary. The first binary electronic computer with a stored program was the Manchester Small-Scale Experimental Machine (or 'Baby') completed in June 1948 by Frederic C. Williams, Tom Kilburn and Geoff Toothill at the University of Manchester (UK), using a cathode ray tube for its memory.

Theoretical developments also contributed to the development of computing. Norbert Wiener's wartime work on anti-aircraft targeting led to his influential, classified 1942 report that first developed a science of 'communication' (defined as 'the study of messages and their transmission') and to his development of a philosophy of 'cybernetics' in his best-selling 1948 book that analysed and tied together the control and communication processes of biological and technological systems within their environment. Claude E. Shannon had already made a contribution to computing in his 1937 masters thesis where he analysed switching circuits using Boolean algebra, thereby showing how binary circuits could be used to perform complex mathematical and logical operations, when, inspired by his reading of Wiener's 1942 report, he developed 'information theory'. Shannon's 1948 essay 'A Mathematical Theory of Communication' developed a linear model of the passage of a message, simplifying the processes of communication to separate out its elements – the information source, the encoder or transmitter, the channel, the decoder or receiver and the destination. His dismissal of the question of 'meaning' and focus upon the message's passage and the avoidance or attenuation of 'noise' was valuable to engineers whilst also finding favour with mass media theorists keen to develop a scientific analysis of communication.

Also important was John Von Neumann's 1945 memo on a planned successor to the ENIAC, 'A First Draft of a Report on the EDVAC'. This drew upon the work of Turing and Eckert and Mauchly to formalise a design model for digital computers that became known as a 'Von Neumann architecture'. Based around five basic components – the memory, control unit, arithmetic unit, input and output units – this architecture has served as the basis for most computers since.

Military uses for computing continued after the war. ENIAC was used to design the hydrogen bomb, EDVAC was used by the US Army Ordnance and MIT's Whirlwind become the basis for the Air Force's real-time SAGE early warning defence system. As importantly, the post-war period saw the take-up of modern computers in the business world. In the UK the Lyon I machine was used from November 1951 to operate the payroll, ordering and distribution for Lyons' tea shops; the same year Eckert and Mauchly marketed their UNIVAC I and in 1953 IBM launched their IBM701. Manchester's Ferranti Mark I and the Zuse Z5 were also available but the business market didn't take off until the 1960s with the success of IBM's 1964 System/360 'family of upgradable computers'.

Computer technology continued to improve. Memory systems such as valves, mercury delay lines and the 'Williams tube' gave way to magnetic core memory, magnetic drum memory and, by 1965 with IBM's 305 RAMAC computer, hard discs. The key development was the invention of the transistor in 1947 by John Bardeen and Walter Brattain working under Walter Shockley at Bell Labs. This was a revolutionary amplifier and switch (first made of germanium, then later of silicon) that replaced the vacuum tube. Inaugurating solid-state electronics it was smaller, needed less power, produced less heat and lasted longer. Its real impact came later when Jack Kilby of Texas Instruments realised they could be combined with other components to create an integrated circuit (IC). Improved technology would shrink them further and increase their power and mass production would bring their prices down leading Gordon E. Moore in 1965 to note that the number of transistors on a chip had doubled every year since 1959. Modified to predict a doubling every eighteen months, 'Moore's Law' has, so far, held true. By 1971 chips were already appearing in everyday gadgets such as Texas Instruments' pocket calculator and Pulsar's digital watch.

By the 1970s computers were still large, expensive machines owned by large organisations and kept apart from anyone but their white-coated operators. Popular 1970s films such as *Colossus: The Forbin Project* (1970) and *Demon Seed* (1977) reinforced this separation, presenting computers as dangerous, anti-human technologies. Computers were getting smaller, with the development of 'mini-computers' such as the PDP-8 (1964) whilst 'time-sharing' allowed more users, but it was the development of the 'microcomputer' that would permanently transform our relationship to the machines. The technological spur for the personal computer was the invention of the 'microprocessor', a single chip containing all the essential components of a computer, the first of which was the Intel 4004 in 1971, but the cultural spur was the growing demand for computing by a 'hobbyist' community. Home-build computers had been available since the 1950s (such as 'Simon' in 1950 and 'Geniac' in 1955) but the breakthrough device was the MITS Altair, available in March 1975. 1975 also saw the creation of the 'Homebrew Computer Club' in Menlo Park, California which, within a year, had over 750 members including Steve Jobs and Steve Wozniak whose Apple I was available in 1976. By the time of the Apple II in 1977 computers were being sold as ready-made devices with built-in keyboards and monitors.

Personal computing took off in the early 1980s with popular machines such as the ZX Spectrum, BBC Micro, Commodore 64 and IBM's PC. In 1982 *Time* magazine made the personal computer its 'man of the year'. Apple's 1984 Macintosh included a mouse and windows-based graphical user interface (GUI), taken from the Xerox-Parc experimental computer the Alto, developed in 1973 as the realisation of Douglas Engelbart's work on computer interfaces and presentation. Adopted by Microsoft, the windows-icons-menus-pointer (WIMP) paradigm would soon become industry standard, aiding in the democratisation of computing. Early PC sales were driven by office applications such as wordprocessing and spreadsheets, the possibility of domestic 'desktop publishing' and by computer gaming.

The earliest games, *Tennis For Two* (1958) and *Spacewar* (1961), were mostly restricted to research communities. The first commercially successful game was *Pong* in 1972, available as an arcade and a console game, but the modern era of gaming began with games such as *Space Invaders* (1978), *Battle Zone* (1980), *Pac-Man* (1980) and *Donkey Kong* (1983). Games were popular on personal computers but the success of the Nintendo Entertainment System (NES) and Sega Master System (both 1985) and the Nintendo Game Boy (1989) saw the take-off of the console and hand-held markets. By the 1990s the games industry was approaching Hollywood levels of investment, production and profitability with games evolving rapidly in their graphics, genre, plot, narrative, characterisation and complexity.

Successive 'console wars' came to define the industry into the new millennium and new releases such as the *Grand Theft Auto* or *Call of Duty* series became major cultural and economic events. By then gaming had diversified onto other devices such as mobile phones, the iPod touch and tablets, aided by the rise of apps, whilst online gaming had also matured. Internet connectivity had transformed domestic console gaming into a shared, communal experience. Early online multi-user dungeons (MUDs) evolved into Massively Multiplayer Online Role-Plating Games (MMORPGs) such as *EverQuest* (1999) and *World of Warcraft* (2004), played globally, whilst social networking sites became the hosts of 'casual games' such as *Farmville* (2009). Gaming was now a central part of everyday digital experience.

All these developments were built on improvements in computing. Consider *Personal Computer World's* summary of their falling cost and increasing power: in 1978, £1,500 would buy an Apple II with 4KB of Ram and a Sony TV to show its colour display; by 1991, £1,500 could buy a 33MHz 386 PC with a 44MB disc and 2MB of Ram; by 1997, £1,500 could buy a 200MHz Pentium MMX multimedia PC with a 4.3GB hard drive, 32MB of Ram and a 17" monitor; by 2001, £1,500 bought a 1.4GHz Athlon PC with 256MB of Ram, 60GB hard drive, CD-RW and DVD-Rom drives, 17" flat-panel TFT monitor,

64 MB video card and surround sound speakers. By 2008, just under £1,000 would get you a HP Pavillion Elite with a 2.2GHz AMD Quad Core 9500 processor, 4GB of Ram, a 1 Terabyte (1000GB) hard drive and 22" TFT. By 2011, for just over £1,000 you could get the Pavillion HPE h8–1070uk desktop PC with a 3.40GHz Intel Core it-2600 processor, 8GB of Ram, a 2 Terabyte hard disc and 23" LCD monitor.

To really understand this changing purchasing power, however, you also have to factor in the rate of inflation. Using the retail price index we can see that 1978's £1,500 was actually worth £4,007 in 1991, £4,727 in 1997 and £5,201 in 2001. By 2013 the actual equivalent of spending £1,500 on computing in 1978 would be to spend £7,791. Not that you needed to spend that in 2013. By 2011, under £300 bought a Compaq computer with a 2.9GHz Dual Core AMD Athlon II x2 245 processor, 2GB of Ram, and a 500 GB hard disc. Compare that with the cost and performance of the Apple II.

Smaller and new machines, better graphics, software and capabilities and the digitalisation of other media content also helped drive a revolution in *use* and *usability* that was the key to unlocking social demand. Computers moved beyond being mere calculation devices to become general-purpose machines simulating all prior media forms, finding a new role as personal media workstations, communications devices and entertainment centres. Central to this revolution was the end of the computer as a stand-alone device. Our contemporary digital ecology is the result of three interlinked developments: the rise of computing, the translation of earlier media forms into digital form and the rise of networked computing that allowed the interconnection of devices and the intercommunication of their content. As all prior forms became digitalised, interconnection allowed content to be sent and shared by anyone.

The paradigmatic example of computer interconnection is the internet. Whilst it is often claimed that its invention was due to the US government's need for a nuclear-proof communications system, the simpler underlying motivation was for computers to intercommunicate. The internet's origins are usually traced back to ARPA, the Advanced Research Projects Agency, created in 1958 as a response to the USSR's 1957 launch of the Sputnik satellite with a mission to fund a community of the best scientific minds and promote 'blue-sky thinking' and research with possible government or military applications. In 1966 Bob Taylor had become the head of ARPA's Information Processing Techniques Office (IPTO) and he became increasingly frustrated by the inability of incompatible computers to communicate with each other. J. C. R. Licklider had suggested an 'intergalactic computer network' in 1962 and Taylor realised that such a network would enable scientists to collaborate and share their work. What began, therefore, as a means to improve ARPA's research actually became ARPA's most famous and important innovation.

The problem of incompatible computers was solved with the idea of IMPs – 'interface message processors' – that would translate between computers, whilst from the work of Paul Baran and Donald Watts Davies ARPA derived the important ideas of a 'distributed network', allowing connection failures to be bypassed, and of 'packet-switching', breaking the message down into 'packets' transferred by any route to be reassembled at their destination. What remained was the development of a 'network control protocol' (NCP), enabling the IMPs and host computers to communicate. In 1968 Bolt, Beranek and Newman (BBN) of Cambridge, Massachusetts, won the contract to construct the 'ARPAnet' and at 22.30pm on 29 October 1969 the first link was established between the University of California, Los Angeles and the Stanford Research Institute (SRI). By 5 December a four-node network was created by adding the University of Utah and University of California, Santa Barbara.

Now communication between users of two different computers was possible. In 1971 Ray Tomlinson sent the first email between two computers, using the @ sign to indicate the receiver was 'at' a different location. Though by 1972 the 29-node network was limited to a scientific elite, email's popularity suggested the network was becoming a personal as much as a professional tool. This was a machine for sociability and community.

With other networks developing, the International Network Working Group (INWG) was set up by Robert Kahn and Vint Cerf to study how to ensure compatibility. Their idea of gateways required a new set of protocols to replace the NCP so in May 1974 Kahn and Cerf presented their paper 'A Protocol for Packet Network Intercommunications' which described messages in 'datagrams' (envelopes, read by the computer), the Transmission Control Protocols (TCP) to send and receive them and the gateways (or 'routers') that would act as conduits between networks. By 1978 they had refined this system so that TCP would act in conjunction with a related set of internet protocols to form the TCP/IP system. The collection of networks began to be called the 'internet' and from 1 January 1983 TCP/IP finally replaced the NCP. More networks developed in Europe and the world and connected to the broader network leading, in 1985, to the US National Science Foundation creating five supercomputer centres plus a 'backbone' network, the NSFNET to link them which together became the basis for the modern internet. By the end of 1989 the original ARPAnet structures were removed leaving the internet in place.

By the late 1970s the broader public was also joining the online world. Ward Christensen and Randy Seuss wrote the MODEM program in 1977 to connect their computers through the telephone line system and they also developed a computer 'bulletin board system' that went online in 1979, storing and forwarding messages sent from PCs. In 1983 Tom Jennings created FIDONET, a bulletin-board network bringing users together. By the early 1990s, however, online communication remained the preserve of a minority, requiring computing expertise and confidence to use. What changed this was Tim Berners-Lee's invention of the World Wide Web (WWW) whilst working at the European Organisation for Nuclear Research (CERN) in Zurich.

Inspired by Vannevar Bush's idea of 'the memex' in his 1945 article 'As We May Think'; Douglas Engelbart's 1962 research into 'Augmenting Human Intellect' and his 1968 demonstration of new computer interfaces and possibilities; Ted Nelson's 1963 conception of 'hypertext' (in print in 1965) and 1981 idea of the 'docuverse', and Bill Atkinson's 1987 development of 'Hypercard', a hypertext system for one's own computer, in 1989 Berners-Lee proposed a hypertext system to link and allow the sharing of CERN research materials. In October 1990 he used the phrase 'World Wide Web' for the first time. On 17 May 1991 the hypertext WWW software was released on the CERN machines, employing a client–server model in which information held on networked server computers was accessed by the client 'browser' program running on other networked machines. To ensure information held on any computer could be accessed he wrote another set of protocols: the uniform resource locator (URL), specifying the location of information; the Hypertext Transfer Protocol (HTTP), specifying how information exchange between machines would work; and HyperText Markup Language (HTML), as a uniform way of structuring and presenting documents to be readable. Though the line mode browser had been available since 15 January, the WWW officially went public on 6 August 1991 when Berners-Lee posted information about it to newsgroups.

The WWW took off with the development of the graphical browser 'Mosaic' by Marc Andreessen. Released for free in March 1993 its ease of use caused the number of net users to increase exponentially. From March 1993 to March 1995 the volume of internet traffic devoted to the web rose from 0.5 per cent to 23.9 per cent – almost a quarter of the total. With Jim Clark, Andreessen released an improved browser, 'Netscape Navigator' in December 1994 which within four months had a 75 per cent market share, a lead that lasted until Microsoft's release of its own 'Internet Explorer' in August 1995, bundled free with its Windows 95 system.

The success of the internet (and in particular of the WWW that became synonymous with it) has been astonishing. By August 1995 there were 18,957 websites online; by August 1996 there were 342,081; by August 2000 there were nearly 20 million; by August 2006 there were 92.6 million, whilst by September 2011 Netcraft were reporting 485 million sites. 2007 estimates put the number of individual web pages at somewhere between 15 and 30 billion and the global number of individual internet users at 1.463 billion, up from 360 million in 2000. By June 2012 2.4 billion people out of a global population of just over 7 billion were using the internet. On 25 July 2008 Google's Official Blog reported that they had indexed over 1 trillion pages (unique URLs) for the first time. As Kevin Kelly points out in his 2005 *Wired* article 'We Are The Web', the most remarkable thing about this is that it wasn't produced or filled by broadcast media companies, but by *us*: by ordinary people, groups, companies and institutions.

By the last decade of the 20th century, therefore, publicly available and easily useable networked computer communication and content joined developments in cheap, powerful personal computing as a cultural force impacting upon the world of mass media and of that broadcast model that had dominated the entire century. As Manovich indicates, these two trajectories had developed from historical roots, taking off in the early–mid-19th century and maturing through the 20th century. What happened next – and what is central to the contemporary digital revolution – was the merger of these two trajectories as older media forms converged upon the digital.

2 The material revolution
Becoming digital

As we've seen, for Lev Manovich 'new media' are the result of the historical development and meeting of two trajectories – mass media and computing. Their merger at the end of the 20th century transformed computers into media technologies and transformed media into computer technologies. In this chapter I want to complete Manovich's analysis by considering how this merger happened. I want to trace how the 'old' media forms of cinema, print, music, home video, photography, video, telephony, radio and television all became digital technologies.

I also want to argue that this meeting of mass media and computing is important not simply for launching the era of digital media but because it constitutes a fundamental transformation in the material basis of our media forms that also changes the capacities and potential of those media. This material revolution serves, therefore, as the basis for a series of related transformations – the ecological transformation of our media; the cultural transformation of the production, distribution and consumption of media; and the personal transformation of individual use and experience. Taken together, these can be considered to have had a revolutionary impact upon the older world of analogue mass media and the broadcast model that dominated the preceding centuries. The ecological, cultural and personal transformations are the subject of the following chapters. In this chapter I am concerned with the passage from old to new media and why this merger and transformation matters: how it changes media and gives us new possibilities of media use and experience.

Old becomes new

By the late 20th century the broadcast ecology was dominated by a small number of separate, mass media forms, with their own established economic models and competing providers, together with established relationships between different industries and with the regulatory authorities. In each case digital technologies were introduced into these industries either to improve their productive or distributive capacity or the quality of their products or services. Digitality was adopted by broadcasting, therefore, as a means to increase efficiency and profits, although the later rise of home computing, the internet and multimedia-enabled personal technologies would ultimately threaten the position of these industries and their business models.

Cinema first experimented with computer graphics in *Westworld* (1973), *Future World* (1976) and *Tron* (1982), though the sequences were expensive and time consuming to produce and met with suspicion: *Tron* was famously refused an Academy Award special effects nomination in 1982 because the voters felt it had 'cheated' by using computers. Within a decade these effects would become central to the industry with films such as *Terminator 2: Judgment Day* (1991) and *Jurassic Park* (1993) showcasing the fantastic and hyperreal possibilities of digital animation and drawing in huge audiences.

Through the 1990s computers transformed cinema production. The common use of digital cameras, digital editing software and digital post-production meant that 'films' were digital long before they were output on film. The industry also began to move towards digital distribution and exhibition, with films being sent on hard disc or via satellite download to the cinema's servers for digital projection. In October 1998 *The Last Broadcast* became the first feature theatrically released digitally, via satellite, to theatres in the USA; in September 2001 *Vidocq* became the first film filmed with high-definition digital video cameras and in May 2002 *Star Wars Episode II: Attack of the Clones* was the first high-profile, big budget film shot on digital video. In October 2011 it was reported that the three major manufacturers of motion picture film cameras, Aaton, ARRI and Panavision, had all ceased production in the last year and would only make digital cameras from now on. Bill Russell, AARI's vice-president of cameras added 'the demand for film cameras on a global basis has all but disappeared'. The same month, British artist Tacita Dean used the turbine hall of Tate Modern for an installation simultaneously celebrating and commemorating analogue film-making. The entire medium was now a museum piece.

The publishing industry was similarly transformed. In the UK, the 'Wapping Dispute' in January 1986 saw the start of a print union strike against Rupert Murdoch's News International, publishers of *The Times*, *The Sun*, *The Sunday Times* and *The News of the World*, sparked by its movement from Fleet Street to new premises in Wapping. Although the causes of the dispute were varied, including the company's attempts to inflict new terms the union found damaging, and hopes to take advantage of new anti-union laws passed by the Conservative government, the publishers' desire to move away from traditional printing methods to more profitable electronic publishing was also a key factor. News International's success by 1987 meant that every major newspaper began to move to new premises and update their production, publication and editing processes with information technology. Through the 1990s every book, magazine and newspaper publisher would move towards digital technology and, like cinema, their objects would be produced, and exist first of all, as digital artefacts.

Journalism's digital transformation continued in the new century. The rise of digital camera and video phones especially opened up a space for public images and 'citizen journalism', as seen for example in footage of the 2004 Asian tsunami. Newspapers also moved onto the internet, launching online content and eventually publishing full digital copies. Aided by free access, their success was phenomenal with *The Daily Mail*'s 'Mail Online' getting 40 million unique monthly users by April 2010. The movement online was perhaps complete in 2007 when *The Guardian* became the first '24/7 Web First' newspaper, with editor Allan Rusbridger telling his staff that now 'all journalists work for the digital platform' and that they should regard 'its demands as preeminent'.

Changes in the book industry were slower but the Kindle launched in 2007 and within a few years e-readers and other reading devices such as tablets would prove successful. Despite warnings that the physical product would never be replaced, ebook sales have soared. In July 2010 Amazon US reported that ebook sales had outstripped hardback sales, in January 2011 they reported they had also outstripped paperback sales, and in May 2011 they reported that for the first time ebook sales were greater than hardback and paperback sales combined.

Music became digital with the launch of the compact disc in 1982, allowing the music industry to profit from consumers upgrading their collections at premium prices. However, it took the evolution of the CD-Rom drive and the possibility of ripping CDs, the rise of the MP3 format and the success of the illegal peer-to-peer network Napster from 1999–2001 for digital music to become freed from its commercial physical form to realise its potential as digital code. The first successful MP3 player, the Diamond Multimedia RIO PMP3000 appeared in 1998 but it was the release of Apple's iPod in 2001, and in particular the 3rd generation model and the opening of the iTunes music store in 2003, that led to the take-off of the digital music player. By 2003 music downloads were second nature to many, whether from online stores, websites or the new wave of decentralised P2P services such as Lime Wire. The take-off of broadband around this time ensured that the downloading of music, films, television, gaming and software became everyday activities for many. The problem of this easy illegal availability and business decisions as to whether and how to provide legal access caused considerable headaches for entertainment industries keen to retain control over their products and profit lines.

Other domestic entertainment media also changed. In the late 1990s home video cassettes were challenged by the new DVD format. The first DVD players and discs were available in Japan in November 1996, March 1997 in the US, 1998 in Europe and 1999 in Australia. As with music, DVDs were profitable for the film and television industries, as consumers upgraded collections and invested in the new product, and DVDs soon replaced videos as the preferred home-entertainment medium. Price falls meant this was only a temporary boom. Within a few years the prices of players and discs had dropped dramatically and by 2008 a 'value range' DVD player could be bought on the high street for under £15. Hard-disc television recording began with the launch of the TiVo HDR 110 in 1999 and within a few years cable and satellite companies were offering their own. The Sky+ Personal Video Recorder (PVR) service was launched in 2001 and its Digital Video Recorder (DVR) was launched in 2005 as was Virgin's TVDrive (later the V+).

During the same period traditional photography began to be overtaken by digital photography. Digital imaging has a longer history but the first experimental digital camera was constructed by Kodak in 1973. Sony unveiled a prototype camera in 1981 and in 1990 Dycam marketed the first consumer digital camera, but it was only from the mid–late 1990s that the market tipped towards digital photography. Within a few years the traditional film camera market collapsed. On 13 January 2004 Kodak announced it would stop producing film cameras in the USA, Canada and Europe. At the same time video camcorders began to be replaced, for both professional and amateur film-makers, by digital camcorders. Sony's mobile 'Portapack' had revolutionised popular video-making in 1967 with its ease of use and JVC and Sony 'camcorders', introduced in 1982–83, had extended this market through the 1980s, but the launch of digital video camcorders by Panasonic and Sony in late 1995 would be even more significant. Over the following years cheaper and smaller products, mobile phone cameras and developments in online video such as the launch of YouTube in 2005 would lead a revolution in popular video-making.

Mobile phones also 'tipped' in the mid–late 1990s. Mobile radio telephony has a long history. The first US commercial mobile radio-telephone service for private customers began in June 1946 in St Louis, Missouri, by AT&T and Southwestern Bell. 'First generation' cellular phone services based upon 'cellular networks' began in 1978 in Bahrain and the USA, in 1979 in Japan, and 1981 in Denmark, Finland, Norway and Sweden. The first UK cellular system began in 1985, though phones were large and expensive and not yet popular consumer items. With the appearance of 'second generation' phones in the 1990s mobile telephony went purely digital. The North American cellular network digital standard IS-54B was adopted in March 1990 and the European digital standard GSM (first proposed in 1982) began in 1992, eventually achieving a worldwide success.

Smaller digital phones allowed the development of SMS ('Short Message Service' or 'texting') as well as the ability to consume digital media content. The mobile phone took off from the mid–late 1990s, becoming a ubiquitous personal communications and entertainment device whose various functions (texting, photography, video, music, etc.) extended far beyond telephony. Its success was aided by new designs such as the first clam shell, the Motorola StarTAC, released in 1996, which transformed the phone into a must-have fashion item. Camera phones had appeared in 1997 but became commonplace by the early millennium, by which time a video capacity was also being added. The first 'smart phone', the Nokia 9000, was released in 1996 but smart phones only took off in the early 2000s as new 'third generation' wireless technology emerged with enhanced multimedia capabilities, especially internet access. New phones such as the Palm OS Treo and the BlackBerry, both launched in 2002, established the market but it was the iPhone in 2007 that ensured its long-term success.

Finally, radio and television also became digital technologies in the mid–late 1990s. The Eureka 147 Digital Audio Broadcasting system (or 'DAB') is a digital radio technology used for broadcasting radio stations. It began development in

1981 with demonstrations in 1985 and experimental transmissions in 1988, though it took between 1994–97 for its protocol specifications to be adopted by various bodies. On 27 September 1995 the BBC began the world's first regular DAB transmissions from five transmitters around the London area. Digital radio has also become available on digital television and over the internet. The first traditional radio station to begin internet broadcasting was WXYC in Chapel Hill, North Carolina on 7 November 1994 whilst internet-only radio services, such as NetRadio, emerged in 1995.

Like radio, television was an electronic medium that broadcast analogue signals. Even cable television (available as early as 1938 in the UK where it carried television signals to places that were unable to receive transmissions) and satellite television (dating back to the first communications satellite, Telstar's transmission of the first live transatlantic television signals on 23 July 1962) both broadcast analogue signals. Like digital radio, digital television – in the form of digital terrestrial television (DTT), digital cable and digital satellite – first became commercially available in the late 1990s.

In the USA, a Federal Communications Commission committee began meeting in 1987 to study the desirability of changing their NSTC standard television to an 'advanced' standard. By 1993 the committee had decided digital television was the future and in May of that year proponents of four competing digital systems agreed to form the 'Digital HDTV Grand Alliance'. Their final system was tested from April–August 1995 and the Advanced Television Systems Committee (ATSC) Digital Television Standard was adopted by the FCC on 24 December 1996. The US digital television service was launched on 1 November 1998.

Digital terrestrial television began in the UK on 15 November 1998, with the launch of the pay-TV service ONdigital (briefly rebranded ITV Digital in 2001), which used set-top boxes to decode the digital signal. Its competitor was the satellite broadcaster British Sky Broadcasting (BSkyB), which had formed in 1990 in a merger of the two prior competing British satellite TV providers: Sky Television (formed in 1989) and British Satellite Broadcasting (formed in 1986). BSkyB launched its Sky Digital service on 1 October 1998. By June 2007 Ofcom research suggested that over 80 per cent of the UK population had digital television on their main receiving set. On 17 October 2007 Whitehaven in Western Cumbria became the first area to have its analogue signal turned off as part of the UK's planned 'digital switchover' that was completed on 24 October 2012.

By the millennium, therefore, every broadcast medium had been transformed by computer technology in some, or all, aspects of its production, distribution or consumption. But it wasn't only media that merged with computing. Across the entire span of everyday domestic, business and industry life a range of technologies had all come to rely on and merge with digital computer processing to create a broader computational environment.

The microprocessor has become integral to modern life, with 'microcontrollers' being found in almost every information and communication process and control device, including everyday appliances (such as clock radios, washing machines, dryers, fridges, microwaves and burglar alarms), transportation (cars, trains, planes), communications devices (phones, pagers, faxes), computer peripherals (printers and scanners), military systems (missiles and torpedoes) shopping devices (vending machines, ATMs, cash tills) and toys (radio controlled toys, robot toys, etc.). RFID (radio frequency identification) chips are increasingly common in shops and even greetings cards have chips that serenade you on your birthday. This is the era of throwaway computing – of disposable power that a few decades ago would have been unavailable except to a select few. With computing becoming near-ubiquitous, our distinction of technologies as 'media', 'tools', 'equipment', 'appliances' and 'toys' is only a functional hangover: they're all computers and they're all part of the digital revolution.

All of this occurred alongside rapid developments in online digital culture. Computers had entered the home from the late 1970s, enjoying a boom in the early 1980s with home gaming, coding and desktop publishing, although their capacities were limited as stand-alone devices and it would take until the mid–late 1990s for internet connections to take off. For the majority of the population the first experience of the internet was probably around 1995. By then the success of the WWW and of graphical browsers and the buzz around the idea of the 'information superhighway' by politicians and newspapers had led to increasing public access in libraries and workplaces and within a few years affordable domestic dial-up services were common. This is the real birth of today's internet: with the tipping-point of mass access. My own experience is typical. I first went online in 1995 on a staff computer at a college where I worked, and by the following year I had my own university computer and email account, though I couldn't afford home access until 2000.

Things moved fast after 1995. Digital technologies and culture increasingly integrated itself into our everyday lives, habits and activities. Whereas broadcast era media evolved separately and slowly, with technological improvements having a limited or a gradual impact, developments in computer processing power and its falling costs now push a different environment and experience. Rapid commercial, technological invention and innovation, combined with the interconnected nature of contemporary technologies, mean that new developments impact upon a range of media forms, constantly remaking their relationships. Interlinked new media forms competing for space, attention and market share and regularly releasing upgrades with new applications and capacities impact upon everyday life and media use, constituting, in the critical mass of their popular success, an ongoing remodelling of the media ecology.

This was seen on the internet. The rise of broadband and the improving multimedia capacities of online individuals fed new developments in online culture. By the early years of the millennium a new 'Web 2.0' revolution of online services and capacities was becoming recognised. Coined by Tim O'Reilly in 2004, the term described the rise of a range of web applications that were built around a participatory architecture, personal content creation by enabled individuals, information sharing and personal networks. These included social media such as Myspace (2003) and Facebook (2005), UGC hosting and community sites such as Flickr (2004) and YouTube (2005), collaborative sites such as Wikipedia

(2001), meta data and aggregation sites such as Delicious (2003) and Digg (2004), as well as other online phenomena such as podcasting and blogging. The net we log onto now is very different from that we first saw in 1995, coming closer to Berners-Lee's original idea of a 'read-write' web.

What we've witnessed, therefore, is the passage of all older media into the digital, alongside the popular take-off of networked digital technologies. The reason why this is important, however, isn't simply in the creation of digital media but in the new possibilities and capacities that this material transformation creates and their effect upon the existing media ecology and experience.

Digital technology

Digital technologies play an interesting trick on us. If you don't want to think about it – if you just want to watch the film; if you just want to analyse the content, its semiological meaning, the characters and their relationships – then it looks as if nothing's changed. It's exactly the same; except obviously it's not just the same – it's actually a bit better; perhaps a bit cleaner, brighter, and easier to use, with added features and scene selection. And there's online material. And fan material and websites. And the chance to watch it backwards. And YouTube spoofs. And others rewriting the story. And the latest series downloaded via a torrent as you can't get it in the UK yet. And the scripts are on the DVD. Along with interviews, storyboards, design features, character summaries and a production footage Easter egg. Everything is still the same, but just with *more*. Nothing's changed; it's just that what's here is more *helpful*. For those who want to simply enjoy this, this is a huge boon. For those, such as media lecturers, who want to understand contemporary media and their effects, this is their Morpheus moment: either they take the blue pill and continue their monograph on *Lost*, or they take the red pill and see how far the digital rabbit hole goes.

Because everything *has* changed and we should know the difference. The passage from analogue to digital technologies is a fundamental transformation in their material basis and functioning. What appears to be an identical object is actually different, with a different material form and different material capacities. No matter how much it looks like what we know, it *isn't* it and doesn't *act* like it.

Analogue media were physical forms created out of a variety of material elements combined together that recorded the trace, the mark, the impression, the image of the original physical input. Books receive ink pressed into paper to be glued or bound in cloth; vinyl records receive the scrape of the cutting needle responding to the diaphragm; the radio microphone signal is an analogue electrical wave of the voice. Digital content lacks this directly traceable path to the referent; this physical connection and tie and obligation. It is a product of the computer.

The modern computer fulfils Alan Turing's 1936 hypothetical description of a general-purpose, symbol-processing 'universal computing machine' – a machine that could be instructed to perform many functions, including simulating other machines. Computers still work by calculation, using powerful microprocessors to process digital code made up of binary numbers, performing a huge number of calculations on these numbers at astounding speed. The computer uses the controlled conduction of electricity through tiny switches called transistors. These can be in one of two states, conducting or non-conducting, which register as a 1 or 0 enabling the passage of electrical signals to represent numbers in binary form. These binary numbers can represent explicit instructions, being the basis of programming languages and thus of all our software, including our operating systems and applications. Just as importantly they can be used to represent any of the major media forms.

Text, sound, still images and moving images (video, television and film) can all be turned into digital code through a process called quantisation or digitisation. Each media form employs a different process of sampling to enable it to produce a binary representation whose values can be reconstituted by the computer. Text is represented by codes such as Extended ASCII which uses 8 bits to represent each character. Sound is represented by vibrations on a diaphragm being turned into analogue electrical signals that are passed through an analogue-to-digital converter (ADC) that samples the wave form to build a picture of its shape and variations. Still images are represented by the sampling of light. Digital cameras contain a charge-coupled device which produces a representation by placing a grid of squares over the image and measuring the levels of light and dark in each square, or 'pixel', as a binary figure on an 8-bit grey-scale. Colour images need more information with each pixel being measured for the level of red, blue and green present. Moving images are an extension of this process with their constituent still frames and sound being digitised and played together.

As Lev Manovich notes in his 2013 book *Software Takes Command*, whilst Turing had the idea of a machine simulating other media, Alan Kay, a computer scientist and educationalist working at Xerox-Parc in the 1970s, was a key figure in the idea of computers imitating *media*, turning what was still primarily a scientific instrument into a 'universal media machine'. Manovich points out:

> Kay's paradigm was not simply to create a new type of computer-based media which would co-exist with other physical media. Rather the goal was to establish the computer as an umbrella, a platform for *all* already existing expressive artistic media.

In a 1977 article Kay and Goldberg described this platform as a 'meta-medium', potentially incorporating all media forms as the dominant technology. The realisation of this process – which required the massive development of processing power and memory and the cheap, easy availability and mass adoption of these technologies and the familiarity of the public with their use – was the basis for the digital media revolution. What we have seen is the widespread passage of mass media forms into the digital. Whilst I've described this as a merger it might better be understood as a digitalphagy: as computer processing eating up mass media.

This explains how digital technology can simulate and consume all older analogue media forms. This transformation in the physical nature of our media is in itself a revolution: where once we lived with analogue media – media 1.0 – now our lives are increasingly orientated towards digital forms, or 'media 2.0'. What makes digitality especially important, however, are the *consequences* of this passage: how the new capacities they possess and the affordances they allow change what our media are, what they can do and how they can interrelate. The key property used to sell the digital to the public was 'quality' and, with a few sub-cultural exceptions such as around vinyl, most consumers would agree that the digital offers a higher quality experience. But better quality isn't inevitable (in depending on sampling rates, the manipulation of the code and the quality of the playback equipment) and it isn't what makes digitality significant.

The most important property of digital forms is instead their manipulability. With no necessary link to their referent and existing only as numerical representation, as Manovich says in *The Language of New Media*, the new media object 'is subject to algorithmic manipulation'. In short, he says, 'media become programmable'. Whereas analogue media are harder to manipulate, requiring physical intervention, digital manipulation is easier and requires less professional expertise. To change an analogue photograph, for example, required an actual retouching of the negative or painting of the image – a physical intervention and marking that was noticeable and destructive. Compare that to my children's Nintendo DSi which takes digital photographs of faces they can manipulate and contort at the press of a button. Today, therefore, simple programs and interfaces allow manipulation to become a common and simple consumer activity, whether in onscreen effects, the personalisation of one's screens or the copying of and new media creation from existing content.

This manipulability is the basis of another property of digital media which Manovich (2013) calls their 'permanent extendability'. Computers don't just simulate older media, they extend them, adding features, capacities and functions that were not possible in their analogue forms. Wordprocessing, for example, doesn't just simulate typewriting, it systematically *transforms* every aspect of textual creation. With it I can cut and paste, change fonts and sizes, insert images or tables and, as I'm typing, immediately go back to the previous sentence and put the word 'transforms' in bold without having to tear the sheet out and start again. Kay, again, foresaw this, Manovich says in *Software Takes Command*, in seeing media simulation as only a part of a broader vision of computing that looked to the creation of 'personal dynamic media' that could be used for learning, discovery and content creation.

For Manovich computing's extendability is aided by its 'modularity': 'a new media object consists of independent parts, each of which consists of smaller independent parts, and so on'. Hence digital technology can be added to. 'The modular structure of new media makes such deletion and substitution of parts particularly easy' – from the hardware to the software level, new components and new programs, applications and content can be added. Hence the quality also of 'variability': the new media object isn't a final product 'but something that can exist in different, potentially infinite versions'. As Manovich explains in *The Language of New Media* (2001), 'new media is always "new" because new properties (i.e. new software techniques) can always be added to it'. Digital media are never finished – the producer-crafted, standardised and finished products shipped in the broadcast era are replaced by mutable forms that can be continually customised, personalised or remade. Every new app changes your phone.

The digitalisation of older media forms, therefore, doesn't simply reproduce these forms *it creates entirely new mediums with new properties*. Manovich (2001) again: 'Computational media uses these traditional human media simply as building blocks to create previously unimaginable representational and informational structures, creative and thinking tools, and communicational options.' The computer as a meta medium acts simultaneously as a media entertainment and information hub; as a communicational device and as a tool for media creation. This definition foregrounds computing's *potential* capacities as a key part of what it is, following Kay and Goldberg's (1977) claim that the content of this meta medium will be 'a wide range of already-existing and not-yet-invented media'.

Manovich's analysis is at pains to limit the definition of new media, rejecting aspects that aren't specific to new media or aren't specific enough: sampling, discrete representation, multimedia, random access, digitality and interactivity, for example, are all found in earlier media forms. Nevertheless if our intention isn't to precisely define new media but to understand their implications for older media then other aspects must also be considered. In particular we need to think about how their properties have been used to challenge existing patterns of media use and consumption.

By themselves, computers need not have changed much. Older media such as print and radio had the potential to be used in a democratic and horizontal peer-to-peer fashion but their incorporation within the broadcast framework was a cultural – a socio-economic and political – choice that restricted their use and dictated the modes of experience they allowed. Although it would have been unlikely, it wouldn't have been impossible to impose a range of restrictions and regulations upon the private use of computers and networks.

Digital technologies, however, were not seen as a threat. The mass media industries saw them as providing a way to improve their production, content, distribution and consumption, thereby improving their efficiency and profits and protecting their economic models into the new century. Even personal computing and networking weren't seen as threatening older industries. Computing was a sympathetic development, giving rise to new broadcast industries based around the mass production of games, software and magazines and books for the home-computer market, whilst time spent on computers was never, it was assumed, going to replace time spent on mass media. 32.30 million people in the UK saw England win the world cup in 1966; 30.69 million people saw the 1969 documentary *The Royal Family*; 30.10 million people saw Den divorce Angie in the 1986 Christmas Day episode of *EastEnders*; and 28.40 million saw Princess Diana's wedding in 1981: it was unthinkable that anything would distract us from the cultural behemoth of television.

What caused this change was the competing desires of other sectors, specifically the computing and consumer electronics industries who created and made available the technologies that would eventually challenge the broadcast media. Personal computers by themselves weren't problematic until their capacities began to develop in the 1990s. Improved performance and new capabilities such as the DVD/CD drive turned the computer into a media centre and soon rewritable drives and commercial network connections meant information could be ripped and stored and communicated, posted, shared and sent at will. With this, as Kay foresaw, the individual became not just a consumer but also a dynamic manipulator, creator and broadcaster of media information and content (including other people's).

For the first time the individual could do something effective themselves. The difficulties of producing physical media, of distributing it and of building an audience for whatever you wanted to communicate that had to date limited individual and small-group production were overcome. The networked personal computer empowered the productive, distributive and consumer powers of the individual, helping to create a sector of media activity, connection and communication outside of the traditional broadcast media and their organisational structures. Developments in consumer electronics fed into this, as mobile phones, digital cameras and digital video camcorders all increasingly synchronised with computers and the internet, improving the tools and capacities individuals could access.

Whilst they may not be defining elements of digital technologies, therefore, certain aspects of networked personal computing became especially important once these technologies were in the hands of individuals who could communicate and connect and produce for themselves. It is at this point that these digital capacities began to challenge and transform existing media practices. First, digital technologies created a new era of productive interactivity in contrast to the dominant technologies of the broadcast era whose interactivity was primarily limited to making them work – to turning them on and tuning them in or changing content. This digital interactivity isn't restricted to functioning but extends to communicative and creative possibilities and that changes the older world of broadcast mass media. As my son's video demonstrates, today one individual can accrue more broadcasting ability than any company had in the pre-internet era.

We could add to this the ease of digital interconnection between devices that enables them to intercommunicate and pass content. The digital form breaks the older 'form barrier' – the physical differences between media that made translation between them difficult (though not impossible). Now information and content pass easily, seamlessly and continuously between devices, without the need for professional knowledge, training and equipment: photographs move easily from camera to Flickr or Facebook profile; music is simply downloaded and moved without effort onto the music player; videos are uploaded in seconds and immediately linked onto one's own blog or profile page; text typed into my phone appears in seconds on my Twitter feed.

The ease of copying is another culturally significant element of this digital change. Copying is central to networked computing. Much of it is automatic: my browser asks for and assembles a copy of a web page on my computer; my computer copies my phone images onto its own drive when I connect it; and when I download a song file from a music service, I only take a copy of their original. Computers not only employ copying technology continuously they also amplify our own ability to copy. Video and audio cassettes were available in the broadcast era but their threat was attenuated by the time they took, by the poorer quality of the analogue recording and by the limited ability of the individual to mass-produce and distribute copies. Networked computers ended these restrictions. Now any media that exists in a digital form can be quickly copied, stored, manipulated, shared and broadcast. This, as the entertainment industries know so well, is a game-changer.

Economic changes are also significant. The effect of 'Moore's law' –increasingly cheaper and more powerful computing devices and capacities – has driven the digital revolution. Though broadcast media also improved continuously this was a slower process and major developments, such as the introduction of FM radio or colour television, were rare. For most individuals the only real effects they saw from technological research were developments aiding media reception and use rather than any enhancing their personal productive capacities. In contrast, developments in digital technologies continuously empower their user. The falling costs are also important. Broadcast technologies got cheaper but theirs was a slow and stratified diffusion through socio-economic groups. To give a personal example, the first colour television broadcasts in the UK were in 1967 and by 1969 the BBC and ITV were regularly broadcasting in colour. Black and white TVs and their licences were cheaper, however, and it took until the early 1980s before my family upgraded to a colour set. Similarly commercial video recorders were available in the 1970s but my family didn't buy one until the late 1980s. Even video tapes were expensive: in 1983 a friend of mine received for his Christmas present the first *Dr Who* video commercially released by the BBC. Edited down to one 90-minute programme, it cost £39.99, the equivalent of £121 in 2013.

Today technologies are not only more affordable they are also more accessible. Few broadcast technologies were generally available or useable without training whereas professional-quality production technologies are today easily found, easy to download and easier to use. And if you get confused there are demon-stration videos on YouTube showing you what to do and forums where your questions have already been answered. To these changes we can also add developments in miniaturisation and storage which, though again not new, have been amplified in the digital age. Digitalisation has enabled a reduction in size from the analogue, broadcast era: compare the microfiche with the USB thumb drive; the 1979 Walkman with the iPod Nano; the video cassette with the DVD; even the CRT with the LCD TV.

The rise of cheap storage has also revolutionised information consumption. With increasing personal storage capacity, cheap external and portable storage devices and free cloud storage available we can all become our own media and informational archivists. Random, non-linear access is another property amplified in digital media. Whilst older forms such as the book could be easily accessed, the process of searching for material within content or finding the point you want is far easier with digital media, whether in a simple find-a-word-or-phrase search or the chapter points on a DVD. This points to a broader phenomenon which is greater usability.

Increasing usability has been central to the computer's success. These developments were themselves closely tied to specific conceptions among the pioneering computer scientists about what the computer was for. The US SAGE system, operational in 1959, was the first computer that wasn't simply used for calculations but for visually presenting information on a screen that could be responded to by an individual user. J. C. R. Licklider had worked on SAGE and in 1960 published his paper 'Man–Computer Symbiosis', which offered a Wiener-inspired vision of a future close cooperation between man and machine. In his subsequent career at ARPA he helped to fund both Douglas Engelbart's research into human 'augmentation' and networking projects that would lead to the ARPAnet. It was Engelbart who developed modern human–computer interaction, with his famous December 1968 demonstration of a graphical-user interface with a mouse, windows and icons and real-time collaborative video-conferencing and editing. His work, together with Alan Kay's vision of a 'personal computer for children of all ages', inspired research at Xerox Parc and the creation of the Xerox Alto, the first available personal computer in 1973. In 1979 Steve Jobs and a team from Apple visited Xerox Parc and took the key ideas of the Alto – the windows-based, mouse system – for their new projects, the Apple Lisa and Macintosh. Within a few years the GUI, WIMP-paradigm system would become dominant in personal computing.

Licklider's cybernetic vision of man–computer interaction joined, therefore, with Engelbart's vision of linked, collaborative problem-solving, Kay's vision of computers as an educational medium and a vision of individual freedom and tool use to create the modern era of usable computers. Where broadcast technologies designed the user primarily as a receiver, reader or audience, digital technologies were built around a user and their active, productive relationship with the technologies and its capacities. This was never about reception but instead, as Licklider and Taylor explained in their 1968 paper, about two-way, interlinked 'creative, interactive communication' that produces new ideas and innovations. At a time when few saw the popular potential of the computer, they were already contrasting its possibilities with the limitations of the entire broadcast era:

> We believe that we are entering a technological age in which we will be able to interact with the richness of living information – not merely in the passive way that we have become accustomed to using books and libraries,

but as active participants in an ongoing process, bringing something to it through our interaction with it, and not simply receiving something from it by our connection to it.

There was a price to pay for this improved usability. Kay foresaw a future in which we could all program our technologies as, after all, literacy in a medium required one to be able to read and write in it. The GUI revolution democratised computing and its productive capacities though it also meant that the more fundamental ability to command the medium and code its abilities was lost. Usability was won at the cost of the loss of writability, but the victory paved the way for computers to fulfil Licklider's vision of 'a common medium that can be contributed to and experimented with by all'. This usability allowed computers to challenge broadcast media and their cultural dominance.

In summary, therefore, the material revolution by which older media forms were subsumed within the digital form fundamentally changed the capacities of these forms. The availability of these digital technologies, the specific ways in which they were taken up and the public embrace of these new capacities disrupted the older industries built upon older forms and led, as we'll see in the following chapters, to the transformation of the entire media ecology, the cultural organisation of informational practices and the individual's own position and powers. It's my claim that together these related transformations constitute a digital revolution.

Since I began to write, blog and speak about the idea of a media studies 2.0 I became aware of certain objections to these ideas. One common response was a complete rejection of any discussion of digitality. There still remain some lecturers who are openly hostile to the very topic of digital media. In this view – as seen, for example, in Dan Laughey's bad-tempered coda to his 2007 student textbook *Key Themes in Media Theory* – there has been no digital revolution and claims of the impact of digital technologies are wildly inflated. Little has changed and anything that can be pointed to isn't new and isn't important whilst older media and practices continue and, in their experience, remain dominant. Here media lecturers sit, Canute-like, dismissing the reality and significance of contemporary developments, regardless of their students' experiences and interests. From one perspective this hostility is easily explained: one would expect professional experts on the broadcast era to be the last group to embrace a world that's left that expertise behind.

A more defensible disciplinary response is the claim instead that digital media are important but aren't revolutionary. From this perspective digital media are an *addition* to existing media rather than a replacement and so can be taken or left according to one's interests. For many lecturers, for example, digital developments are irrelevant, having little to do with their interest in the oeuvre of Martin Scorsese or the gender politics of *Sex and the City*. Digital media appears here as an optional knowledge and specialism within media studies, rather than as a force transforming all aspects of media production, distribution and consumption and the discipline itself. Less important than traditional media and approaches, they are merely an option to be studied in the final year or a final chapter of a textbook, noting more recent developments. And in the round of conferences broadcast era media researchers put on for each other these developments are of limited relevance or significance.

Even lecturers interested in digitality still commonly see it as merely an addition to the existing media ecology and discipline: its appearance complementing existing assumptions and requiring only an extension of existing analyses to incorporate its developments. Hence the DVD commentary is just an 'extra' for film studies; more channels allow more television studies; YouTube offers ever more 'texts' to be semiotically analysed; online activity is only more proof of the importance of 'fans' and the IMDB is a useful tool for lectures and papers. And if the digital is only an extension of existing media then this justifies approaching it from the same existing perspectives rather than in its difference as a digital object with a different form and capacities.

Underlying this view is the idea that digital media represent an evolutionary rather than a revolutionary change. As I've suggested, academics have long bristled at claims of historically revolutionary processes. Their most common criticisms centre around the extent to which the 'new' has its own history and traces within the 'old'; the ongoing influence of the 'old', suggesting a far less radical or sweeping change than the concept of revolution implies; and the way in which changes are experienced at a micro level as gradual and hence as far less disruptive or epochal. The greatest academic contempt is reserved for claims of a contemporary revolution and the author's apparent privileging of their own time as the most important. From this perspective the concept of 'revolution' lacks proper academic caution and historical detail.

My actual position answers most of these objections. In following Manovich's claim that digital media arise from the meeting of two separate traditions with their own historical trajectories then we can simultaneously recognise *both* the historical evolution of mass media and computing technologies and a distinct revolutionary moment – that point of merger which transforms our media into digital forms and remakes the entire existing ecology, practices and experiences. As I'll argue, taken together these changes do indeed constitute a revolution but this claim is also backed up by the pace and timescale involved in this merger.

We need to be clear about this: it *is* a revolution we have lived through. Technologies become revolutionary not at their point of invention but at their 'tipping point' – their point of popular take-off, dissemination and success and integration into the everyday lives of the population. Although digital technology has a long history it had a remarkably short tipping point for its popular commercial availability and success. If we look again at the changes discussed earlier in this chapter we find that most of them occur within a time period that lasts for little over a single decade, from 1995. Although each medium has a longer history of experimentation with digitality, it is from the mid-1990s that we see the major commercial transformation of cinema, newspapers, music, home video, photography, video camcorders, telephony, radio and television and the take-off of the internet and online life. In little over ten years every major broadcast form and industry, all media practices and every individual informational experience in the advanced western economies was digitally remade.

This represents an astonishing collective transformation of media forms and experiences at a scale, pace and global reach that has few precedents. As I'll argue, the material revolution gives rise to an ecological revolution: a transformation, realignment and remodelling, to a greater or lesser (though still real, ongoing and significant) extent, of *all* the major existing media forms, their interrelationships, industries and experiences. Most earlier media innovations only remodelled part of the media ecology, however, making minor waves through the rest of the informational ecosystem. Perhaps only the invention of writing remade the entire existing communicational system and that revolution took generations or centuries to change societies and millennia to achieve a global reach. Compare that to the timescale of the digital transformation. No media form before or since has so thoroughly or rapidly remade the entire existing material media ecology.

Of course one may rightly object that older media still exist. David Edgerton's *The Shock of the Old* (2006), for example, argues for the continued importance of older and commonly overlooked technologies amidst all the hype of the new. The point, however, is not the *extinction* or physical abolition of older media. Rather what is important is that every major broadcast media form has moved down this path; that it continues to be their path of development and that the digital either has already or almost certainly will attain an effective dominance of the market and user experience. Hence the continued existence of printed books doesn't disprove the digital transformation of print or its possible dominance and nor does the market for vinyl disprove the digital transformation of music, etc. From an ecological perspective we can see that many diverse forms continue to exist and survive within niche environments but this doesn't detract from the broader ecological changes that have occurred.

A second major objection is that digital technology is not equally spread around the world – that a huge proportion of the world exists with only rudimentary technology, and that 'digital divides' exist both within nations and globally. This is certainly true, and such divides – and the media ecologies formed within different parts of the world – need exploration, but it doesn't alter the revolutionary impact of digital media. First, as examples such as Africa show, the development and success of technologies isn't linear: there the mobile phone is more successful than the landline, and even within western societies different forms have different rates of take-up among different economic classes. In addition, the fact that some countries don't have certain technologies doesn't invalidate an interest in these technologies, just as the continuing existence of pre-literate societies doesn't demand we renounce an interest in literacy. Equally, the lack of technological take-up in some areas doesn't prevent a technology from being revolutionary: few would argue that the existence of non-literate tribal societies means writing wasn't historically revolutionary. Finally, given that no society on earth today escapes the impact of digital technologies, being subject to the electronic information, surveillance and weapons systems of the wealthier and more powerful nations and the economic, material and mineral demands of its technology industries, then a media studies 2.0 isn't invalidated by global concerns. On the contrary, it may help to explain their contemporary form better.

So far, therefore, we have established a material revolution in the physical basis of our media has occurred and considered how this changes the nature of our media and its capacities. Next we need to look at how these technologies and capacities remake the 'media ecology'.

3 The ecological revolution
Convergence and hybridity

It's becoming increasingly common among journalists, commentators and academics to refer to the contemporary 'media environment' or 'media ecology'. The terms have become popular metaphors, equating the diversity and life of our technological creations with that of the natural world. For most who use these terms, however, that is as far as the analysis goes and there have been few attempts within the mainstream discipline to consider in detail what a media ecology might actually be and how it works. This is because media studies has historically approached media from a different perspective.

Reflecting the dominant broadcast model of communication, media and communication studies has focused upon *the communication process*: seeing content and messages being created by large media companies or institutions, being distributed along particular channels through particular media forms, and being received and interpreted by their audiences. Hence debates in the 1920s about the mass media's role in the formation of public opinion and the rise of empirical academic studies to explore this question of the effect of transmitted messages upon behaviour. Hence also the popularity of Claude Shannon's 1948 engineering model of communication in the nascent discipline as its linear, teleological model – running from an information source producing a message, a transmitter encoding it into signals, a channel for those signals, a decoding receiver and a destination for the message – was a perfect expression of the unilateral broadcast process (see Shannon and Weaver, 1963). Though media scholars would tweak this model over the following decades the broad approach would remain the same.

Stuart Hall's influential 1973 paper 'Encoding/Decoding' (see Hall, 2006), for example, reconceptualises the model as a complex structure comprised of distinctive 'moments', such as production, circulation, distribution, consumption and reproduction, each of which retain their own modality and conditions of existence. What Hall adds to Shannon's model is a Barthesian focus on the semantic element of the message (seeing them as sign vehicles), a Gramscian emphasis upon hegemonic struggle over its meaning, and thus a privileging of the moment of reception. Whilst encoding and decoding are each determinant, a 'work' is required to enforce the 'preferred' decoding of the message and thus the receiver has the ultimate power to develop different or oppositional 'readings' of the message. Hence, though superficially critical of the linear model, Hall's conclusions reinforce its validity.

Few media scholars really leave this linear model behind. Most still conceive of media as primarily about the mass production, distribution, reception and meaning of a message and most specialise accordingly, focusing upon one privileged element of the model, most commonly media production and regulation, media content (film and television studies) and media reception (audience studies). There are, however, other ways to approach the media and 'media ecology' is one of these.

The sources of this ecological perspective have a long history, predominantly in traditions and ideas that mainstream media studies has overlooked or marginalised. Yet it is these traditions that offer one of the most valuable ways of understanding contemporary changes. The popularity of the ecological metaphor is a recognition that something is happening today that has transformed the simpler structures of the broadcast era and led to a more complex and continually evolving system whose levels and relationships are on a similar scale to those of the natural world and which can only be grasped in a similar, holistic way. The aim of this chapter is to introduce the idea of media ecology and sketch the contours of the digital ecological revolution.

Media ecology

Within media studies the idea of 'media ecology' is most closely associated with the 'Toronto School' of media theory, sometimes described as 'medium theory'. In the early 1950s the Toronto economic historian Harold Innis developed a theory of the competitive historical interrelationships of media forms and their impact upon social and political organisation but it was Marshall McLuhan who established the broad principles of an ecological approach. Indebted to Butler, Mumford and Wiener, McLuhan developed an organic philosophy of technology as an 'extension', 'amputation' and 'amplification' of the human body, senses and central nervous system, seeing these as creating specific 'sense-ratios' and as forming an all-encompassing habitat. *This*, he says, was the breakthrough of his 1964 book *Understanding Media*: that 'each new technology, be it house, or wheel, or radio, creates a new human environment'. But McLuhan also offered a vision of how these environments were transformed. 'No medium has its meaning or existence alone, but only in constant interplay with other media', he wrote, and he saw them evolving through their 'interface' – through a rubbing up against each other that led to a 'crossing' or 'hybridisation' and the release of a 'great new force and energy as by fission or fusion'.

In *Understanding Media*, therefore, we find an image of the environmental interaction, competition, evolution and energetic exchange of media life-forms and a vision of a media studies that ignores content and audience reaction and instead takes a broader, systemic, holistic view of how media environments are created and work. Hence the book's remarkable contents pages, where, alongside chapters on newspapers, radio and television, etc., we find chapters on roads, houses, money, clocks, weapons, the wheel, bicycles, airplanes and cars. This is a fundamentally *different* conception of media; one that the mainstream discipline still can't follow, let alone countenance. The aim of this media studies was to make entire environments and their biases and processes visible and to follow their changes. Later McLuhan would explicitly refer to his 'media ecology' and refine his evaluation of its transformation, leading, finally, to his 1977 article 'Laws of Media' (see McLuhan and Zingrone, 1995) and its 'tetradic' analysis of forms that asked what they 'enhanced', 'retrieved', 'obsolesced' and 'reversed' into.

If McLuhan gave expression to media ecology, it was Neil Postman who gave it an institutional form and character as an academic field. He began using the term in 1968 and in 1972 established a media ecology graduate program at New York University. He returned to the idea of media ecology throughout his career, defining it, in *Teaching as a Conserving Activity* (1979), as 'the study of information environments. It is concerned to understand how technologies and techniques of communication, control the form, quantity, speed, distribution and direction of information; and how, in turn, such information configurations or biases affect people's perceptions, values and attitudes'. Postman's influence was widespread, leading to the creation of the Media Ecology Association in 1998 and a range of publications by former pupils including Paul Levinson and Lance Strate.

But this ecological approach isn't limited to medium theory. Lance Strate's 2004 essay 'A Media Ecology Review' attempts to survey the range of thinkers who contribute to the approach but his list barely scratches the surface. This is because the ecological perspective has a much broader scope, with its origins discoverable throughout western religious and philosophical thought. As David Channell's *The Vital Machine* (1991) demonstrates, the 'organic' and 'mechanical' have always been thought together, comprising two distinct, but related, symbolic worldviews competing for dominance through western history. Channell traces the history of the mechanical worldview, from Greek atomism and astronomy through its height in the 17th and 18th centuries, considering its materialist claim that the organic can be interpreted as a machine. Against this Channell identifies another perspective, one interpreting technology as imbued with or directed by an inner, vital force, substance or principle, a philosophy he traces from Greek thought to the present. His conclusion is that we have never historically separated life and technology, conceiving repeatedly of life as mechanical and the mechanical as organic.

Perhaps the best 20th-century examples of this prior to McLuhan are the theories of ecology and cybernetics. The term 'ecology' (from the Greek for the study of 'the home') was coined by Ernst Haeckel in 1866, though the idea of studying the organism's environmental relationships had a longer history. Ecological science developed out of advances in biology, chemistry, botany and geology, leaving older vitalist–mechanist debates behind to emphasise new organic, systemic approaches. These drew upon broader philosophical debates such as Smuts' idea of 'holism' and Whitehead's 'Process philosophy' whilst Bertalanffy's emerging 'general systems' theory would also prove influential on the field.

Roy Clapham coined the term 'ecosystem' in 1930 and in 1935 Arthur Tansley refined this concept. The text which brought these ideas together, creating the modern science of ecosystems, was Eugene and Howard Odum's *Fundamentals of Ecology* (1953) which drew heavily upon Norbert Wiener's *Cybernetics* (1948). 'Cybernetics' was an organic philosophy equating biological and technological beings, drawn from biology and inspired by Wiener's wartime work on anti-aircraft guns and the system they formed with their operator. His post-war best-seller explored how organic beings, as well as new, emerging technological forms, employed 'communication and control' – or information, messages and 'feedback' – to regulate its relationship with the world. The emerging post-war field of ecology was drawn to cybernetics, recognising its emphasis on systems and sub-systems and environmental relationships helped it understand the natural world.

Cybernetics also influenced McLuhan but it was the combination of the two approaches that led to the most systematic early attempt at a media ecological analysis by the 'Raindance Corporation' – 'an alternative media think-tank' founded in 1969 by Frank Gillette, Michael Shamberg, Louis Jaffe and Marco Vassi whose ideas receive their classic expression in Shamberg's *Guerrilla Television* (1971). Shamberg's cybernetic McLuhanism sees man and media as coexisting symbiotically and evolving together, with the technological forms creating a complete system: a 'media ecology' or 'information environment'. For Shamberg these environments are either 'healthy', in enhancing life, or 'unhealthy' if they limit its forms and expression. Broadcasting, he argues, was a perfect example of an unhealthy system in being dominated by a small number of aggressive forms, in restricting diversity, in concentrating power and in refusing feedback, limiting the expression of self.

Hence Raindance's call for a revolution in production – in the distribution of video cameras to ordinary people – and in distribution, hoping even for a computer bank of videos that could be added to and accessed by anyone. As in cybernetics, the aim was a homeostatic 'media ecological balance': our 'survival' depends, Shamberg argues, on understanding how to orchestrate our technologies to create a life-enhancing ecology.

What we learn from this history are two things. First, although the idea of media ecology is commonly associated with 'medium theory' this is only part of a broader and richer perspective; one whose foundations lie deep within our historical understanding of humanity and which has intimately informed our experience of and relationships with both technology and nature. Second, almost all these traditions have been ignored by mainstream media studies. We have the remarkable situation of a discipline devoted to studying media that has little interest in technology or the history of the conceptualisation of the organic–mechanical relationship throughout western civilisation. Whilst media studies treats medium theory for the most part as a marginal and even erroneous approach (as promoting a simplistic technological determinism that is easily rebuffed), placed within this broader intellectual context, media studies itself appears as the marginal and erroneous approach in its separation of technology from its debates.

So when we see the terms 'media ecology' and 'media environment' we must be cautious, as these ideas have a very specific application. Although there is no single, agreed ecological approach most contemporary uses employ, or can be linked back, to either cybernetics or McLuhanism – Fuller's *Media Ecologies* (2005), for example, draws upon Felix Guattari's *Three Ecologies* (originally published in 1989; see 2008) which was inspired by the cybernetics of Gregory Bateson; whilst Bolter and Grusin's *Remediation* (1999) takes up McLuhanist ideas of media evolution – and, through these ideas, they can be linked back to broader ideas of nature and technology. Thus this ecological approach is largely incompatible with the mainstream discipline and its specialised study of communication, of particular media forms or of isolated elements of the linear model. Media ecology is not a term that can be used lightly. It implies a worldview: *it evokes a world.*

The complexities of this approach can't be adequately explored in this brief chapter, but if the aim is only to show that one ecological arrangement – that of analogue, broadcast media – has been transformed by the development of digital technology, then the task is relatively easy. To do this all we need do is set out a basic overview of the elements of the ecology and consider how these have changed. What follows here, therefore, is a relatively simple discussion of a media ecology and a consideration of its digital revolution.

At its simplest, 'media ecology' can be seen as employing the concepts of biological ecology as a metaphor to understand the media environment, analysing the elements that comprise these systems and their interrelationships. It might begin, therefore, from the idea of media 'ecosystems' – of 'communities' of media 'life-forms', interacting within a system and engaged in competitive energy exchange with the aim of establishing their own niche position or dominance. These ecosystems will vary by region and it is likely that different parts of the world will differ so greatly as to justify the identification of different media 'biomes'.

Each system will include particular media life-forms, with the dominant media creating specific epistemological environments: extending our senses in particular ways that bring the world to us in different forms, impacting upon and directing our experience and knowledge. But media forms can also be analysed as their own separate systems; as systems constituted by the physical elements they comprise and their internal layers. This deep materiality plays a significant part in what a medium is and how it works. This design is intentional, incarnating the desires of the creators as well as broader social and cultural values, since the designers are embedded in a specific economic and social milieu. Each medium can also be seen to incarnate an imaginary, manifesting within a cultural environment a specific cultural drive or dream that compels its creation and use. This is the hope of what the medium will achieve, what experiences it will give or knowledge or experiences it will reproduce. Each medium has a cultural aim, representing the fulfilment of a perceived need.

Media are also obviously carriers of content – the specific informational experiences encoded in their form – though this concept is curiously neutral, downplaying its ability to affect us. McLuhan noted precisely this power, describing content in *Understanding Media* (1994) as like a 'juicy piece of meat carried by a burglar to distract the watchdog of the mind' and historically we have long understood the ability of content to form realities for us. Content is a mode of simulation and our media constitute efficacious images or simulacra whose modes of reality (even in abstract levels such as language) capture us, move us, control us, prompt us and compel us. Theirs is a phantasmatic force that impresses itself upon us, organising our reality and experience through the worlds they create.

Each medium also possesses its own form of interface – the physical form that is experienced and the elements that are manipulated to activate the medium's content. These may remain fixed for long periods of time, evolving incrementally with technical improvements to their functioning, or they may undergo periods of rapid transformation, with new paradigms of user experience. As the meeting point of technological and biological life, the interface has a major role to play in the form's experience and simulation. Each media form, therefore, constitutes a system of elements and internal relationships in its own right, whilst also taking their place within a broader ecosystem and web of relationships. These include their relationship with their user: as cybernetics suggests, the biological and technological forms co-exist as a symbiotic form and system. Media forms also exist in relationships with each other, as new or upgraded forms appear in the ecosystem and compete with older forms to establish their own niche or dominance.

This broader ecosystem includes the organisational forms and structures that produce the technologies, arrange their technical distribution and direct their operation. Organisations and institutions create technologies and deploy them within the existing cultural and economic systems for many reasons (including, especially, market dominance and profit). This organisational system includes both the public and private collectivities that produce technologies and content and all constituted authorities that control the ecosystem's existence, whether at a local, national or international level and the economic, legal and regulatory frameworks that they create and enforce. Organisational forms and structures exist with different aims and intentions and compete or create alliances to further these. At a more abstract level this system takes its place within a specific cultural system that expresses the history and values of that society and gives rise to forms of life that interact with, determine and are directed by other ecological elements.

An ecological approach such as this has certain benefits over traditional media analysis. First, it explores the relationship of biological and technological life, considering how specific technical extensions create specific environments which produce particular ontological experiences and epistemological effects. Second, it takes a holistic approach, considering the entire technical environment, rather than just that portion labelled 'media'. Third, it rejects linearity and specialisation, emphasising instead a web of forces and agents and the study of the relationships within this ecosystem. It focuses simultaneously upon the material layers of the form, the system formed with its user and the radiating spheres that situate it within other systemic contexts. In place of a linear model of communication it presents a three-dimensional model of a world.

Fourth, this approach emphasises multiple determinisms. The problem of determinism only exists within a linear model where identifying a deterministic element means that it automatically influences every following element in the chain. For contemporary media studies, with its humanistic privileging of the sovereign power of the receiver, this is unacceptable, hence its hostility to economic and technological determinism. But this is less of an issue for an ecological approach which recognises that within a web of agents, forces and relationships multiple determinisms exist and can be traced. Each 'end' of the communication process – production and reception – is thus re-immersed within the broader systems they exist within and which determine or influence their form.

Fifth, this ecological model is a dynamic one. It recognises that media forms adapt, evolve and succeed in relation to other forms and elements and it emphasises the cooperative and competitive relationships within the ecosystem. It employs biological metaphors to understand the ecosystem's transformations – the establishment of media populations and communities; the issue of ecological diversity; the modes of regulation and balance within the system; species competition; the food chain, or modes of energy exchange; the creation of niche habitats; the different trophic levels within the system, and its sustainability and viability or risk of extinction and ecological collapse.

Sixth, this is a systems approach. It sees lower-level systems as having their own modes of interaction, following these through to higher-level systems and their relationships. It sees higher-level processes as more than the sum of their parts, recognising the process of emergence – the appearance of complex phenomena from lower-level rules. Media ecology thus explores emergent phenomena and their impact. Finally, we can also see that the idea of 'media ecology' isn't just a metaphor. Just as man is an animal in the world, operating within and impacting upon ecosystems, so all our technical productions exist within the same natural ecosystem and should be understood as part of it. Technology is natural: it is composed of natural elements and is part of humanity and is a real agent within the global ecosystem.

The digital ecology

In the last chapter I discussed the material revolution of digital technology – the passage from analogue to digital physical form – and traced the digitalisation of the older media forms. I argued that although digital technology has a longer history it rapidly transformed the analogue media forms from the mid-1990s in almost every aspect of their production, distribution and consumption. This material revolution underlies, therefore, an ecological revolution in media: a revolution in the elements of the media environment and their interrelationships. The starting point for investigating this ecological change is the concepts of 'convergence' and 'hybridity'.

The idea of convergence became popular through the 1980s–1990s as a buzzword within the information communications sector. Though widely used it had no simple, agreed definition, being applied to a range of developments from digitalisation to networking, the use of IT or the internet, the rise of cable TV and economic changes in the IT sector. Business debates were dominated by the anticipated merger of IT, media telecommunications and consumer electronics and this idea fuelled numerous corporate mergers and aggressive diversifications. For our purposes convergence is best understood as process by which all older media forms now converge upon the digital form – a development that was already being highlighted by thinkers in the 1970s.

Shamberg's *Guerrilla Television* pointed out in 1971 that cable could carry digital signals that could deliver 'all and any electronic information', and foresaw a 'wired nation' of 'broadband communications' whilst Ted Nelson's *Computer Lib/Dream Machines* (1974) argued that computers would soon contain every media form, incorporating 'the entire mental and working life of mankind'. The coming merger of 'electronic screen presentation and audio-visual technology with branching, interactive computer systems' would lead, Nelson said, to 'a revolution in how information is handled'. By 1977 Alan Kay described the computer as a 'meta-medium', potentially including within it all media forms, but this was only an extrapolation of ideas he'd already developed in a 1972 paper on a hypothetical 'dynabook' tablet computer able to hold and access all information and media.

This digital convergence isn't complete, and nor will it ever be as older forms find a niche life within communities such as collectors or specialists, but every analogue form has been transformed to a greater or lesser extent by digitalisation and the trend is only towards increasingly digital forms and experiences. What's important is that this isn't the *addition* of digitality to an older form but *the end* of that form. Everything that was a separate form in the analogue era is now only a type of digital content accessed on digital devices. Every older form is now software running on digital hardware. Even media lecturers find this hard to grasp. Discussing these ideas recently elicited one comment from a media lecturer that this talk of a digital revolution was ok but television still existed and was more popular than ever. I replied that after the digital switchover television *didn't* exist and that people were watching computers. What we call television is a cultural not a media form: specifically the cultural ghost of a material form surviving as the content of digital technologies.

Whereas convergence was once thought of as leading to homogeneity – to one device to rule them all – in fact the opposite has happened, with digitality sparking a remarkable hybridity. For McLuhan this meant the crossing and evolution of forms through their interface but here it represents the dominance of the digital form and the crossing of the devices that employ it. Hence we have no single, dominant device but rather an array of intercommunicating technologies competing for use including desktops, laptops, notebooks, netbooks, tablets, mobile phones, e-readers, music players, digital television and its set-top boxes and recorders, game consoles and generic media players. Though some devices (such as digital radio) remain designed around a core functionality, most take advantage of digital multi-functionality to develop far beyond their original uses.

The mobile phone is the best example of this hybridity, in expanding far beyond telephony to include texts, emails and messages; photography and video production and storage; and music, radio, map, GPS, calendar, note-taking, watch and alarm functions. Smartphone internet capability and apps means that it can now access any content and perform a bewildering array of tasks. I can read books, newspapers and documents, watch videos, TV and film, stream music and shop online whilst apps allow me to take hearing and vision tests, test my urine, track aircraft flight paths, play a virtual lighter at concerts, use a torch, drink a virtual pint and destroy complex porcine architectural arrangements using avian missiles.

Whilst analogue media were distinct and separated by a form barrier – by the difficulty or impossibility of translating or sharing content between forms – the dominance of digitality leads to a fluidity of content, information and experiences that is constrained only by interoperability. Devices exist in a 'permanent beta', tested in the market place, with continual upgrades either with software updates or revised iterations. Developments come from research or competition (BlackBerry, for example, were pressured into adopting touch screens by their market popularity), hence evolution isn't linear but also involves a lateral crossing between devices as they collide with each other. The proliferation of multi-functional, multimedia hybrid digital devices, competing and crossing leads to an era of *chimerical media*.

This digital convergence and hybridity, therefore, helps us understand the changing media ecology. The most obvious ecological transformation is, as we've seen, the replacement of the variety of analogue forms by computational technologies, a process that has both real and metaphorical ecological effects. Entire eras of media have been built on specific materials. The mid-19th-century replacement of pulped rags with pulped wood, for example, transformed both paper production and the nature and sources of the material form, whilst the insulating properties of gutta-percha created a revolution in undersea telegraphy in the 1850s and the industrial exploitation of the genus of tropical trees that were its main natural source. In the same way a new communications infra-structure is remaking the world today, based upon computational technologies, its component parts and the support and services it requires.

Consider the materiality of digital technology. Computers are made of metal, ceramic and plastic, with memory, microchips and integrated circuits made of silicon, oxygen and traces of arsenic, boron and phosphorous. Component connections are soldered using metals such as bismuth, silver, copper and tin, whilst liquid crystal display screens include glass or plastic, plus rare-earth minerals. The motors powering the hard drive use magnets made of a neo-dymium-iron-boron alloy, or metal mixture. The electricity is part of the computer's materiality, as are the lithium batteries and the wires that connect it together and that link it to external networks. The global information network employs fibre-optic cable to carry messages long distance and to this we could add the material form of all the landing points, and the internet exchanges, data centres and server-farms that route the internet and store the equipment.

One example of the effect of the global demand for computing is the mining of 'rare-earth' minerals. The iPhone, for example, uses Yttrium, Lanthanum, Cerium, Praseodymium, Neodymium, Europium, Gadolinium, Terbium and Dysprosium for its colour screen, glass-polishing, phone circuitry, speakers and vibration unit. The changing needs of the technology industries thus impact upon different regions, creating new opportunities as older ones close down. Ninety per cent of rare-earth minerals are mined in China, though other regions have become important for their contributions such as the Democratic Republic of Congo. Its mining of Tantalum, used for electrical capacitors in mobile phones, has fuelled local warfare and impacted upon the region's social and political organisation and economy.

The digital era has also given rise to its own imaginary. Digital technology was initially characterised by claims of its higher-quality reproduction, durability or even permanence and these ideas were prominent in early marketing campaigns. Early online life developed its own imaginary, seeing 'cyberspace' almost Gnostically as a disembodied realm of mind superseding the physical world and as a space of personal reinvention and new, virtual communities. As digital technologies evolved so did this imaginary. With increasing internet access and its mobile penetration of everyday life the cyber-utopian dreams of transcending the world gave way to a new interest in the ability of digital media *to remake it* and the potential of empowered individuals to refashion social and political structures. Cyber pessimism similarly evolved, moving from earlier fears of the loss of humanity, reality or relationships to more concrete attacks on the quality of digital culture and for digital media's negative effects (from pornography and cyber bullying to malicious communication and inciting riots).

This empowered individual has become a central part of the digital imaginary, fuelling a consumer dream of freedom and choice. In the always-on world individuals have come to expect information and content to be immediately available on demand, often at little or no cost, and struggle with technical or economic arrangements that impede this. The season three premiere of *Game of Thrones*, for example, became the most simultaneously shared torrent ever, due in no small part to its limited broadcast availability and the year-long wait for a DVD release. Not only the organisation of the digital world, therefore, but its imaginary too becomes realigned around the individual.

Digital technologies have also transformed the ecology of content. Most obviously whereas the broadcast era was dominated by professional products, the digital era has seen the expansion of personally produced content, an empowerment of individual creation that represents an epochal transformation of the structures of media communication. All professional content now exists in a competitive relationship with the individual's own content and peer-produced information.

Whilst digital technologies have impacted upon the production of professional content (allowing an improvement in quality and effects), the most important effect has been freeing content to move across earlier form barriers and platforms and devices. Television provides a good case study here. Whilst analogue TV was available on a small number of channels at times of the broadcaster's choosing or on commercial or home-recorded VHS, today that limited experience has expanded through the proliferation of channels, new time-delayed channels ('plus one'), buttons to access extra content, programmable electronic programme guides, live rewind capacity, hard-disc episode and series recording and a range of catch-up and on-demand services.

TV has also migrated across the digital ecology. I can watch it via apps or browser on my phone, laptop, tablet or game console; I can watch it on company or channel websites and players (the iPlayer, 4OD, HBO); on free or subscription-based streaming services (Netflix, LoveFilm) and on video-sharing sites such as YouTube, whether in illegal, fan-uploaded episodes or through official broadcaster 'channels', and I can even watch uploaded or streamed television on the internet via my digital television. Alternatively I can illegally download TV from torrents, P2P software or other file-sharing communities to view on a device of my choice.

The online world has also grown around TV. Many shows include web-only content ('webisodes'), whilst official and fan sites build background, new and explanatory content around a series. Shows are also discussed live, whether on fan forums, social media or through the mainstream media (newspaper sites host episode blogs that the readers can contribute to). Add to this the systemic loop created as this content is remixed and remade and shared and linked to across social sites and we can see that the simple structures of the analogue era have given way to a more complex set of ecological relationships around every aspect of its production, distribution and consumption.

Every older medium has changed in this way. *The Guardian*'s online paper, for example, had little relationship to its hours-old print edition. In contrast to its static and limited form the online paper presents a scrollable mosaic whose stories are continually updated and moved around the page. New stories are added or emphasised, a breaking news feed runs along the top; stories now include videos, photographic slideshows and audio as well as links to earlier stories or external sites; reader's comments build up conversations and the 'Comment is Free' section offers a range of reader-generated opinion pieces; new albums are streamed; TV programmes have a video review; and live blog pages follow sporting, cultural and news events, aggregating information, social media outputs and user comments. Whatever this is, the word 'newspaper' doesn't even begin to cover it.

User interfaces have also been transformed. Whilst the small number of dominant forms of the analogue era had established and relatively stable interfaces (with developments mainly devoted to increasing performance), the digital era has seen the development of a new ecology of interfaces, producing new experiences of content and information. The haptic touch screen became commonplace after the success of the iPhone; voice control has appeared with Apple's Siri; augmented reality (AR) apps on the phone employ GPS and the camera to overlay digital information onto the world; cinema and television have rediscovered 3D and game consoles have pioneered gestural command systems (the Wii) and full-motion body capture (the Xbox 360 Kinect). Some progress has been made on brain–computer interfaces (BCI); Samsung have introduced eye-tracking software on mobile phones and Google Glass promises to bring new voice-activated, online and AR experiences.

This changing ecology, therefore, changes our informational relationships. The tablet touch screen allows a new gestural system including tapping and double-tapping, pinch-to-zoom, rapid finger-scrolling, moving pages and images around, panning, flicking and rotating, all of which create a different bodily and experiential relationship with information and hence epistemological relationship with the world. I don't just read a web page, I throw it around and abuse it, grasping and controlling its form.

All of this highlights the key shift from the 'audience' to the 'user'. As I'll argue later, media studies has misunderstood this shift, seeing the 'user' as merely the realisation of its broadcast era concept of the 'active audience', but the change is more fundamental, in the passage from a limited receiver with few practical capacities to an empowered user able to control, challenge and direct their own activities in real time. This is not a receiver but a producer of their own experience and content, reorganising their entire media relationship around themselves and their interests and networks.

Alongside this the digital era has led to significant changes in the media's organisational forms and structures. Most obviously media production has been structurally transformed by the expansion of producers. Now anyone with an internet connection and mobile phone is able to create and globally post content – platforms such as YouTube have allowed individual superstars to emerge whose viewing numbers can eclipse broadcast shows; individual bloggers have been able to broadcast their experiences and opinions to the world and 'citizen journalists' – ordinary people producing and sharing video, images, opinion and stories – have transformed journalism. Modes of production have also changed, with online collaboration and 'crowdsourcing' of activities emerging as viable and important modes of content creation.

The transformation of journalism is especially significant. Digital technologies have transformed access to stories and the processes of story creation and reporting as well as, obviously, news production and distribution. These developments have often aided journalism, bringing new sources of information for it to employ or exploit and allowing new symbiotic relationships that strengthen its investigative role (such as the international broadsheet collaboration with WikiLeaks in 2010 or *The Guardian*'s publicising of the 2009 death of Ian Tomlinson leading to the discovery of amateur video footage undermining the police explanation). In other ways, however, digital technologies have been a threat. The internet has sucked away precious advertising revenue and readers; the industry has struggled to cope with the general availability of free information; and the journalist class's privileged status as informed and quali-fied professional commentators has been overturned by a more democratised concept of informational expertise. Who now needs *one* music magazine review of a new CD, for example, when the internet is awash with a range of reviews and shared opinions? At the centre of a range of economic, political, social and cultural changes, therefore, the broadcast model of journalism has had to significantly adapt to remain viable or even significant in a digital ecology.

Digital technologies have also transformed the operation of the market, aiding the emergence of a global financial system and the processes of globalisation and global production and distribution. The Neo-Liberal marketisation of global relationships and opening of global markets depends on digital technologies for its coordination, decision-making and everyday functioning. On this level digital informational and media technologies underlie the operation of the entire economic system and disruptions to these technologies can impact upon businesses, profitability and market judgments. In April 2013, for example, the 'Syrian Electronic Army' hacking group accessed the Associated Press Twitter feed and posted breaking news about explosions at the White House and President Obama being injured; fake news that immediately impacted upon the New York Stock Exchange which dropped 150 points in under three minutes, erasing US$136 billion in equity market value.

Digitality has also changed the ecology of media companies, with the rise of particular technology companies (whether major companies such as Apple and Samsung or smaller app-creation software companies); new telecommunications industries (ISPs, digital media providers and cloud, data and server centre providers); new content producers (media production companies, game design studios, effects companies, etc.); new digital service providers (such as analytics companies); new online service or platform providers (Google, Facebook, YouTube); and new online businesses (such as Amazon and The Book Depository). Companies such as Apple, Facebook and Google now play a significant part in our everyday media experiences and their interrelationships, business models and competition throw a light upon the changing digital ecology.

Whilst Microsoft was once a dominant technology company, based upon its control of the desktop software market, legal challenges to its monopoly and new developments led to its eclipse. Though Windows still provides its main income, the company has tried to diversify, becoming a major video game player with its Xbox console (2001) and its accessories and games and trying to move into cloud-computing with 'Azure' (2008) and search with 'Bing' (2009). Its music player, the 'Zune' (2006) failed to challenge the iPod and music was instead integrated into its Xbox package. The 'post-PC paradigm' (with mobiles, laptops and tablets replacing desktops) hit Microsoft hard, making it imperative it establish a position in these markets. Hence the 2012 release of its Windows Phone OS, its Nokia-developed Windows Phone 8, its 'Surface' tablet and its Windows app store, though to date its success in these areas has been limited.

By August 2010 Apple's market value had surpassed Microsoft's and that August it temporarily became the world's most valuable company as its value surpassed Exxon's. Apple's business was built on computer hardware and the software to run on it. Although initially successful, the company removed its founder Steve Jobs in 1985 and struggled over the next decade until his return in 1996 and his revitalisation of its product lines with the launch of the iMac in 1998. Jobs reorientated 'Apple Computing' as a consumer electronics company (it would change its name to 'Apple Inc.' in 2007). He revolutionised computer retailing with the Apple stores in 2001; changed music playback and consumption with the iPod (2001) and iTunes Music Store (2003); revolutionised the mobile phone industry with the iPhone (2007); created an app store (2008) that also created an entire app industry; and created a new commercial electronics sector with the success of the iPad (2010).

Hence Apple's powerful position in computing, consumer electronics, the mobile phone and music industries as well as retailing, enjoying a diverse income stream from product sales, software sales, music sales, phone subscriptions and app sales. Their primary income, however, is from high margins on hardware: in 2012, for example, the iPhone's profit margin was 49–58 per cent with its sales accounting for two-thirds of Apple's profits. Apple's success owes much to its model of control – of vertically integrated production dictating every aspect of the technology and the user experience and the control of every relational partner (such as the third-party developers and owners of app content). Their aim is to enclose the user within a closed ecology of Apple products, all linked to an iTunes account for a seamless user experience and incorporation.

This closed ecology can be contrasted with Google's open approach. Founded in 1998, Google was a software and advertising company, relying on the efficiency of its search engine and its monetisation through 'Adwords' and 'Adsense'. By 2011 96 per cent of its income came from advertising. Google diversified into location services such as Google earth, Google Maps and Street View, and the digitalisation of texts with Google books as part of its project to organise the world's information but its most important ecological moves came online and in the phone and tablet market.

Relying on advertising for its profits Google recognised it needed to be where eyes were, hence its 2007 purchase of YouTube and its attempts to monetise this service through advertising and broadcaster deals. Hence also its development of the Android OS, launched in 2007 and becoming the leading platform by 2010. Fearing a lock-out of the phone and tablet market by Apple's early dominance the success of its open-source OS, usable by any company, has ensured a space on mobiles and tablets for its search engine, maps and other services, protecting its post-PC revenue, whilst also allowing it to develop 'Google Play', an app and content store for Android devices that provides another income stream. Google was already a significant hardware player, in its development and use of server equipment, investment in fibre optics and creation of major data centres, but it also moved into consumer hardware with the development of its Nexus 7 and 10 tablets in 2012 and Google Glass in 2013–14. This was, again, an ecological move, motivated by the need to prevent competitor lock-out and maximise its own position and profits.

Facebook was also a software business – one based on the provision of a social networking platform. Available in February 2004, it expanded its user base, overtaking its competitor MySpace in April 2008, reaching 1.1 billion active users by May 2013. It became a public company in May 2012, with an initial value of US$104bn and although this dropped after the share offering its share prices rose by 55 per cent in 2013 so that, by August 2013, Facebook was again worth over US$100bn. Its major problem was how to monetise a free service, with its main profits coming from targeted advertising with additional income from virtual currencies and payment on in-site games. Its greatest potential value lies in the information it stores and controls, though there are serious privacy issues over its commercial exploitation and Facebook must balance reasonable exploitation with threats of legal action and the risk of alienating the user base that provides almost all of its content.

Though successful in its own niche, Facebook too has attempted to expand its sphere of operation. It tracks logged-in users across websites to harvest broader information about user activities and it is embedded in many sites, enabling one to sign into, like or share directly to it. On one level it has coped well with the post-PC paradigm, with its free app and easy mobile and tablet use securing its place in the digital ecology. Its desire to reinforce this position and lock-in users led to its movement into consumer electronics with the April 2012 launch of a HTC 'Facebook Phone', with a Facebook 'Home' app as its primary screen. Initial sales, however, were low and delayed the European launch, and it wasn't the mobile game changer the company planned.

Finally Amazon have also become an important digital media player. Founded in 1993 and online in 1995, they began as a book retailer. They went public in 1997 though took until 2001 to make a profit. Their success owed much to the features they added to their experience, harvesting automatically generated data such as page views and purchases to make precise recommendations and using voluntary user-generated information such as public reviews to increase the value of the site and to make it a major source of consumer research. The company diversified beyond books to become a general retailer and added a 'marketplace' allowing anyone to register as a seller, bringing in more income.

Amazon also diversified into consumer electronics, with the launch of the Kindle e-reader in 2007, releasing continually upgraded versions of this as well as a new Android tablet, the Kindle Fire in 2011. These are automatically linked to Amazon accounts, are sold at near cost and allow one-click purchases and are obviously designed to lock users into Amazon's retail ecology and sell their content. Amazon also diversified into DRM-free music downloads in 2007 and into TV and film on-demand in the USA in 2006. In January 2011 they purchased the 'LoveFilm' online rental and streaming service, consolidating their role as a central digital entertainment content provider.

Amazon has also become a significant hardware player, with its excess capacity making its EC2 service an important cloud-computing provider. As its removal of cloud services from WikiLeaks under political pressure following the December 2012 leak of diplomatic cables showed, however, its hosting service isn't neutral. Ecological position always translates into real-world power. In March 2011 it expanded its cloud services for consumers, offering a 'cloud drive' and 'cloud player'. This was an extension of its Kindle model, aiming again at consumer lock-in to its own linked ecology of cloud storage and streaming – content store – registered account and payment card – immediate downloads – Amazon device. Its in-depth knowledge of user activities and purchases is used to target adverts and push sales whilst it retains a control over your licence to use this content, as evidenced by its remote deletion of an unlicensed copy of Orwell's *1984* from users' Kindles in January 2009.

What all these companies demonstrate is the significance of the individual in a digital age. Whereas the broadcast era marketed to a generic mass audience, with little fine-grained information about users and their activities, the digital era allows the systematic harvesting of information. This is now a key source of economic value, with the analysis of behaviour, views, clicks, likes and purchases being used to target advertising and improve services. The more the individual can be locked in to a company's ecology the greater the information that can be gathered and the more direct or indirect profit they can produce.

Distribution has also been digitally transformed. Most major broadcast forms have moved to digital signal processing and distribution whilst the internet has emerged as a major delivery form. Now many media industries including books, newspapers, music, film and even television embrace digital downloading, not least for the economic benefits as the user is transformed into the retail assistant (in selecting, serving and purchasing products); into the delivery driver (in paying for the connection and the equipment that brings it to their home); and the factory worker (in controlling the way the product is output, whether on a hard drive or burnt to disc).

Purchase, of course, isn't essential, beyond illegal downloading much is available to stream for free (such as on the BBC iPlayer) or through subscription or free services (such as Spotify). Distribution of content on the internet extends across P2P software, online services and stores, embedded media players, on social networking and sharing sites and blogs, through digital archives and on official and unofficial content pages. Unlike in the broadcast era information is potentially available instantly and globally and, as sites such as WikiLeaks highlight, this has implications for the management of information and its release across borders and jurisdictions.

These ecological changes have increasingly clashed with existing legal and political regulatory structures. Though early pioneers such as John Perry Barlow in his 1996 'Declaration of the Independence of Cyberspace' saw the internet as beyond government control, in fact governments have taken an increasing interest in cyberspace and have developed a range of methods to implement their will including controlling ISPs, search engines, platforms and private companies operating within their territory; the use of their own filtering systems, and the arrest of individuals and seizure of assets. Censorship for moral, political and religious reasons is common internationally. Formal censorship is rarer in the west but laws still exist for personal protection (laws against child pornography, libel and malicious communication) and to protect existing copyright holders. Hence the range of legislation designed to control digital developments such as the 1998 US Digital Millennium Copyright Act, the 2000 EU Electronic Commerce Directive and 2001 Copyright Directive, the 2006 French DADVSI and the 2010 UK Digital Economy Act.

The rise of social media highlights the clash with existing laws. Its success and the ability it gives to ordinary people to publish their opinions and share information has led to government, parliamentary and mass media attacks on social media and debate as to whether new laws are needed. Twitter, for example, has been used to libel public figures, to break court super injunctions against naming companies or individuals, to name rape-case victims and for racial and celebrity abuse, whilst Facebook has been blamed for numerous crimes including incitement to violence. As a result of escalating social media investigations the UK Crown Prosecution Service was forced to issue new prosecution guidelines in December 2012.

National and regional systems may also be the expression of specific cultural systems and one effect of digital technologies is to increase the globalisation of media forms, contents and experiences and thus the relationships between these ecosystems. The global availability of content has a long history but as international distribution required considerable investment and organisation it was primarily mediated by major broadcast companies, private companies and institutions. Now the internet has made cultural exchange simpler and faster and individuals can post globally and can access information, cultural products and services from different parts of the world relatively easily. This has often led to a backlash – YouTube, for example, has been banned in several Muslim countries because of its controversial content. In September 2012 its hosting of the film *Innocence of Muslims* led to bans in Afghanistan, Bangladesh, Iran, Pakistan and Sudan.

Global access by individuals has also been blocked for political reasons. Global social media have been used by protest movements such as those in Burma in 2007, Moldova and Iran in 2009, Tunisia in 2010 and Egypt and across the Arab world from 2011, often leading to attempts to ban specific services or the effective shutdown of internet access, such as the Mubarak regime attempted in Egypt on 28 January 2011. In an ecological counter-manoeuvre, protestors often found ways to circumvent blocks and their messages and videos have done much to inform the global community about protest movements and government actions.

Western media use is similarly global. Most UK internet users, for example, exist in ongoing relationships with US companies, with their search histories and personal data controlled by foreign companies and, as the June 2013 revelations about the US 'Prism' surveillance program revealed, this data is also accessible by another government's security services. The websites and services we use can be hosted in any country and many sites and companies take advantage of the internet's geographical architecture to protect themselves. The 'digital locker' provider Megaupload Limited was a good example of a global internet service.

It was founded in 2005 in Hong Kong and run by New Zealand resident Kim Dotcom using servers located around the world (for example, in the USA, Canada and the Netherlands) and by the time the US Department of Justice closed it down in January 2012 it had 180 million global members, with 50 million users a day accessing stored files.

Content also has a new power to move between cultural ecosystems. The success of Psy's 2012 K-Pop single 'Gangnam Style' is one of the best examples here, becoming the first video to gain over a billion views on YouTube (reaching 1.63 billion by June 2013), facilitating its commercial success in the west, topping the charts in 30 countries including the UK, Australia, Canada, France, Italy, Germany, Russia and Spain. Fluidity isn't absolute and is still constrained by technical issues, language, culture and knowledge, but the transformation from a broadcast era when even accessing your own country's products was often difficult is remarkable. The internet unleashes a global 'long tail' of media and informational consumers and producers, often outside of traditional media institutions and organisations.

This, of course, barely begins to map the digital ecology, offering only a quick sketch of the agents and forces and relationships in operation today. It succeeds, however, in suggesting the scale of the changes we are dealing with and even its failure – in being unable to adequately model this entire ecology and survey every aspect of its ongoing transformation – supports its general thesis, that the material revolution from analogue to digital media has led to a revolution in the entire media ecology and its relationships and operation. Another way to approach this revolution is from a cultural angle, to consider how digital technologies have impacted upon the broadcast system and model of media production, distribution and consumption whose emergence and success we traced in chapter one. In the next chapter, therefore, I want to consider the cultural revolution from a dominant broadcast model to a post-broadcast mode of media creation and experience.

4 The cultural revolution

The post-broadcast era

In the last two chapters I explored aspects of the contemporary digital revolution, looking first at the transformation in the material basis of the medium in the passage to digitality and then at how this had remade the analogue era ecology. In this chapter I want to explore the cultural aspects of this revolution: specifically those relating to the socio-economic and political organisation of the production, distribution and consumption of information and entertainment. As we saw in Chapter 1, broadcasting was a cultural model of the mass production, mass distribution and mass consumption of content with no necessary relationship to any specific technology. Broadcast media didn't have to be used for broadcasting: each media form could have developed in ways that foregrounded other models of communication. Radio, for example, was used at first for point-to-point communication and later by amateurs for personal broadcasts and messages, whilst telephony had an early broadcast application in entertainment and news services and in its use by network radio.

Here, therefore we are talking about the cultural practices that develop around technologies, specifically the difference between how the production, distribution and consumption of content was socially organised in the broadcast era and how this has changed in the 'post-broadcast' era. As we saw in the last chapter, in 1971 Michael Shamberg's *Guerrilla Television* included a critique of the broadcast ecology and in particular of its restrictions on who could produce and distribute information – as he argued, 'growing up in America on television is like learning how to read but being denied the chance to write'. In 1971 such criticisms were the province of idealists and fantasists: few seriously thought the media system would ever change and that ordinary people could be empowered as media creators. Today, however, we're finally getting a complete media education. In the post-broadcast era we're all learning to write.

The broadcast model

The historical overview offered in Chapter 1 allows us to understand the development of broadcasting and of the 'broadcast model' – a specific mode of media production, distribution and consumption. Here, I first want to draw from this history the main features of this broadcast model to understand how it functioned. In particular it can be seen to rest upon a number of key elements.

First, broadcasting was traditionally dominated by what Dan Gillmor, in *We the Media* (first published 2004), calls 'Big Media'. The term emphasises the size of the industries and their drive to monopolise their audience or readership. These were, and still are, major commercial companies or publicly funded institutions, with a considerable economic investment in premises, technology, production, distribution and staff. They have long-established relationships with the governing and regulatory authorities, technology companies, advertisers, retail outlets and other organisations or intermediaries as well as their audiences. Their aim is to broadcast their product or service to the local or national region and, if possible, to lucrative international markets. Big media, therefore, mass produce entertainment or information for mass distribution and mass consumption. As Yochai Benkler writes in *The Wealth of Networks* (2006), in the broadcast era, 'a very small number of production facilities produced large amounts of identical copies of statements or communications, which could then be efficiently sent in identical form to very large numbers of recipients'.

Broadcasting is also a 'top-down' mode of delivery. As in agricultural 'broadcasting' in which the sower walks along the ground, throwing and scattering the seed onto the earth below, so, from the apparently magical heights of their television, radio, film and recording studios – packed with stars and celebrities – a select group decide, commission, arrange, craft and produce the programmes, films and records they think we desire, scattering their seed upon the waiting population. Theirs is a vertical model of dissemination, cascading the product or information down to those below and separate from them.

Broadcast media also utilise a 'one-to-many' method of production and distribution in which individual companies or institutions produce programmes or products that are sent out to as large an audience as possible ('the many'). Benkler visualises this as a 'hub-and-spoke' structure with lines running out from the centre to each consumer. Implicit in broadcast era one-to-many communication is a concentration of productive and distributive capacity in the hands of the few and the existence of a majority population outside this whose role is to receive the product and whose own interrelationships and connections are limited.

Broadcasting is also characterised by macro production. The products of broadcast media are expensive and complex to produce and distribute, requiring a large-scale investment of money, resources and man-hours. Consider the process of recording an album, TV or radio programme or the production of a film: the premises, equipment and skilled staff required and the complex process of turning the recording into a product that each of us can experience. The scale of these demands means that 'big media' were previously best placed to deliver these products and serve these markets. Small-scale, amateur and independent production was possible but it suffered from significant limitations and rarely offered a serious economic challenge to the major companies or institutions. Their macro production also applies to the volume of their product. A major record company produces enough physical copies of an album to be in all major retail outlets; a major studio produces enough prints to run in all major cinemas; and major radio and television stations have the technical capacity to broadcast to the nation or even sell, distribute or broadcast internationally. Macro production, therefore, refers to both the scale of resources a company can bring to bear and the volume or capacity of production and distribution they are capable of.

Broadcast media also traditionally produced standardised, uniform, finished products. They craft, produce and deliver to us a message, content or product. They invest in creative personnel whose ideas are turned into specific end products, whether films, television programmes, newspapers, books, radio programmes or albums, etc. Following market research these products are commissioned and designed to appeal to specific target markets and are made generally available – being mass produced and mass distributed for mass consumption – to maximise their economic return. These products are standardised, following specific design conventions for easy market insertion (westerns, thrillers, hip-hop, R 'n' B, etc.); they are uniform (each example of the product is identical) and they are finished (consumers receive a completed product, both in terms of the form itself and its content). Each consumer pays for, takes home and enjoys the same finished product.

Broadcast media also follow a scarcity model in both production and consumption. Economic and physical considerations limit what and how much they produce: publishers limit newspaper and book sizes to keep costs down; film studios can only make so many films; and even radio and television stations are still limited by broadcasting costs and the hours in a day. Because of this scarcity everything the broadcast media produce must be as successful as possible. Ideally it would all be successful, but as long as there is enough success overall then the broadcaster or publisher is profitable or has justified its funding.

In order to maximise this success broadcast industries rely upon pre-production filters: commissioning and editorial decisions that determine what gets made, what it will look or sound like and who it should appeal to. Hence the central role of market research and audience or readership figures in the broadcast model. Close analysis of consumption patterns allows the broadcast industry to build up a picture of who each product appeals to, enabling them to tailor products to specific audiences and maximise their chances of succeeding. This has the benefit of giving the audience more of what they 'like', though it restricts what gets made and critics argue it leads to a repetition of formulaic products, appealing to the lowest common denominator.

The broadcast era was also a world of consumer scarcity: despite providing the basis for company profits or institutional success, informational goods and products used to be surprisingly hard to get. As they were primarily distributed in a physical form products had to be made available and remain available. Rural areas, for example, had fewer retail outlets and often had problems of reception but even in cities access wasn't perfect. Stock was still limited by the physical space available in shops, resulting, as Chris Anderson notes in *The*

Long Tail (2006), in a bias towards the most popular items or 'hits'. In addition broadcast material wasn't necessarily available for long. Newspapers disappeared from the shops the next day; radio programmes were long gone after broadcast; films rarely reappeared in the cinema and took years to arrive on television and even television programmes were rarely repeated. Comics and magazines were rarely republished and books and music could all go out of print or be deleted from the catalogue.

Decisions about availability depended upon the companies who owned the content and individuals who wanted to keep material or access older broadcast material faced numerous problems. Eventually video tapes allowed home recording and audio tapes could record radio and even TV programmes (many old episodes of which only exist now as audience home audio recordings). Hence the significance of libraries in the broadcast era. They were our internet: the only source of free, abundant, searchable information and entertainment, though they remained constrained by geographic positioning and size. Their stocks of books and newspapers remained limited and only specialist libraries, museums and archives stored audio, audio-visual or specialist print material. For collectors or researchers the only other options were second-hand or antique shops, specialist journals, fan clubs and collector communities but all of this required considerable effort.

Even buying a book was difficult. First of all you had to know it existed and without online catalogues that meant you probably needed to have read about it in another book. Then you had to find a copy. Bookshops would order books they didn't stock but the experience of queuing for service, waiting whilst a staff member found it on microfiche and waiting weeks or months for a telephone call from the shop to say they did or didn't have it was off-putting. Customers couldn't consult the microfiche themselves and enquiries as to other texts available by the author or involving a list of books didn't endear one to the staff. For a system built upon mass production and consumption this was remarkably inefficient.

Broadcasting is also dominated by 'push media'. Needing to reach as large an audience as possible their efforts go not only into distributing their products but also convincing and coercing their audience they want or need them. Hence large-scale advertising is used to promote and push their products at a mass audience, trying to create a momentum for their product that makes it seem essential for the consumer. Though the audience decide whether to pull the product towards them, the idea of 'push' media emphasises the broadcast focus on directed distribution and aggressive promotion.

Broadcasting also employed closed, elitist, hierarchical professional structures. Through most of the 20th century, media production has been dominated by 'professionals' with fewer opportunities for amateur production and distribution. Access to the major facilities is limited to those working in the industry and employment requires specific educational or vocational training and qualifications, relevant experience or specialist knowledge or skills. In short, mass media production is a closed and elite phenomenon. Within each industry there is a complex division of labour and professional hierarchies that dictate one's position and power to produce content. Entire professions such as journalists, editors and producers, etc. have been created by mass media industries with strict rules of entry and progression and although anyone can train for them only those who succeed have any decision-making and productive power.

The broadcast industries were also characterised by their monopoly position but this was a monopoly held not against organised competition but against the public. Very simply it was mass media that produced media content not the public. This was, first, an economic monopoly in so far as the public couldn't afford to set up and run a newsroom, print works, or their own film, TV or radio station. Second, it was also a technological monopoly as the public had no under-standing of what equipment was required for broadcasting, where to source it (specialist equipment was only available through specialist outlets) and how to set up and use it. Third, it was also a political or professional monopoly in so far as television and radio broadcasting required a licence and adherence to government regulations and most forms of broadcasting benefitted from established rela-tionships with official bodies and trade organisations as well as with distribution companies and retail outlets. Finally – and perhaps most importantly – it was a social and cultural monopoly over media production and distribution. The public expected the mass media to provide them with content, news, information and entertainment. In the broadcast era it was taken for granted that the mass media monopolised the social production and dissemination of information. Amateur and peer production was accorded little cultural significance.

Broadcast media were also built upon the lecture. They produced content and the consumer's role was to receive, watch, listen, enjoy and buy. As Benkler says, 'there was no return loop to send observations or opinions back from the edges to the core of the architecture in the same channel' and 'no means within the mass media architecture for communication among the end points about the content of the exchanges'. Communication among individuals at the ends was shunted onto point-to-point media such as telephones whose social reach 'was many orders of magnitude smaller than that of mass media'. As we'll see, media studies grew resentful of this unilaterality, emphasising the 'active' role of the audience and their decisions about content but it's arguable how much power the audience really had in the broadcast era. Media industries produced what they thought we wanted based upon their creative urges, ideals, or, more typically, their knowledge of what had already proven successful and profitable. As in a lecture theatre this was a unilateral relationship: the 'one' talked at 'the many' and opportunities for feedback were limited. Letters to the editor, radio phone-ins and television appearances were possible but these were limited to the few, dependent upon the decisions of editorial staff and closely controlled. More recently more opportunities have been created for viewer participation, most obviously in reality TV and in the use of audience feedback, emails and discussions, but this hasn't significantly altered the power structures involved.

The mass media don't just lecture us, they explicitly adopt the voice of the expert. Their information is based upon expert research or draws upon and includes expert commentary. News programmes are presented by authoritative-sounding figures backed by a newsroom of supporting journalists and researchers and contributions from invited subject specialists; documentaries are written by experts, backed by the research of the producing company; and even entertainment presenters tell us definitively what they think and what's of value. Radio presenters seem to have an encyclopaedic knowledge of the music they play and newspaper correspondents, columnists and editorials leave us in no doubt as to what they think. In all these ways broadcast media adopts and utilises the expert voice: the privileged and institutionally supported voice of authority. Expert culture, or at least its crafted simulation, dominates broadcasting.

Finally, broadcasting was traditionally marked by the positioning of its audience as a receiver. The public's role in the communication process was to consume the messages, content or products offered by the broadcast industries. Whilst media studies developed the idea of the 'active' audience to counter the common industry and popular assumption that the audience was uncritically accepting the information and material given to them it over-emphasised the audience's power. The fact that this branch of the discipline called itself 'reception studies' highlights how entrenched the broadcast media's positioning of the audience was and how removed the audience remained from the processes of production and participation. As media studies showed, the audience may do many things with the messages they receive, but in the broadcast era the circuit of communication began with the broadcast industries and the audience's primary role remained, like the radio set they were named after, that of 'receiver'.

The post-broadcast model

As we have seen, for most of the 20th century the mass media developed, honed and followed this model of media production, distribution and consumption. This was the era most media lecturers grew up within, consuming the mass-produced products of the impossibly remote and seemingly all-powerful media industries with little or no access to them for themselves. With the rare exception of editorially overseen audience participation, the overwhelming majority of people spent the majority of their media life as receivers, watching, reading, listening and purchasing. That world, however, has ended: my son's expectations and experiences are completely different to my own at his age. My students have also grown up not only watching this transformation but taking part in it, helping, in their own media use and activities, to create the new media ecology: the post-broadcast era.

The passage from analogue to digital media is, as I have argued, central to this movement from broadcasting to post-broadcasting but the relationship isn't a necessary one. Early digital media such as CDs and video games, for example, were developed within the traditional broadcast model, being mass produced and distributed by large companies and much contemporary digital media still involves the mass distribution of content. Nevertheless, the ongoing development and success of digital technology was the key force remaking the older media ecology and propelling us into the post-broadcast era. In particular we can see that the developing capacities of computers in the 1990s, the popular take-off of networked computing and the internet from the mid-1990s, the digitalisation of the major media forms, the success of personal digital devices and the transformation of the older media ecology had, by the new millennium, transformed the individual's capacities, relationships and informational expectations and hence the entire societal communicational structure. Together they necessitated a realignment of the broadcast industries' model of production, distribution and consumption within a very different culture of media consumption and technological use.

The concept of 'post-broadcasting', however, needs careful clarification. Its use doesn't signify the end of broadcasting. Broadcast media still exist and many are thriving in the digital ecology, but they now take their place within a much more complex and rapidly changing environment, defined by fundamental transformations in media technology, new alignments of creative and productive power, new modes of communication and interrelationship and new modes of reception and use. The post-broadcast era is defined, therefore, not by the end of broadcasting but by *the end of the dominance of the broadcast model* – the end of the dominance of one particular, historical mode of producing and distributing content and doing business.

Today the broadcast industries have been forced to adapt to new technologies; to rethink their media operations to accommodate this changing media culture; and to find new ways to monetise their products and services and ensure their popularity, security and success. This has necessitated adjusting to a world whose capacities and processes often run counter to those that characterised their traditional business and production model. What new elements, therefore, have been added to our media worlds that characterise our post-broadcast ecology?

If broadcasting was dominated by 'Big Media' then the post-broadcast era is characterised by the rise of 'small media'. From one perspective this is a misnomer: these technologies are developed by major technological and communications industries and, in their networked and global nature they are 'bigger' than broadcast media. 'Small' here, however, refers to the scale and cost of media production today. Whereas in the broadcast era 'Big Media' were necessary to collect the economic, technical and social resources for the mass production of media content and its mass distribution for mass consumption, in the post-broadcast era these powers can be held by any sufficiently digitally equipped individual. As I've argued, in the single, simple act of posting a comment online I accrue to myself and demonstrate more publishing power than any broadcast media company or institution had prior to the take-off of the internet.

Even in its 'golden age' broadcast radio and television could not publish instantly, globally and permanently. Attempts at live, global broadcasting were reserved for major events, required the marshalling and ongoing organisation of huge resources and still suffered from limitations of reception. This rise in 'small media' is built upon a fundamental change in media economics. Whilst the digital technologies take their place within a broader technological and telecommunications economy, for the individual producer at least the cost of the equipment, connection and publication is small. Big media production requires large-scale resources, but small media production potentially achieves the same reach with a small-scale operation.

The increase in the individual's productive and distributive capacity undermines the dominance of the broadcast industries' 'one-to-many' model of media, amplifying alternative modes of communication. Whereas broadcast era media production was concentrated in the hands of a minority, with individual companies or institutions producing the majority of the content for the majority of a population who lacked that productive capacity, post-broadcast production is marked instead by the potential participation of the whole public in their own and each other's media experience. If we factor in our own personal and peer communications as well as our public contributions and productions we can see that the dominance of one-to-many has been shattered by an increasingly complex network of communicational possibilities – by many-to-many, everyone-to-everyone, someone-to-anyone, each-of-us-to-others communication.

All of this adds up to a significant collapse of the broadcast industries' dominance of communication and control of production, distribution and consumption and consumption. In the post-broadcast era the barriers are down: the monopoly of production held against the public has ended. Economic barriers to media production have collapsed: all you need is internet access to post online (which is often free in libraries, schools, colleges and universities and relatively cheap in cafés and at home) and the cost of hardware and software is also relatively low (entry-level prices are generally affordable; hardware may be given free with certain contracts and much software is available free, is freely shared or illegally downloaded). Ever-cheaper processing power also brings features and capacities that were previously the province of the professional into the hands of amateur media producers. Hence technological barriers have also come down as the tools of media production have become more easily available than their broadcast counterparts, more easily understandable, more portable and easier to use. A significant technological democratisation has occurred in access to and the use of tools. Even a decade ago you needed some computer programming knowledge and skills to produce a web page. Today blogs and social networking sites offer templates that anyone who can type can use.

Political and professional monopolies have also ended. Though national laws still govern digital publication, the individual is under far less regulation and oversight than the mass media industries. More importantly, they are under no obligation of being suitably qualified or experienced, of being employed, of being part of a profession or adhering to its codes of practice or ethics, or of occupying a particular position within the industry's division of labour before they have any productive or decision-making power. Finally, social and cultural barriers have come down. Whereas we once looked to the broadcast media for our information and entertainment with little value attached to anything originating outside of their sphere, today that has changed. Indeed today we are more interested in and trust more the opinions and responses of our peers. Instead of automatically turning to the mass media we now seek out multiple views and give more credit to the opinions and reviews of our peers rather than the production company's public relations material and advertising or the 'expert' views of professional reviewers or commentators. The closed, elite, trained, hierarchical professional world of mass media exists today alongside another more open, structureless world of individual and collective creators collecting and contributing towards shared knowledge and ideas.

One of the defining elements of the post-broadcast ecology, therefore, is the rise of 'user-generated content'. In his book, *The Third Wave* (1981), Futurist Alvin Toffler coined the term 'prosumer'. Whereas the industrial revolution separated the spheres of production and consumption, electronic technology, he argued, would blur that difference once more, involving more of us in the productive process as 'prosumers'. As Axel Bruns (2008) points out, Toffler was really describing 'the emergence of a more informed, more involved consumer of goods who would need to be addressed by allowing for a greater customisability and individualisability of products' rather than the full flowering of real creative power. Hence Bruns prefers the term 'produsage' as a way to describe the 'new hybrid form of simultaneous production and usage' found in 'today's emerging user-led content creation environments'. The traditional industrial and broadcast-era value chain of production, distribution and consumption fails to describe contemporary, informational age, digital practices, he argues, where:

> the production of ideas takes place in a collaborative, participatory environment which breaks down the boundaries between producers and consumers and instead enables all participants to be users as well as producers of information and knowledge – frequently in an inherently and inextricably hybrid role where usage is necessarily also productive: participants are *produsers*.

For Bruns, produsage involves the move to a broad-based, distributed generation of content by a wide community of participants; the fluid movement of produsers between different creative or organisational roles; the creation of products that are always unfinished and continually under development, and the use of permissive regimes of engagement based on merit.

What Bruns is describing is, once again, the amplified capacity of individuals or groups to produce media content, communicate, win an audience, collaborate with others and respond to events and media with their own voice, opinions and creations. The result is we're no longer simply 'receivers', nor are we even still 'audiences' – a term that only describes a small part of our contemporary media experience and activity. This is rather the age of what Henry Jenkins, in *Convergence Culture* (2006) describes as a 'participatory culture', defined by the interaction of participants in creating and sharing their own media experiences and worlds.

In contrast to the broadcast era's model of top-down media production today, therefore, we're seeing the rise of 'bottom-up' communication. It was, of course, possible to join the broadcast world, either by working for the industries or trying to produce your own alternative. Scissors, glue, pens, typewriters, 'banda machine' (spirit duplicators) and photocopiers were essential tools for individuals producing their own fanzines and group newsletters but public participation in media production was structurally limited. Today, that's changed. The previously voiceless public now have the opportunity to throw their own ideas, opinions and experiences back up the communication chain. This is a bottom-up, 'grassroots' revolution, transforming the unilateral, vertical cascade of broadcast information and products. Now we can join the debate, responding to, talking back to and even challenge mass media opinions, broadcast decisions and content.

Critics find it easy to dismiss this bottom-up, individual broadcasting as its audience is typically small but this is a mistake. Self-produced content can reach larger audiences and have a greater cultural impact than broadcast products whilst, taken collectively, the volume of product and the volume of attention it receives poses a significant challenge to the broadcast industries. More importantly the size of the audience doesn't matter. Personal broadcasting is undertaken for the pleasure of creation, the experience of sharing and feedback and the reputation it brings. A large audience would be nice but a niche, interested audience is fine. Whereas in the broadcast era a company without an audience would not survive, today the producer's personal survival and continued content creation doesn't depend upon profits or justifying public funding. As Jeff Howe writes in *Crowdsourcing* (2008), 'This calls to mind the updated twist on Andy Warhol's maxim: in the future everyone will be famous to fifteen people.'

In addition to the new broadcasting power of the individual we're also seeing the development of 'horizontal media' – or communication between peers outside of the broadcast one-to-many or hub-and-spoke structure. As John B. Thompson points out in *The Media and Modernity* (1995), 'For most of human history, most forms of social interaction have been face to face. Individuals interacted with one another primarily by coming together and exchanging symbolic forms, or engaging in other kinds of action, within a shared physical locale'. The development of communication media separated social interaction from the physical locale and from face-to-face contact, Thompson says. In particular he identifies two new forms: 'mediated interaction', in which a technical medium stores information that is passed to and deciphered by another individual (as in letter-writing or telephone calls), and 'mediated quasi-interaction', which 'is monological in character and involves the production of symbolic forms for an indefinite range of potential recipients' (as in the major broadcast media).

The former mode of 'mediated interaction', or horizontal, mediated one-to-one communication, has always suffered from limitations. Telegrams and telephones were expensive; the success of phone calls depended upon whether someone was in the building when the phone rang, and most people only had one family household phone, typically shared amongst all the members. Letter-writing and postal communication was slow, whilst walkie-talkies, amateur radio and citizens' band (CB) radio had only a limited or faddish appeal.

Traditionally, therefore, media studies has dismissed this horizontal communication as of little interest, concentrating almost exclusively on public mass media content but one of the most remarkable consequences of digital media has been the explosion of personal, horizontal communication and its creation of new worlds of communication, new opportunities, modes and forms of expression and new forms of interaction. What Manuel Castells, in *Communication Power* (2009), calls 'mass self-communication' has become central to the media ecology and hence also to any valid contemporary media studies.

As I'll argue in the next chapter, today what happens *outside* the mass media, between ourselves and our peers, is of huge significance. First, it is economically significant, if we consider the technology and telecommunications industries that provide and service our personal communications. Second, it is culturally significant. Add up the time each day spent on our phone calls, texts, personal messages, shared videos and photos, emails, IMs, contribution to chat rooms, forums and mailing lists; our posting, sharing, status updates, tweets, messaging, photo comments and wall messages on social network sites; our contribution to social sharing websites such as Flickr and YouTube, fan sites and collaborative wikis; videos and texts; our blogs, reviews, comments, lists, recommendations, responses, forwardings, linking and tagging, and it's probable that horizontal media communication now constitutes the majority of our media use. This is a world of me-casting, of *me*-dia, or *we*-dia, centring upon *ourselves*, *our* lives, activities, relationships and meaning. But this isn't a solipsistic world – it centres around the self but it's directed at others and creates and utilises a network of peers, being actualised in ongoing conversations and communications. Today we're too busy talking to be talked to: we're more interested in our own and our friends' news than the mass media's. Broadcasting is less interesting than peer-casting.

Whilst broadcast era production was standardised, uniform and finished, production in the post-broadcast era is marked by the rise of customisation, personalisation and 'the perpetual beta'. First, it needn't follow the standardised marketing conventions, not needing to fit into specified genres or appeal to specific demographics. Without a reliance on profits it can afford to have a smaller audience and appeal. Second, it need not be uniform. Products and services can be customised by companies for individuals (such as 'the page you made' offered by Amazon), or personalised by individuals themselves (I fill my phone with whatever apps, images and content I choose). Third, nothing exists in a finished form. As we've seen, digital technologies are manipulable, variable, modular and unfinished. The technologies and their content never settle in the way broadcast media did, for whom significant new developments or model upgrades were rarer and more disruptive. Instead developments and upgrades are continuous in terms of new models, makes, capabilities, services and content. Tim O'Reilly, in his influential manifesto 'What is Web 2.0?' (2005) describes this as 'the perpetual beta'. Whereas products were once tested in a 'beta phase' on a select group before being put on the market, today everything is released as a beta product, being tested in the real market, as the basis for ongoing development and new, improved releases.

In the post-broadcast era even the official products of the media industries are unfinished. If we like them we can remake, remix and pastiche them; if we don't like them we can respond to them in blogs and videos. In September 2007 ITV broadcast 'Ann Widdecombe vs. the Hoodies' as part of their current affairs series *Tonight With Trevor McDonald*. The local community, angry at being stigmatised as an out-of-control estate terrorised by teenagers, organised a campaign that raised £7,000, enabling them to hire a film-maker to make a 10-minute documentary, 'Beyond the Hoodie', that they placed on YouTube which garnered more than 2,000 views in two weeks. Whilst a community film would always struggle against the power of a major broadcaster its real meaning was perhaps different: that today the broadcast industry no longer has the final word.

Whereas the broadcast media had to contend with physical and economic limits on how much could be produced, the post-broadcast era is marked by post-scarcity or even abundance. Physical limits on how much can be produced and distributed are less important; economic constraints upon the individual producer are reduced whilst the extension of productive and distributive power simultaneously results in far more content becoming available. For the price of a computer, internet connection and electricity, an individual can post their idea immediately, as often and at as much length as they want; they can email one friend or thousands of contacts across the world; they can host as much information as they want for comparatively small cost and upload as much video or as many photographs as they can produce onto sharing sites. To date no one has yet received an email message from Facebook, YouTube or their blog-hosting company telling them they have produced too much. This ability to continue producing and publishing cheaply and rapidly with few restrictions represents a challenge to broadcasting's scarcity model.

As Chris Anderson argues in *The Long Tail* (2006), the digital era also inaugurates an age of relative abundance, unleashing the pent-up demand of the broadcast era in allowing desires that move beyond the 'hits' to niche interests to find their expression. Now communities of obscure interests can form and any individual can easily research and collect information and material. Legally more is available: digital retailing means that music catalogues can be kept available, books can be digitally printed-on-demand, and online newspaper and radio archives are easily accessed and searched. Second-hand purchases are also easier, for example through Amazon's marketplace and eBay or online collectors' groups or pages. Online information and archives have proliferated and services such as Google Books make many texts fully or partially available. Out-of-copyright material is often collected and shared – such as UC Santa Barbara's huge online archive of previously hard-to-find early music cylinders – whilst meta-data – information about information – is also amplified, making it much easier to find out what was produced and whether it is accessible. Commercial catalogues such as Amazon and non-commercial services such as fan sites and Wikipedia all increase our knowledge. Access is also faster. Music is downloaded in seconds; books appear instantly on the Kindle; TV programmes and films take only a short while longer or can be streamed in real time; text, video and music are all instantly available online and even physical purchases have faster delivery options.

Then of course there is illegal availability. Peer-to-peer sharing technology makes most digital content – especially music, television and films – easily accessible. Music blogs use digital lockers to make out-of-print or bootleg material available and international music download stores of disputed legality offer album downloads for a fraction of the mainstream store's price. Copyrighted content is easily found on video sites and fan and collector sites and their forums can make more material available to those who want it. Even legal outlets can aid illegal activity. eBay sellers used to offer DVDs packed with hundreds of CDs. I've still only listened to a fraction of the *Northern Soul* DVD I bought.

As Anderson notes, this abundance is itself a problem. With the easy availability of so much content the emphasis shifts from 'pre-production filters', such as the editors who decided what was published, to 'post-production filters': the search engines, recommendations, lists, reviews that help us sift through the volume of material to find what we are looking for. Filtering moves from stopping something becoming available to sorting through what is available. Online, pre-production filters are less important: more can be produced, appealing to fewer people, containing content that would never have made it past commissioning editors, increasing the diversity of the informational ecology and almost always appealing to someone. Andrew Keen complains in *The Cult of the Amateur* (2007) that the internet has led to a deluge of poor-quality product but his argument misses two key points. First, content quality is not the exclusive monopoly of one form of production, as the banal and formulaic products of the mainstream media demonstrate. Second, whereas in a world of scarcity all broadcast product played an important cultural role, in the post-scarcity world unwanted product can easily be ignored, with targeted searching, tagging and book-marking enabling us to sift through irrelevant material to find what we want, producing personalised worlds of media experience.

This sifting and searching results in the rise of 'pull media'. The broadcast era model of aggressively 'pushing' and promoting products has had to cope with a changing ecology. The explosion of information production and content means that today our 'pulling' of media and self-creation or personalisation of our media worlds and experiences has become dominant. The scarcity model has been overturned by the easy, cheap, and seemingly limitless ability to produce and distribute content and if we add horizontal media to the sphere of available media it's obvious that the mainstream media are competing much more for our time and attention. Individual choices as to our informational and cultural engagement now become much more significant.

All of this also means that the broadcast era lecture is transformed into a world of conversations. Reception isn't the final moment in the circuit of communication: we have the ability and inclination to respond. Interactivity allows continuous feedback across a range of technologies, services, sites and platforms.

Conversations are created between friends, peers, or larger groups and broadcast product is re-immersed in this world of debate and feedback. As we've seen, the broadcast era had few opportunities for feedback. This was especially seen with complaints. Mass media could easily ignore limited criticism and the judgement of regulatory authorities took a long time to be decided.

Today the individual as producer and solo media industry reverses this unilaterality. Instead of receiving a finished, polished product from the broadcast factories, media outputs are provisional and unfinished, remaining open for discussion, commentary, argument, repudiation, revision, re-use and criticism. Some contemporary forms such as wikis exploit this. As Clay Shirky argues in *Here Comes Everybody* (2008), the best-known wiki, Wikipedia, is best understood as a 'process' rather than a product. Everything in it may be added-to, rewritten, vandalised, repaired, corrected, edited and improved in a permanent cycle without any final, accepted version being produced. A media studies that has traditionally studied finished products and their meaning will therefore need to change for an age in which media content is so fluid.

If the lecture is now a contested form, so too is the broadcast industry's expert voice. As commentators such as James Surowiecki, in his 2005 book *The Wisdom of Crowds*, point out, we have, for a long time, accepted the idea that individual experts exist and that their intellectual genius, inspiration, ideas, leadership and decision-making are the source of our progress. In contrast 'the mass' has historically been synonymous with random, irrational, thoughtless and stupid action and behaviour. Although media studies eventually adopted the idea of an 'active audience' implicitly able to decode and understand media messages this new admiration for the audience retained an implicit rejection of the concept of 'the mass' as too broad, too deterministic and as possessing too many negative connotations. In the digital era, however, the collective has a new position; one in which its collective action, conversations, thought and behaviour are seen as more intelligent than any individual or expert. In Chris Anderson's phrase, within 'the long tail' of the whole population there are more experts than any institution or broadcast company can gather and more collective, collaborative intelligence too. In the digital age the single, authoritative expert is easily challenged.

All of the above begins to describe some of the most important transformations in individual media experience and use in the post-broadcast age. In so many ways, it seems, this era is marked by an astonishing democratisation of productive and distributive power compared with the processes and avenues that marked the broadcast era. Whilst it would be easy to assume from this that digital media are purely beneficial, the question of changing power relationships in the new ecology is more complex as digital media simultaneously empower traditional companies, producers, broadcasters and authorities in new ways.

We can see that the most important change is in the level of control and surveillance enabled by this technology. Lawrence Lessig emphasises the role of the 'architecture' of cyberspace – its 'code' – as a constraint upon activity. From this perspective, those who decide and program this code have the power to dictate our interactions and the modes of experience offered. Governments and corporations, therefore, have the capacity to direct and control our behaviours through control at the level of hardware and software. One example of this is the digital rights management (DRM) protective software companies build into many devices and media forms such as commercial DVDs which dictates the uses they find acceptable or desirable. Another is the control over their own technological ecosystem and its use exerted by contemporary technological companies.

Beyond this overt control, however, is the possibility of exploiting the fact that digital connections and activities leave electronic traces. This data is useful, with information about product and service use and user activities becoming an important currency in the post-broadcast era. This information couldn't previously have been collected as audience and consumer activity remained beyond the knowledge of the media producers. Audiences and viewing figures could be estimated and the sales records of print, cinema and music industries were available but the age of mass media brought relative anonymity within the mass. Today's amplification of individual capacities comes at the price of greater individual visibility as our search, use and purchase activities are all accessible to companies and the authorities. The processes of control and surveillance and issues of privacy become central, therefore, to the digital ecology.

In other ways, however, control over media production, distribution and consumption has been lost. Whereas the broadcast industry was heavily regulated by governments, official supervisory and regulatory bodies, consumer groups and pressure groups and legal oversight, the majority of individual digital era production and distribution successfully avoids this oversight. In principle one's online activities are identifiable and one remains legally responsible for one's online behaviour and publications – hence the lawsuits brought against file-sharing individuals by the US music industry from 2003 and the prosecution and jailing of individuals in the UK in summer 2011 for posting incitements to riot. In practice, however, the sheer numbers of users involved means most illegal or offensive behaviour has no formal consequences. Whilst some of those who incited violent behaviour on Facebook during the summer 2011 riots were imprisoned, those who set up and contributed towards pro-violence groups such as 'Shoot the London rioters' and 'Using real bullets on rioters because their parents didn't use rubbers' escaped legal notice.

Information and content consumption also avoids legal controls. Hardcore pornography, banned material and violent imagery that could not be legally published are easily found and viewed with relative impunity. Users can be traced but this is most likely to happen only for extreme cases involving terrorism or paedophilia. Illegal information sharing is also easy, making a mockery of corporate or judicial attempts at control. In April 2007 the Motion Picture Association of America (MPAA) and the Advanced Access Content System Licensing Administrator, LCC (AACS LA) began issuing demand letters to websites publishing a 128-bit number which was one of the cryptographic keys for HD DVDs and Blu-ray discs under the US Digital Millennium Copyright

Act (DMCA) and the following month issued a cease-and-desist notice to Digg to prevent the posting of articles about the controversy. Their actions produced a cyber revolt in which the number was reproduced across the internet.

This mass protest has become known as 'the Streisand effect' after Barbra Streisand's failed attempt in 2003 to suppress photographs of her Malibu coastal house generated mass publicity and interest in the photographs. Another example was seen with the UK footballer Ryan Giggs' May 2011 court 'super injunction' that prevented newspapers reporting on his affair with television celebrity Imogen Thomas. Leaked online his name was spread over Facebook and Twitter until the super injunction had become meaningless. The paradox of the digital age is the replacement of the ignorant mass with both a potentially greater, connected, collective intelligence and a hyper-individualisation that simultaneously empowers and monitors every one of us.

This brief survey highlights some of the most significant shifts taking place today but the post-broadcast era is more complex than this simple list of elements might suggest. As I suggested earlier, the idea of 'post-broadcasting' requires careful definition. We aren't witnessing a simple passage from the first list of elements to the second but rather the emergence of a new competitive ecology in which elements of the broadcast model survive within and recast themselves for a different ecology. Broadcast print, cinema, radio and television obviously survive and even thrive in the new ecology, although this has required substantial changes at the level of form, as they either incorporate digital technologies into their production, distribution and consumption or become fully digital forms. It has also necessitated significant and ongoing transformations in their modes of distribution and retailing, their relationship with other media forms, and with changing cultures of use and consumption and new user expectations, demands and patterns. Equally many new digital modes of media production follow or include elements of the broadcast model: blogging and podcasting, for example, are built upon the broadcasting of content to a widespread potential audience.

The best way to understand the post-broadcast era, therefore, is as one in which the dominance of the broadcast model has ended and been replaced by a different ecology in which the number and capacity of the producers of content and information, the distributive channels and modes, and the practices of consumption have all become infinitely more complex. Broadcasting's dominance has been superseded by a different set of relationships between individuals, groups, companies, industries and institutions and a multi-layered competition at the level of form, models, distribution, content and use.

5   The me-dia revolution
The second reformation

So far I've covered key macro aspects of the digital revolution – the transformation of the material basis of our media, our media ecology and our cultural organisation of social information – but the micro level of personal media use and experience is also central to this revolution. I've already noted the amplified productive, distributive and consumer capacities of the individual in the digital age but this is only part of the story. What's more important is the broader phenomenon of the re-orientation of the entire media ecology *around* the individual.

By way of background, a few years ago I considered adding a lecture on the telephone onto a module on media history. The problem was, apart from Ronnell's *The Telephone Book* (1989) – which was hardly suitable for first year undergraduates – I couldn't find any books in media studies on the telephone. Although there was a growing literature on mobile phones, media studies seemed to have had little interest in the history and use of the telephone. I thought there were four probable reasons for the oversight.

First, it was a technology and media studies isn't that interested in technologies. Second, there was no public content to analyse: telephone conversations were private, unavailable and couldn't be analysed as texts unless they were recorded and typed up. Third, the telephone wasn't a mass medium. Admittedly nor was the electric telegraph and there were texts on that but they were mainly produced by McLuhanists, science journalists and historians of technology not media lecturers. Mainstream media studies was only interested in mass media: with mass-produced, publicly disseminated and available content. Hence it also ignored letters: despite their importance as a means of personal communication and their significance for history, literature and biography they were of no interest to media studies. Finally, the telephone wasn't important because it was a trivial medium. Whereas newspapers and radio contained important content, television contained culturally important programming and film, well … film was an *art form*, the telephone contained only personal chat, gossip, plans, trivia and catching up.

What I realised was that media studies has intentionally ignored an entire mode of media communication. As a product of the broadcast era, media studies has always been a reflection of the forms and processes of the broadcast model, concentrating upon the dominant forms of print, cinema, radio and television and on mass-produced, mass-distributed content mass-consumed by a large audience. What this misses is mediated interpersonal communication: the entire realm of peer-to-peer, horizontal, personal communications. Admittedly this has always been a limited sphere – letters, telegrams and telephone calls account for the majority of mediated interpersonal communications prior to the development of digital media – but it nevertheless remained an important one.

One of the most significant aspects of the rise of digital media has been the explosion of this realm of horizontal, peer-to-peer, mediated interpersonal communication. As that's a bit of a mouthful I suggest calling it 'me-dia'. I like this term because it emphasises the fact that *I* am at the centre of this communication. And that *I* isn't solipsistic. That *I* really means me, myself, we, my friends, my contacts, my network, and our messages and communication. It encompasses all media content and information produced and shared among ourselves outside of the traditional structures of public mass media broadcasting. If before media studies could ignore this me-dia, its ubiquity, scale and importance make that increasingly difficult. Today me-dia are at the centre of our personal media ecologies.

The history of digital media and its uses has only been partially written. Every new possibility of digital media requires us to discover a new history to situate it within. Some of these lineages will be technological, some economic or cultural, and others philosophical. New forms and phenomena force us to rethink and rewrite our histories, disrupting the simple, linear analyses of single forms that mark the broadcast era. It's in this spirit that I want to approach the possible history of me-dia. This history is multi-stranded, centring around oral networks, images and later interpersonal forms such as letters, telegrams and phone calls, but it also possibly includes another influence. There is one particular historical resonance I want to explore here: the claim that the rise of me-dia constitutes a 'second reformation'.

The roots of me-dia

As I've argued, broadcasting is not necessarily linked with any specific media, rather it is a cultural form, employing available technologies in a particular way. Although media studies typically traces its origins to the development of printing, one might find examples of the broadcast model in use before modern mass communications. If we look back to the medieval world, for example, we can see that the Catholic Church had a dominant position in the lives of the European population and that it can itself be thought of as a *medium* in two senses. First, it was a means of communication – an institutional form that distributed a single, uniform doctrine to the mass of the population, operating in a top-down, hierarchical fashion, employing the technologies at its disposal (monasteries, manuscripts and the local church) to mass-distribute its message. Here the Church operated as a broadcasting form, employing the typical hub-and-spoke structure that linked people to it rather than to each other. Second, the institution acted as a medium for the individual's relationship with the divine as the appointed mediators of God's message.

By the early 16th century the Catholic Church faced a new reformist movement protesting its doctrine, rituals, ecclesiastical structure and practices. Its success would lead to the 'Protestant Reformation' and the end of Catholic theocratic dominance of Europe. The symbolic moment of its origin was on 31 October 1517 when the German monk Martin Luther wrote to his bishop, Albert of Mainz, enclosing a copy of his 'Disputation of Martin Luther on the Power and Efficacy of Indulgences' which came to be known as the 'ninety-five theses'. Luther's points protested at the sale of 'indulgences' – remissions of punishment for one's forgiven sins in the after-life – which were a popular means of Church fundraising. In 1516–17 the Dominican monk and papal commissioner for indulgences Johann Tetzel had been sent to Germany to sell indulgences to raise money to rebuild St Paul's Basilica in Rome and his materialism and gross claims appalled Luther. Luther's theses spread and were widely published, propelling him to the forefront of the reformist movement.

The printing press played a key role in the Reformation, being used to print and distribute ideas, democratising information and allowing a broader public to form opinions and participate in previously restricted debates. As John Man says, Luther became 'a household name' as 'according to one estimate, a third of all books printed in Germany between 1518 and 1525 were by him'. Luther's objection to the sale of indulgences was motivated by the belief that only God could offer forgiveness. What lay behind that was his belief in the centrality of faith: of one's own, individual relationship with God. It was that relationship that determined one's fate after death rather than one's works, the purchase of indulgences or the decisions of the Church and its priesthood.

Of his three famous pamphlets from 1520, 'On the Freedom of a Christian' clearly expresses his position. He asserts here two contradictory claims: 'A Christian man is the most free lord of all, and subject to none, a Christian man is the most dutiful servant of all, and subject to everyone'. Explaining the first part Luther argues that 'As regards kingship, every Christian is by faith so exalted above all things that, in spiritual power, he is completely lord of all things'. Faith brings a spiritual power and 'this is the inestimable power and liberty of Christians'. In principle, therefore, the Christian individual is free: 'the inward man' is under no earthly authority, even if 'the outward man' is. We are, he concludes, equal before God on earth: we are 'fellow priests' with Christ.

Here we find Luther's famous assertion that 'we are all equally priests', a claim opposed to that 'injustice' that saw the word 'priests' taken from every man and given to the few. As his 1520 pamphlet 'Address to the Christian Nobility of the German Nation' argues, the office-holding priest is only a functionary, no different in kind from the laity. As John Witte, Jr observes (2005), Luther clericises the laity and laicises the clergy, establishing an equality before God that rejects the official priest's status, special privileges, immunities and exemptions.

So Luther's opposition to the sale of indulgences was motivated by a broader theological critique of the Church and its practices. At its core we can identify two defining elements of this critique. First, there was an opposition to an organisational form – to an institution and its privileged hierarchies and its top-down production and distribution of an approved and completed message. Second, there was a new defence of the individual: upon the interior and 'inward'; upon one's own faith and personal relationship with the divine. No priest or pope could absolve you and no man stood above you before God or between you and God. At the heart of Luther's critique, therefore, was an attack on both senses of the Church as a medium.

Luther's opposition was unthinkable for an organisation that insisted upon shackling the individual to its structures and doctrine. The claim that everyone was their *own* priest attacked the entire ecclesiastical structure and its control of the production, legitimation, distribution and even the modes of consumption of the highest information and knowledge. Against the one-to-many, hub-and-spoke, centralised structure of the Church, mediating the divine, Luther offered a flattened structure based upon the one-to-one communication of 'the inward' with God and the many-to-many networked structure of a community of equal priests. As Tarnas (1996) says, with this critique, 'the Church could no longer be reverenced as the sacred medium of Christian truth'. First and foremost the Reformation was, he argues, 'an assertion of the individual conscience against the established Church framework of belief, ritual and organizational structure': 'The individual believer's interior response to Christ's grace, not the elaborate machinery of the Vatican, constituted the true Christian experience.'

Of course, the Reformation didn't lead to the end of the Catholic Church. Instead it brought about a religious pluralism with the fragmentation of the Church into many churches. One could now choose one's priests and there was more room for one's personal interpretation of biblical meaning, but the organisational form itself survived, albeit in different ways, within a changed theological ecology. Nor did it lead to the freedom of the individual Luther had envisaged. From one perspective the following centuries saw a range of forces develop and spread this individualism. Cartesian philosophy's enshrinement of the cogito; the emerging scientific worldview that claimed one's experience as the foundation of empirical knowledge; Liberalism's valorisation of the natural rights of the individual; the Enlightenment's privileging of the individual's intellectual and moral reasoning; the nascent capitalist culture that spurred the industrial revolution; and the spread of print culture and a secular reading public all weakened the Church's position as a cultural organisation organising the minds and behaviour of the people.

Printing itself has been claimed as a powerful individualising force. Marshall McLuhan famously saw print as breaking man from the communal bonds of oral culture, leaving them as private owners of texts and private readers of the opinions of an individual author with their own personal viewpoints. But whilst print as a medium was individualising, its cultural deployment was not: the individual's mind may have been free but their voice was stifled. Though the print revolution transformed the mechanics of production and distribution and democratised the consumption of information, cultural factors still limited the number of producers. In the broadcast model very few could own and operate their own printing press or afford to hire one. Hence Luther's revolution in the position of the individual and their internal communication had no effect on their *external* individual communication. The direct interior communication with God wasn't joined by a new interpersonal communication with one's peers – with one's community of priests.

Although it didn't promote one message and had a secular, commercial basis, the emerging mass media system, therefore, had many cultural similarities with the Church's organisation. It adopted the same broadcast, top-down model, employing faster and more powerful technologies to distribute its content to the modern masses to become, like the Church before it, the central source of social knowledge about the world. It inhabited the same ecological position and ultimately instilled a similar fear of 'excommunication', albeit now of a social rather than a spiritual nature. The mass media, therefore, came to replace the Church as the dominant broadcast form.

Media studies has implicitly understood these connections between the mass media and the Church. There is a long Durkheimian tradition of analysis of 'media events' as social 'rituals', linking the communion of the religious experience to that connection offered by television. Dayan and Katz's *Media Events* (1992) offers the most famous example of this, in describing collective 'festive' television-watching as equivalent to a religious ceremony. Broadcast television, they suggest, functions as our church, offering a similar level of communion. McLuhan had a similar idea about the real, unifying aspect of contemporary electronic media, seeing an electrically extended humanity fusing into one in a 'global village'; a vision that, as many commentators have noted, owes much to his own Catholicism.

In replacing the Church as the dominant broadcast form the mass media increasingly replicated its effects. As print culture matured, the same system that had fostered the enquiring individual mind that lay behind the Reformation, the scientific revolution, modern philosophy, the Enlightenment and industrial invention began to have the opposite effect upon the individual. By the mid-19th century newspapers had become popular, cheap mass media with a large readership and were increasingly seen as a homogenising force impacting upon the individual and their interior life. The best critique of this reversal is found in Soren Kierkegaard. His 1846 book review, *Two Ages: A Literary Review* (since republished as *The Present Age* – see 1977) offered a reflection on his own age – a time that saw the increasing impact of industrial mass society upon Copenhagen and the rise of popular newspapers. Inspired as much by 'the Corsair Affair' – his ridicule in a satirical newspaper and in the streets by a delighted public – Kierkegaard responds with a remarkable polemic against the press and their readership.

This 'public' doesn't even exist, Kierkegaard says – it is a 'phantom'; 'a monstrous abstraction, an all-embracing something which is nothing, a mirage'; 'a monstrous nothing'. Only in an age in which the power of association is too weak 'to give life to concrete realities' can the press 'create that abstraction "the public", consisting of unreal individuals who never are and never can be united in an actual situation or organisation – and yet are held together as a whole'. This abstract public 'becomes everything', exerting such a pressure that we desire to join it, to become part of its phantasmatic power 'in comparison with which concrete realities seem poor'.

More and more individuals, Kierkegaard says, aspire to join this nothing, to *be* nothing, forming an 'indolent mass', a 'gallery' that is 'on the look out for distraction' and that 'abandons itself to the idea that everything that one does is done in order to give it (the public) something to gossip about'. Hence the concrete reality of the individual and their inwardness is abolished in the desire to join this media abstraction. 'The really terrible thing,' Kierkegaard concludes, 'is the thought of all the lives that are or easily may be wasted ... the many who are helpless, thoughtless and sensual, who live superior lazy lives and never receive any deeper impression of existence than this meaningless grin.'

Kierkegaard's critique of broadcast media is founded on a philosophy of communication valuing, above all, the subjective individual and their inwardness – understood as a mode of being and of communication, with oneself, with God and with others. Against the vulgar 'sensual' world of gossip, cheap pleasure and sensationalism he emphasises the value of the individual and the ethical and religious dimensions of their existence. What Kierkegaard raises against the press, therefore, is the Lutheran individual. He recognises in the mass media the same organisational forces that oppose the 'inward man' that Luther recognised in the Church. Print culture employed the same broadcast model to achieve the same dominance.

Similar fears of the mass media are found in contemporary Liberal and Conservative thought. By the mid-19th century demographic, social and economic changes had led to an urban society that Liberals increasingly saw as a threat to individuality. Hence Alexis de Tocqueville's warning in his two-volume work *Democracy in America* (1835/1840) against 'the tyranny of the majority' and John Stuart Mill's attack in *On Liberty* (1859) on the 'social tyranny' of 'public opinion' and the 'ape-like faculty of imitation' that erased individuality. By the century's end Conservative thinkers had picked up on the same theme, as seen in Friedrich Nietzsche's defence of the self-mastered individual against the 'herd' mentality he saw as defining the age and Gustave Le Bon's 1895 attack on the 'crowd', each member of which 'descends several rungs in the ladder of civilisation', becoming an unthinking barbarian. Simmel's 1903 analysis of the impact of 'the metropolis' on mental life similarly focused upon the threat to individuality of the city and their attempts to avoid 'being levelled, swallowed up in the social-technological mechanism'.

Mass society, public opinion, the crowds of modernity, the metropolis: all, therefore, impacted upon the individual and increasingly the mass media were seen as a central part of these powerful social forces. In the early 20th century, the apparent success of propaganda in WWI, the rise of mass-circulation newspapers, the popularity of cinema with women and children and the lower orders, the rise of radio and the development of the modern advertising and public relations industries all brought a renewed urgency to the question of the impact of mass media upon the individual.

By the 1930s the broadcast era, with its assembly-line production of cultural produce, was in full flower, assembling the combined forces of the 'culture industry' against the individual, under the precise guise, the Frankfurt School claimed, of expressing their individuality. A direct line can be drawn here from Theodor Adorno and Max Horkheimer's critique in *Dialectic of Enlightenment* (first published 1944) of the uniformity of broadcast content and its 'pseudo-individualisation'; through Marcuse's 1964 critique of industrially manufactured and manipulated false needs in *One Dimensional Man*, to Guy Debord's 1967 *Society of the Spectacle* with its critique of the alienation and separation of mass mediated popular culture and its unilateral pleasures. This unilaterality of broadcast media highlighted its refusal of all individual meaning and relations; an idea Jean Baudrillard would soon develop at length in his own radical Durkheimian, 'symbolic' critique of the 'semiotic'.

Not everyone has seen this sphere of broadcast mass media as producing homogeneity. Popular opinion often sees the realm of media-consumer society as a source of real individualisation, with one's personal choices and tastes taken as representing core aspects of oneself. There is here enough variety even in mass-produced and consumed content for a personalised selection and enough common currency for others to recognise one's choices. Media studies has developed a similar valorisation of individual behaviour and responses. The discipline has reacted strongly against the critical tradition, developing a consensus around the idea of 'the active audience', rejecting ideas of the over-arching power of the media and studying and promoting audience and fan behaviours.

Except what media studies identified in its analysis of the broadcast-era fan use, and what they ultimately valorised in the 'active audience', is more the desire and demand for a mode of personal expression and individual meaning and response than its reality. Desperate to assert this activity they over-valued responses even though, structurally, the broadcast era offered few significant opportunities for individual expression and communication. Productive, reproductive and distributive capacities remained limited and the audience's 'activity' was of comparatively little social, cultural, economic or political significance. With the rise of digital interactivity, audience studies thought its claims of an active audience were fully realised, though, as I'll argue later, this new sphere of activity revolved around 'the user': a figure that, unlike the audience, was designed as an active manipulator and creator of their own experiences and outputs. The mass consumption of broadcast product by audiences now gave way to the rise of me-dia and the explosion of the user's own personal sphere.

The age of me-dia

By 'me-dia' I mean the realm of mediated interpersonal communication in a digital age. It encompasses our mobile texts, videos and photos; emails, PMs, IMs; our contribution to chat rooms, forums and mailing lists; our social networking and micro-blogging activity (posting, sharing, messaging, writing on walls, updating statuses, tweeting, linking); our contribution to social-sharing sites (YouTube,

Flickr), fan sites and collaborative sites (wikis); our amateur porn videos and sexts; our blogs; our media productions (music, images, software), plus all our comments, lists, recommendations, and responses. That's a standard list of everyday digital media but what's interesting is how little attention these forms have received and also how much me-dia there is. Compared with the limited sphere of letters, telegrams, fixed-line telephony and niches such as amateur and citizens-band radio available in the broadcast era, this constitutes an explosion of horizontal, mediated interpersonal digital communication.

This also constitutes, I believe, a 'second reformation'. Like the Lutheran assault upon the Church, what we're living through is a seismic shift in which one hitherto dominant organisational model of the production, distribution and consumption of information and arrangement of social connections gives way to a more complex ecology which allows the creation of one-to-one and one-to-many links and networks centred around the individual and their relationships, operating outside, alongside or with the older structures. Just as the ideal of 'every man his own priest' represented a fundamental assault upon the system, institutions, rules, hierarchies, interests, roles, economic and social privileges and the epistemological framework of an entire age, so too the idea of every man with his own video camera, cam phone and personal newsfeed represents an assault upon a system, a set of institutions, rules, hierarchies, interests, roles, privileges and the social epistemology and reality that dominated for the last century.

There are, of course, many differences between the two eras, not least the secularity of contemporary changes, the underlying philosophical impetus, the economic and cultural context and the technologies that facilitate this shift. Nevertheless just as the printing press aided a reformist movement whose success would transform the informational structures of the medieval era, so the rise of digital media facilitated a similar democratising movement placing the individual similarly at the centre that has, in a short time, transformed our own informational structures. Except this second reformation goes further in empowering not just the individual's interior relationships but also their external peer-to-peer relationships. The limits of the print revolution are overcome in the digital revolution with the democratisation of productive and distributive capacities that give anyone the power to create and communicate.

As in the first Reformation, this isn't leading to the final end of the mass media broadcasting organisational form but, once again, to a fracturing and fragmentation: a proliferation of new 'churches' – of places, institutions and platforms of expression (Facebook, YouTube, Twitter, etc.) – and a funnelling of individual expression, interiority and personal relationships into new ecological forms. Following Kierkegaard's critique of 'talkativeness' one might query how 'interior' this interiority is when every aspect of the individual mind is made visible and broadcast over one's own network, but the new centrality of that individual mind is irrefutable. Seen in the light of the Reformation, me-dia appear now not as secondary technologies but part of a broader historical trajectory, with a meaning and significance that places them at the core of the new media ecology. In particular their importance lies in six areas.

First, as we have seen, me-dia is important as it represents a transformation of the dominant organisational modes of communication that defined recent western history. Previously these were the most marginalised modes of communication: rarely taken seriously, not being seen as having any greater social significance and with limits on their functioning that prevented their expansion. In a heliocentric mediaverse ruled by the central sun of the broadcast industries around which we all orbited as receivers of its light, this is our anti-Copernican revolution. Now the mediaverse is brought to earth to revolve around us as the centre of our own experiences and information. And where once the powerful, celestial forms of broadcast media governed our lives, now it is the humbler forms and modes of communication that assume that role. The mangled grammar of quickly thumbed texts, the photos of a night out, the video of the children in the park, the lover's sexts, the PMs and IMs and updates and 'likes' and retweets, the comments and the changing profile pictures – all these represent the most important forms today.

Second, therefore, me-dia are important because of their emphasis upon the individual. Their personal focus and meaning gives them a real intensity for us. As our own expression, *me-dia are more important to us than anything the mainstream media can provide*. However much I enjoy their programming I am just more interested in my own personal ecology of contacts and messages: a 'like' on my status is more important than *Avatar* (2009); a text from a friend is more important than whatever's on television; a link shared with me is more important than anything the advertising industry can show me. Today we orientate ourselves around me-dia and its relationships rather than around mass media.

For most of our students the contents of their phone are far more important than the contents of *The Times*, BBC Radio, or BBC 2's *Newsnight*. We might think this is their failure but it isn't so simple. Me-dia *are* more important in being about us and our relationships. Their real-time, always-on pull that creates the need to continually check them for messages, definitively eclipses the world of impersonal mass-produced, appointment mass media. Though we may hold on to a lingering belief that television, newspapers and cinema must really be more important, as shared social forms, all our behaviour contradicts this. For each of us our personal, personalised ecology dominates. Where once mass media knew we would come to them now they have to chase us across whatever platform or application we favour today. Hence even mass media are integrated within our me-dia, as part of our personalised ecology, secondary for the most part to our own messaging and reorganised around our own desires, temporality and needs.

The third reason me-dia are important is for their promotion of the social bond; a claim that appears odd as they seemingly create a solipsistic, anti-social world where the importance of media is determined only by one's embrace of it. Whereas the 'social' in 'social networking' derives from one's individual 'social life', the broadcast era held onto a different conception of 'the social' as the abstract body – the public, the population, the citizenry, the masses – that the media unified, incarnated and informed. Their role was to create the connective tissue that linked and educated the public and made democratic participation possible. Seen from this perspective anything that broke this social bond seems to represent a mode of withdrawal, disinvestment and de-politicisation.

The reason why this isn't the case lies in the original meanings of the term 'social': the Latin 'socius' meant 'companion or associate'; 'socialis' meant to be 'united with or living with others', whilst by the 16th century the term 'social' had also come to mean 'characterised by friendliness or geniality'. Social networking, therefore, offers a return to *this* 'social' – to an associative, congenial realm that was eclipsed by mass society and mass media and ignored by broadcast media studies. Me-dia represent the recovery and amplification of this mode of sociality, incarnating it through our own individual web of micro relationships, associations and interests. Instead of a deficient mode detracting from understanding and participation, it represents the potential expansion of these.

This is because the world of me-dia is always a shared one: me-dia is always *we-dia*. The self is the centre of the network but it is not its end or limit. The reversal of the older organisational structure doesn't lead to the end of communication but only new modes of organisation. As the Reformation demonstrated, the Lutheran critique freed the individual for new modes of organisation beyond the Catholic Church, although contemporary technology failed to empower the exterior relationships as much as it had the interior individual. Contemporary me-dia are different in amplifying the connective and communicative power of each individual and their relationship; hence it reduces rather than increases solipsism as we share our experiences and interests.

Hence we have a far more social future than many expected. In his *Being Digital* (1995) Nicholas Negroponte suggested a coming electronic newspaper – 'call it The Daily Me' – which would deliver personalised content to each of us. Still caught in broadcast-era assumptions he wasn't radical enough: what happened was the rise of me-casting, or my-casting – a mode of social networking in which we become self-journalists, investigating our own lives, collecting information about ourselves and our opinions, responding to each other and the world and broadcasting this to our own subscribed readers. Whilst broadcasting piped the world to us, in post-broadcasting the world pours back.

Using the same model of decentralised, distributed networks that underlie the internet, our me-dia allow any node to connect with any other. Hence they are more social than the one-way pipes of mass media, creating more connective tissue and allowing continuous responses to and conversations about the world. As Evgeny Morozov demonstrates in *The Net Delusion* (2011), such connections don't necessarily lead to more democracy, but they do represent the empowerment of a mode of sociality that had shrunk under mass forces and an increased avenue of engagement with the world.

Liberal commentators have made much of this sociality of digital media. Clay Shirky's *Here Comes Everybody* (2008) discusses how new digital tools lead to 'a remarkable increase in our ability to share, to cooperate with one another, and to take collective action, all outside the framework of traditional institutions and organizations'. By changing the conditions of assembly, contribution and management, he says, 'these tools have radically altered the old limits on the size, sophistication and scope of unsupervised effort'. The result is the end of barriers to collective action, creating an age of 'ridiculously easy group formation'. The same ideas reappear in Charles Leadbetter's *We-Think* (2008) which describes an emerging, collaborative and creative 'mass innovation economy'. His concept of 'we-think' is important in emphasising the connected aspects of our lives though his contrast of this term with the individualistic Cartesian 'I-think' is overdrawn. It is still *our node* which is the centre of our networks. Me-dia always move beyond us, but they begin *from us*, as we take our own opinions, interests, relationships and responses as their starting point.

The fourth reason me-dia are important is for the time they occupy: containing our most personal messages and content and occupying the centre of our own ecology, they absorb our attention. Indeed, if we add up the time we spend checking and following our me-dia messages and content then it's likely that broadcast media come a poor second. Broadcast media only ever consumed part of our time: we only liked a selection of its products and had to wait for each new episode, film or album. Me-dia, in contrast function in real time, always pulling our attention back: there is always the chance of another message or update since we last looked, or of our own comment or response. Me-dia even win over media. Few today sit through a film or TV programme without a laptop or phone to check. Me-dia multitasking ensures our attention is always on our own productions.

Whereas broadcast media required only reception, me-dia require a more active response. Digital me-dia require continual management, taking up time and attention. Devices need to be continually synched, backed-up and updated; apps need updating; emails, messages and texts need deleting or moving; music players invite the creation of playlists; downloads and files need housekeeping and we have to remember to take out the digital trash. Me-dia, therefore, aren't simply liberating, they *involve* the individual: they commit us to an ongoing digital labour. Add to this the time we spend fixing them, checking what's wrong, finding out why things haven't sent, carrying out security scans, rebooting, reconnecting, cleaning touch-screens, finding where we put devices, checking batteries, finding chargers and keeping equipment working, and we find a Sisyphean labour that didn't exist in the broadcast era.

Me-dia are also always with us, increasing the time we spend with them. Whereas few broadcast media were mobile or truly personal, today we carry immense communicational capacities with us. The mobile smartphone has become the paradigmatic me-dia technology: it is this device, perhaps more than any other, than we privilege today with our *concern*, as our most intensely personal device. Arguably today the mobile phone has become more important than any of the older broadcast media forms and any media studies that doesn't begin from the mobile has nothing to say to its students.

The fifth reason for their significance is the volume of communication they produce. It's worth thinking for a moment about how much content we produce, individually and collectively, all day. To give an example from a single Web 2.0

company, by 2010 YouTube were reporting 'more video is uploaded to YouTube in 60 days than the three major US networks created in 60 years' – the equivalent of putting over 150,000 new 'full-length movies in theatres every week'. By October 2013, 100 hours of video were being uploaded to YouTube a minute, with 1 billion unique users watching 6 billion hours of video a month. On Facebook alone 500 years' worth of videos are watched every day, they claim. This is an astonishing scale and although YouTube is increasingly hosting professional content, the majority of its video remains user-generated. Add to this all the content we produce on other social platforms and the numbers rapidly eclipse the output of the largest professional broadcast companies.

The final reason for the importance of me-dia is their value for companies and institutions. This value is first of all economic. The digital transformation of the media ecology has led to a concomitant transformation of the economic ecology. Whilst some companies have seen their business models threatened, others have risen on the back of new digital consumer technologies and their uses. Social networking, for example, has risen from nothing to become a significant media force. By September 2011, Facebook had over 800 million users, with Facebook Inc. having an ad-based revenue of US$4.27bn. By April 2012 it had reached over 900 million and the following month its IPO valued the company at US$104bn. Though its share price dropped it recovered through 2013 and most see it as having a highly profitable future. Founded in 1998, Google is another relatively new media force built upon its individual users and developing a portfolio of services and interests that have led to rapidly rising profits. Its revenues increased, for example, from US$29.321bn in 2011 to US$50.2bn in 2012.

The success of the mobile phone has made it one of the most important contemporary sectors. By 2011 there were 5.2 billion mobile phones globally, with 3.7 billion unique users, constituting 54 per cent of the global population. There were already more mobile phones than cars (1 billion), television sets (1.6 billion) and radio receivers (3.9 billion). The total value of the global mobile phone industry in 2011 was estimated at US$1.18 trillion, twice the value of the global pay-tv industry (US$53bn) and four times the value of the global film industry (US$29.9bn in 2009). The technology companies producing the hardware, software and consumer electronics have also been phenomenally successful. On the back of 73.5 million iPhones sold in total by the end of 2010 and over 25 million iPads sold by June 2011, in August 2011 Apple toppled Exxon as the most profitable public company in the world with a market valuation of US$338bn. By August 2013, when it again swapped places with Exxon, its valuation stood at US$414.89bn. Though Apple's fortunes are volatile they remain one of the most significant global commercial interests and brands.

The value of me-dia is also informational. The explosion of me-dia doesn't just empower the individual, it also empowers companies and institutions. As I argued above, the emphasis by thinkers such as Shirky and Leadbetter upon the collective networks produced by digital media obscures the centrality of the individual and this is affirmed by the new ability of digital technologies to individualise users, to track their activities and to directly tailor communications to them or hold them responsible for their behaviour.

In the broadcast era the point-of-sale marked the limits of the producer's knowledge: newspaper publishers, cinema studios and record labels knew only how many units or tickets had been sold and where, whilst radio and television employed sophisticated market research companies and technology to effectively guess at their audiences. Digital media, however, go beyond the point-of-sale, bringing companies into the home and giving them precise information and records. They not only empower the individual, they empower others against the individual, allowing a monitoring, penetration and control of individual behaviour. From hardware design, to the structure of code, to the ability to trace, track, store and sort electronic records of use and purchase, the individual pays for their electronic information with themselves: with a fine-grained, personally provided, real-time, informational archive that feeds back into the business model, service or functioning of its recipient. Often this is presented as necessary and beneficial, aiding customer service.

Examples of this individualisation are easy to find. Every time I visit Amazon its cookies construct a page of 'recommendations' based upon its catalogue of my purchases. This same record is used to improve its recommendation model, with all activity helping create pages of what people viewed or bought. Every click adds more information and hence more value to their service, being aggregated to improve its model and profits. Google similarly uses the user. Every search is individually recorded and retained and user activity – the production of pages and linking between pages – is used as the basis for its PageRank search algorithm. In December 2009 Google also introduced a personalised search, ranking sites according to what one's previous history suggested one 'liked'. Its popular Gmail service similarly scans emails to produce personalised adverts directly linked to keyword content, in much the same way that Facebook adverts on the side of your profile mirror your status updates.

A personal record is created, therefore, for every company whose services we use: our ISPs retain information about our data traffic; our search engines store internet protocol (IP) address based records; web pages recognise us and online retailers have a full account of every view and purchase. One might request the deletion of information, or assume this automatically happens after a period of time, but the individual has no way of checking that this happens. As Viktor Meyer-Schonberger argues in *Delete* (2009), the economics of information have changed with the decreasing cost of storage: today it's less economical to delete information, hence our individual records are more likely to be retained. The default setting has changed from forgetting to remembering.

These records also act, therefore, as a mode of surveillance with legal implications: one's own records can be used against you. In September 2003 12-year-old Brianna LaHara of New York became the first person targeted by the Recording Industry Association of America (RIAA) after illegally downloading children's rhymes and pop records, having been identified through her IP address. In January 2010, Paul Chambers, frustrated at delays at Robin Hood Airport in the UK, joked on Twitter 'You've got a week and a bit to get your shit together, otherwise I'm blowing the airport sky.' Though he'd later be acquitted, his home was raided, he lost his job and he was initially convicted of sending a menacing message. The same micro-surveillance was seen after the Summer 2011 UK riots. In August two men were sentenced to four years in jail after posting Facebook messages encouraging riots in their home towns, even though no riots ensued. In each case me-dia implicated their producer.

Knowledge about 'you' is, therefore, important. On 5 July 1993 the *New Yorker* published a Peter Steiner cartoon of a dog at a computer saying to another, 'On the internet nobody knows you're a dog'. The cartoon became a famous commentary on the anonymity of online life though today it's no longer necessarily true. Today your ISP and most of the companies you've used not only know you're a dog, they know your preferred brand of dog food, where you like going walkies, which dogs you've sniffed, where, when and for how long and whether they sniffed you back.

As Eli Pariser comments in *The Filter Bubble* (2011), 'The race to know as much as possible about you has become the central battle of the era for internet giants like Google, Facebook, Apple and Microsoft.' Their free services, he says, are 'extremely effective and voracious extraction engines into which we pour the most intimate details of our lives'. There is 'a massive new market for information about what you do online' that is used to offer more precisely targeted adverts or services but their effect, however, is to limit our experiences. Their internet filters:

> are prediction engines, constantly creating and refining a theory of who you are and what you'll do and want next. Together, these engines create a unique universe of information for each of us – what I've come to call a filter bubble – which fundamentally alters the way we encounter ideas and information.

We each exist, therefore, in our own personalised 'bubbles', created from our online choices using filters that are invisible to us that select and tailor information just for us.

The result is an 'informational determinism' in which the past determines what we see next, trapping us 'in a static, ever-narrowing version of yourself – an endless you-loop' that has social and political implications. The more we consume this 'invisible autopropaganda' of our own filtered feeds that indoctrinates us with our own ideas, the less we're exposed to different ideas or broader issues and the less able we are to understand and participate in the complexities of the world. Whilst social media create a lot of 'bonding capital', he says, they create less 'bridging capital' – that kind that creates our sense of the public, 'the space where we address the problems'.

Pariser overstates this. Websites and social media exist in a broader informational ecology which doesn't lack bridging capital and even online network theorists point out how our 'weak ties' do indeed take us beyond our limited sphere to introduce new possibilities and experiences. But in other ways it's possible that he doesn't go far enough. A clue as to why is provided when I log into my Windows Live email, which continually begs me to connect with others, to include all other aspects of my messaging and networking within *its* sphere. What Google, Microsoft, Facebook and Apple aspire to is a new model of integration and advertising that goes beyond the simple model employed by broadcast-era media.

The film industry, for example, achieved a 'vertical integration' of finance, production, distribution and exhibition but it could not extend it to the consumer who remained outside their sphere of control. Equally, as the Northcliffe revolution showed, modern advertising was built upon the delivery of specific mass demographics to advertising companies, though the only element of the individual that was recognised was readership. Today the aim is to go further, to integrate every individual within a new digital model that wants to achieve a 'lock-in' not simply, as we assume, to products and services, but the lock-in of the individuals themselves – of their time, attention, activity, networks, friendships, relationships, interests, searches, messages, sharing, productions, experiences, opinions, views, clicks, ideas and their entire online mode of being and its expression. The aim is to integrate and own the individual in ways that the broadcast era could never dream of. Similarly, personalised advertising moves beyond the broad demographic to infiltrate every aspect of the individual. Mass capture of readers and viewers by mass communications gives way to the capture of the fine-grained, fully rounded and highly personal life of each individual: the new unit of value in the digital ecology.

Facebook is typical here in its aim of capturing all of an individual's life. It was based upon the aggregation of a range of previously unconnected tools such as IM, email, photos, shared linking, shared interests, group activities, etc., to enclose the individual within one service. The once-derided 'walled gardens' of providers such as AOL now return, bolstered by the network effects of every person joining adding more value and increasing the efficiency of the service. In September 2011, Facebook announced the culmination of its 'Open Graph' initiative, encouraging an ecosystem of developers to create media applications that – unlike the spam-like applications to date – would be tightly woven into the system. The result would be a new 'frictionless' sharing – the near-automatic updating for others of your activities and media consumption habits, combined with a new profile that Chris Cox, the Facebook VP of Product, called a 'foundational narrative timeline'.

Now one will automatically write one's own autobiography in real time, self-curating your own activity so that you will be able to refer back to it in years to come and creating a deeper picture of one's life. As *Wired* explains:

> Cox says that instead of that brief conversation you used to get by scanning the previous version of the profile, visiting the profile will be the equivalent of going to a bar to have a long overdue five-hour soul exchange. 'It's that conversation where you play the jukebox till it runs out, the bar closes, and you walk about and say, "Man, that was really deep,"' he says.

The result for Facebook is a quantum leap in the information they record, store and employ to attract advertisers, allowing a new age of nano-targeting or depth-targeting in which every aspect of the individual becomes even more important.

What's interesting here is that Luther's hopes for his own reformist movement were multiple. His assault on the organisational structure and communicational hierarchy of the Catholic Church was intended to emphasise instead the individual and in particular their dual relationships – their internal relationship with a God that would know them intimately, in their full interiority; and their horizontal relationships with each other, with that equal community of priests that was their peers. In the 'second reformation', that latter realm of horizontal communication has finally been amplified and empowered, allowing the one to communicate with another or with the many at will, but it has also amplified and empowered a new internal relationship.

This is a relationship in which it is not God but one's ISP, one's search engine, web mail provider, social networking site, favourite bookstore or pornography-site-of-choice, that now knows that intimate interior 'you'. As Luther was clear – and as Kierkegaard's personal theology emphasised – to be an 'inward' man before God was not a liberation but a mode of surveillance and responsibility that, unless we fled into inauthentic modes of communication, resulted in an anxiety and anguish. The age of me-dia avoids such anxiety by offering us the pleasures of our self and friends and interests, but somewhere underneath this remains a moment of understanding and a fear of what precisely this omnipotent, inward vision of ourselves might mean for us. Today it is Google that stands above us knowing our every guilty thought.

6 Mass media studies
The rise of duck science

So far we've traced the material, ecological, cultural and personal transformation of the analogue broadcast era with the rise of the digital post-broadcast era. If my argument is that media studies as a discipline needs to change to reflect these developments then we first of all need to know what media studies is and why its current form is inadequate. That's the aim of this and the following chapters. Here I consider the history of media studies and its contemporary success; in Chapter 7 I explore why the discipline failed to deal adequately with the study of media; and in Chapter 8 I explain why the discipline needs to be upgraded to deal with the digital era. To begin then, we first need to ask what media studies actually is.

Academic disciplines are not natural objects, but cultural products reflecting the concerns of their age. They emerge out of the shifting intellectual currents and problematics and political structures of their times. Their formation is the product of a range of decisions separating the new field off from cognate areas, helping to establish its coherence and identity and place in Higher Education and its own avenues of publication. Then there is the question of what the discipline should contain: what is outside its parameters; what perspectives, authors, texts, knowledge and approaches are permitted and what methods of knowledge acquisition and legitimation are acceptable. As Michel Foucault helps us understand, the concept of a 'discipline' involves a *disciplining* – a disciplining not only of the subject matter but also of its practitioners. Those who enter the discipline are also disciplined – by undergraduate and postgraduate study; by lecturing in the subject; and by their research and accumulation of publications that establishes them as an approved expert and 'academic' who understands the academic system and its expectations.

Media studies is no different. It is an academic discipline that, through the 20th century, struggling with its multi-disciplinary roots, had to establish its own place within the academy, create its own departments, found its own journals and formulate itself as a distinct entity with its own chosen traditions of research, methods, perspectives and knowledge. What then is media studies and where did it come from?

The origins of media studies

What we now call 'media studies' or 'media and communication studies', was once simply known as 'communication studies', a term that remains popular in the USA. There the study of mass media and its impact was placed within a broader field of 'communication', encompassing all human symbolic production and relationships. As well as the study of mass communications, therefore, this included the realm of intrapersonal and interpersonal communication, language and speech communication and group communication (including small group communication, organisational communication and public or rhetorical communication). US communication studies, therefore, is a truly interdisciplinary field, drawing upon the classics, rhetoric, linguistics, psychology, anthropology, philosophy and cybernetics, as well as the socio-cultural dimension.

This communication studies traces its roots to ancient Greece and Rome, where the study of rhetoric was considered central, and to the European middle ages and Renaissance, where the study of grammar, rhetoric and logic comprised the 'trivium' which formed the basis of the educational system. It began to coalesce as an academic discipline from the late 19th to early 20th century, developing out of schools of rhetoric and speech as well as journalism, social psychology and sociology, uniting their disparate elements within a new, overarching concern with human 'communication'.

Perhaps the key influence on its contemporary emergence was the US pragmatist tradition which developed from the 1870s through the work of Charles Sanders Pierce, William James and Chauncey Wright. By the late 19th century thinkers such as Pierce, George Herbert Mead and Charles Horton Cooley were all emphasising the construction of meaning in shared situations and interactions and the fundamental role of communication – of languages and symbols – in the formation of human relations and in society itself. Thus they approached mass communication as only a small part of a more fundamental human process that was, as Dewey said, 'the foundation and source of all activities and relations that are distinctive of internal union of human beings with one another'. Cooley summed up this view in his 1909 book *Social Organization*:

> By Communication is here meant the mechanism through which human relations exist and develop – all the symbols of the mind, together with the means of conveying them through space and preserving them in time. It includes the expression of the face, attitude and gesture, the tones of the voice, words, writing, printing, railways, telegraphs, telephones, and whatever else may be the latest achievement in the conquest of space and time. All these taken together, in the intricacy of their actual combination, make up an organic whole corresponding to the organic whole of human thought; and everything in the way of mental growth has an external existence therein.

The pragmatist tradition, therefore, was interested in a broader philosophical conception of communication. Though their ideas, and the 'symbolic interactionism' they would give rise to, would become an essential element of US 'communication theory', and eventually of mass-communication research, they didn't yet take mass communication as their specific focus.

Hence although Czitrom, in his survey of the origins of modern media studies, *Media and the American Mind* (1982), identifies the sociologists Cooley and Robert E. Park, along with the philosopher John Dewey, as developing in the 1890s 'the first comprehensive reckoning with modern communication in toto as a force in the social process', this needs clarification. More precisely, we can say that late 19th-century developments in US mass communication (especially in the print industry), as well as in point-to-point communication (telegraphy and telephony) were influential upon the philosophical and sociological traditions, helping push the concept of communication to the fore as an important contemporary force and facilitating the eventual emergence within the academy of communication as an interdisciplinary field of research. It wasn't until the 1920s, however, that we see a clear focus upon mass communications.

There are two reasons why we have to wait until then for this research to emerge. The first is the changed media environment: the first two decades of the 20th century saw the development of mass-circulation newspapers; the take-off of cinema and recorded music as international commercial industries; the development and success of radio broadcasting, and the emergence of the modern advertising and public relations industries. This was the era when broadcasting came of age. The second reason was the fear these developments caused. This was a different world from the 1890s and there was a growing unease about the power of these broadcast forms and industries over the individual mind and their potential ability to sway the opinions and behaviour of large groups in a 'mass society'. There were repeated worries, throughout this period, of the moral impact of cinema; of the success of newspaper propaganda in WWI; of the possibility of radical agitation of the working classes using broadcast media and concern at the successes of the nascent advertising industry. With mass media becoming a pervasive force, the question of their influence and persuasive effects became an urgent one.

Although it emerged out of broader debates around communication and would retain a close relationship with it throughout the century, media studies, therefore, begins here – in the focus upon mass communication and the fore-grounding of the question of their effects upon their audience. Modern media studies research begins in the 1920s as a product and reflection of broadcast mass media, originating at that moment when a fear *of the masses* – of the irrational, animalistic, violent 'mob' or 'crowd' and the real possibility of its political revolt – gives way to, or is supplemented by, a fear *for the masses*: a concern for this physically separate but connected national 'public' and their potential manipulation and control through these seemingly omnipotent media technologies.

The 1920s saw the publication of a series of texts dealing with these issues. Walter Lippmann's *Public Opinion* was inherently pessimistic about the individual's cognitive ability to make sense of the complex world around them; hence their resort to 'stereotypes' and other simplifications, a fact he saw as having important implications for democracy itself. People acted increasingly not on their own knowledge, he argued, but in response to 'pseudo-environments' produced by mass media. As they were unable to learn enough about the world from media to make informed decisions there was a need for 'the manufacture of consent': for those in a position to know to formulate the framework for public understanding and unity. Lippmann's ideas were influential upon the founder of public relations, Edward Bernays, who similarly argued, in *Crystallizing Public Opinion* (1923) and *Propaganda* (1928) that democracy required 'the conscious and intelligent manipulation of the organised habits and opinions of the masses'. A 'smoothly functioning society' required active, media-created mind control.

Other, more progressive, authors coming out of the pragmatist tradition such as Park and Dewey saw more positive uses for the media. Robert Park's *The Immigrant Press and its Control* (1922) emphasised the role played by foreign language newspapers in helping assimilate immigrants to the USA, whilst John Dewey's *The Public and Its Problems* (1927) was a response to Lippmann's *The Phantom Public* (1925), rejecting his pessimism and retaining a faith in the ability of people to make sense of their world and construct shared understandings. Though he recognised the power of mass media entertainment, he believed that improved communication and education would enable the public to resist propaganda and distraction to become informed enough for democratic participation. Harold Lasswell's conclusions in his *Propaganda Technique in the World War* (1927) also differed from Lippmann and Bernay's. Though he chronicled the power and success of propaganda mechanisms and strategies used by governments against their own populations he acknowledged their success was not automatic. A range of factors such as the state of mind of the audience and economic, social and political conditions all influenced the receptivity of the public.

This idea of social conditions determining reception would be developed by the 'Chicago School' at the University of Chicago, who also pioneered the turn away from speculative analyses towards more academic, empirical media research. Media such as cinema and radio were causing concern and the Payne Fund supported a series of twelve research studies from 1929–32, including qualitative research by the Chicago School's Herbert Blumer, to investigate the effects of movies upon children. Published in *Movies and Conduct* (1933) and *Movies, Delinquency and Crime* (1933), Blumer's conclusion highlighted cinema's 'emotional possession' of the child, getting 'such a strong grip on him that even his effort to rid himself of it by reasoning with himself may prove of little avail'. As a symbolic interactionist, however, he followed the pragmatist, Chicago School's belief that identity and meaning were formed through interaction and personally rejected simple ideas of media effects, emphasising the complex contextual nature of reception and of the audience's relationship with the content.

As Czitrom reports, however, although most of the Payne studies similarly pointed to individual differences in reception and the difficulty of singling movies out from other cultural influences, 'still, through popularisation and selective quotation in books and articles, the Payne Fund studies provided ammunition for vigorous attacks on movies and the movie industry' and the findings were overshadowed by political wrangling over their interpretation.

In addition to public opinion, propaganda and social-psychological research, Czitrom also points to the rise of market research through the 1920s–30s, with independent surveying organisations emerging to service publishers and broadcasters and becoming widely used in industry, the media and politics. Hence, although the term 'mass media' didn't gain widespread use until the 1940s, by the late 1930s there was already a recognition by social scientists of newspapers, cinema and radio as a social force and 'as a subject matter around which a new research field ought to be organized'. Communications research as 'a unified area of study' was attractive as empirical research into audiences attracted support and funding from media companies, private foundations and government institutions. In each case a more precise understanding of media effects and how to create them would lead to economic or social and political benefits.

No one did more to establish this new, industry-facing empirical 'behavioural' field of academic mass-communications research than the sociologist Paul F. Lazarsfeld. Settling in America around 1935, by 1937 Lazarsfeld had become Director of the 'Office of Radio Research' at Newark University, a Rockefeller-funded study of the effects of mass media continued at Columbia University's 'Bureau of Applied Social Research' after his move there in 1939. As part of what would become known as the 'Columbia School' of mass communications research, Lazarsfeld oversaw scores of studies (mostly on the effects of radio), pioneering the systematic use of quantitative research methods to produce a behavioural science of communication that would become the most influential model of the 1940s. He would summarise these radio studies in a special edited issue of the *Journal of Applied Psychology* in 1939 and his *Radio and the Printed Page* (1940). In 1939 he participated in the Rockefeller Foundation's 'communication seminar' and contributed towards their 1940 'Research in Mass Communication' memorandum that did so much to define and consolidate the nascent field of communications research.

John Marshall's letter of invitation to the twelve selected seminar participants was one of the first uses of the term 'mass communications' and, under Lasswell's influence, the memorandum famously defined the subject of communication according to four categories: who, says what, to whom, and with what effect, with the last question being seen as the most crucial. The memo listed the five major methods to be used to study this question – the poll, the panel, the intensive interview, community studies and content analysis – and called for the national organisation of this research. As later research has shown, however, the aim of the Rockefeller-organised seminar and its memorandum was not only to define the new field of mass-communications research but also to promote this field to the government, as potentially helping it to create official propaganda to mould the public mind to secure consent at a time of growing international crisis.

With the outbreak of WWII this aim was realised, with communications research being pressed into government service. The government's need for information about attitudes and influence brought many communications scholars to Washington where they worked as consultants or employees of government agencies. One effect of this wartime work was to establish the dominance of the term 'communication' by the late 1940s above earlier concepts of 'propaganda' and 'public opinion research', though this was primarily accomplished for ideological reasons as 'communications research' was more politically neutral and it obscured the scholar's pro-governmental role. From now on 'propaganda' was only what the enemy did. A second result of this wartime work was the development and enshrinement of empirical research. The quantitative communication research of Lasswell's Library of Congress-based 'Experimental Division for the Study of Wartime Communications', of Sam Stouffer's US Army 'Survey Division', and of Carl Hovland's US Army 'Experimental Section', for example, proved highly influential on post-war social science and communication studies.

But perhaps the most important effect of this war work was in laying the basis for the institutionalisation of communication studies. Lazarsfeld, Lasswell, Stouffer and Hovland, as well as Kurt Lewin and Wilbur Schramm, all worked for the government and their interaction led them to conceive of an inter-disciplinary field of communication studies. As Jefferson Pooley points out, in Park and Pooley's *The History of Media and Communications Research: Contested Memories* (2008), wartime work on 'psychological warfare' created social networks and an intellectual framework that would create and shape the post-war communication field.

In 1943 Schramm returned to the University of Iowa as the Director of the School of Journalism where he tried to implement his vision for the field of communication, establishing a PhD. programme and a centre of mass commu-nication research. He had more success at the University of Illinois where, after his move there in 1947, he established the Institute for Communications Research. He also produced some of the first textbooks in the field, such as the edited collections *Communications in Modern Society* (1948), *Mass Communications* (1949) and *The Process and Effects of Mass Communication* (1953). By the time he moved to Stanford in 1955 the field of communication was becoming well-established, spread by his own graduates, and by 1960 more than a dozen US universities boasted mass communication research centres and doctoral programmes.

One reason for this success was official support. The propaganda expertise that had served the government in WWII was in even greater demand during the Cold War and CIA, military and State Department funds poured into communications research centres. In the 1940s Lazarsfeld had defined his own work as 'administrative research', in contrast to the 'critical research' developed by Adorno. He had meant it positively: scholarly work in communication could serve the needs of the industry and of policy whilst developing its own field. By the time of the Cold War, however, this service had taken on an ideological role. Communications research bought its place in the university by its official service.

With its broadcast focus and emphasis upon the empirical study of audience behaviour, mass-communication studies paid only limited attention to other contemporary developments. Lazarsfeld was a participant at the inaugural Macy conference, an interdisciplinary meeting that introduced new scientific approaches such as 'cybernetics' to a broader audience, including social scientists. Although Norbert Wiener's *Cybernetics* (1948) was a best-seller, establishing a prescient vision of human–machine relationships that would inspire 'human computer interaction' (HCI) research, communication studies was more interested in Claude Shannon's 1948 paper 'A Mathematical Theory of Communication' whose publication in book form the following year was arranged by Schramm for the University of Illinois Press. Shannon's 'scientific' model of communication, of an information source, transmitter, channel, receiver and destination, served as a perfect framework for understanding the linear, teleological, unilateral processes of broadcast media. In his 1948 essay, 'The Structure and Function of Communication in Society', Lasswell immediately altered his description of communication to incorporate a fifth element – 'who, says what, *in which channel*, to whom, with what effect', and the following decades saw numerous attempts to improve and develop Shannon's model of communication.

Another approach that found only a limited purchase within communication studies was the critical theory of the 'Frankfurt School'. Relocated from Frankfurt to the USA due to the Nazis (being based at Columbia University from 1938–41 and then Los Angeles until 1949), their 'Institute .of Social Research' synthesised a range of philosophies within a Marxist critique of early mid-20th century broadcast media and consumer culture. Initially Adorno attempted to integrate his own approach within the 'administrative' framework of Lazarsfeld's Columbia Bureau of Applied Social Research, but his systematic cultural critique had little place in such an industry-facing empirical project. Instead the Frankfurt School placed that industry into question. Their 1947 classic *Dialectic of Enlightenment* launched a systematic assault upon 'the culture industry' – an evisceration of the processes of capitalist mass media mass-production; of the standardisation and uniformity of content, and of the incorporation and moulding of the individual that left them with only the 'pseudo-individualisation' of schematised and rationalised consumption. Predictably, such ideas had little effect on the dominant pro-government and industry, empirical communications research.

Disciplining media

As Pooley argues, despite its institutional gains, post-war US communications research suffered from 'a legitimacy deficit'. It was in order to solve this problem, he says, that a 'body of disciplinary history' was drafted in the early 1960s. One source for this was the work of Lazarsfeld and Katz. Lazarsfeld, Berelson and Gaudet's study of voter choice in the 1940 presidential election in Erie County, Ohio, published in 1944 as *The People's Choice*, was one of the most important wartime studies, proving influential in the emergence of the 'two-step flow' model of communication. Its key contribution, the discovery of the mediatory role of key opinion-leaders on individual opinions, inspired a series of post-war studies including Lazarsfeld and Katz's research in Decatur, Illinois, published as *Personal Influence* (1955).

In this book's opening sections Lazarsfeld and Katz traced a brief history of communication research, creating a straw-man of an earlier generation of scholars under the influence of European mass-society theory, who implicitly advocated what would become known as a 'hypodermic needle' or 'magic-bullet' theory of media influence. Their debunking of this idea of an all-powerful media in favour of the role of interpersonal relationships is usually interpreted as presenting a history of communication studies as a movement from naïve, speculative, direct-effects theory to a sophisticated, empirical 'limited-effects' theory.

This 'history' remains widely repeated in the literature through to the present but it is, however, misleading on three levels. First, there was never a real 'hypodermic needle' theory in the pre-war era: debates of the 1920s were less about media power than about the question of democracy and the public, and statements about both the power of mass media and of individual responses can be found in a range of authors and even within the same text. Second, as Glander points out, Lazarsfeld's *Personal Influence* was actually based upon a strong faith in the power of media propaganda, with the discovery of the role of interpersonal relationships helping suggest a way to improve the success of these mass media. Thirdly, this idea of 'limited effects' can itself be questioned.

Recent work by Glander and Simpson has shown how the US government's agenda funded and dominated wartime and post-war communications research. In a Cold War played out amongst the nations and battlefields of the southern hemisphere, communications experts had an important propaganda role to play. As Glander concludes, the US military and CIA 'represented the most significant source of funding for social science research during the post-war period'. Hence, Pooley argues, 'even while "limited effects"-style conclusions were published, in *Personal Influence*, for example, research outfits like Lazarsfeld and Katz's Bureau were under federal contract to design effective propaganda campaigns overseas'. In reality, therefore, media studies didn't believe in the 'limited effects' it was apparently arguing for.

The other sources of communications history were the work of Bernard Berelson and Wilbur Schramm. Berelson had begun analysing the origins and state of communication research in the 1954 'Conference on Research in Public Communication' and in 1959 he published 'The State of Communication Research' in *Public Opinion Quarterly*. He identified here 'four major approaches to communications research' – Lasswell's 'political approach'; Lazarsfeld's 'social survey approach'; Lewin's 'small-groups approach', and Hovland's 'experimental approach' – though his overall feeling was one of the exhaustion of these traditions: 'the innovators have left or are leaving the field, and no ideas of comparable scope and generating power are emerging'. It was Wilbur Schramm, however, who did most to promote communication studies' status and write its history. From 1963 he began to create an origin-myth for the field, taking Berelson's 'four major approaches' and enshrining Lasswell, Lazarsfeld, Lewin and Hovland now as the four 'founding fathers' of communication. Over a series of articles and publications throughout his career Schramm formulated and codified an acceptable history of the field.

Berelson's pessimism was misplaced. The 1960s saw the take-off not only of television but also of new perspectives on media. Their power over the individual was re-asserted by 'medium theory' which emerged in the 1950s. Associated with Harold Innis, Eric Havelock and Marshall McLuhan and known as 'the Toronto School', its authors were united by a belief in the historical significance of the form of the media – the technology itself – rather than its production, content or reception. Innis's *Empire and Communications* (1950) and *The Bias of Communication* (1951) traced a remarkable macro-history of the impact of technologies and the effects of their relative 'time-bias' or 'space-bias', whilst Havelock's *Preface to Plato* (1963) offered an analysis of the implications of the shift from 'oral' to 'literate' culture in Ancient Greece. McLuhan's ideas, however, garnered most attention, first in his discussion of the effects of the development of print culture, *The Gutenberg Galaxy* (1962) and then in his best-selling analysis of the new electronic world, *Understanding Media* (1964, see 1994).

McLuhan's public popularity, media-status and highly personal style of writing and thinking didn't endear him to the academy and was far removed from the empirical functionalist communications research that dominated US universities. Ironically, although much of later media studies was explicitly framed as a rejection of his ideas, his role in the discipline's creation was significant, especially in the UK.

The year 1959 was a key date in UK communication studies, when Joseph Trenaman left the BBC's Further Education Unit to become the first holder of the Granada Research Fellowship in Television at Leeds University. Trenaman and McQuail's research on the role of television in the 1959 election was published in 1961 as *Television and the Political Image*. In 1960 James D. Halloran put on the first course on the sociology of mass media at Leicester University as part of his extra-mural adult education evening classes. His notes for this led to his 1963 publication, *Control or Consent: A Study of the Promise of Mass Communication*. With fears at the time that television was contributing towards youth aggression and violence Halloran was appointed secretary to the Home Office's newly created 'Television Research Committee' in 1963. Persuading the committee that it was important to establish a broader study of media beyond the issue of delinquency he helped establish the first 'Centre for Mass Communication Research' at Leicester University in 1966. Though the committee also funded media research at other universities, David Morrison rightly described Halloran in his 2007 obituary as 'without doubt, the founding father of British mass communications research'.

The UK study of communication, however, owed more to the new poly-technics. Created by Labour following the 1963 Robbins report, the polytechnics aimed to expand HE provision, focusing upon vocational, professional and industry-based qualifications. They began by offering practical courses in media before expanding to include a theoretical dimension. David Cardiff was one of the pioneers, joining Regent Street Polytechnic (now Westminster University) in 1969 to help set up a diploma in communication studies that became, in 1975, an honours degree in media studies that was, as Paddy Scannell recalls (2006), 'the first, and for some years the only, undergraduate course on this topic in Britain'.

As Scannell remembers, Regent Street offered print, radio and television journalism, taught by professional staff, 'while a small number of people like myself provided the obligatory "liberal studies" bit of added value'. With no institutional history of communication research or established intellectual corpus, lecturers were forced to create their own syllabus and McLuhan's *Understanding Media* became one of the most widely taught books whilst also helping to name the subject area. As Scannell argues: 'I was very much under the influence of Marshall McLuhan at this time. He was the only person I'd read that seemed to have anything interesting, relevant and new to say about "the media" as we were learning to call them, thanks to him'. Thanks to McLuhan, therefore, the UK field began to coalesce around the concept of 'media' rather than the broader US model of 'communication'.

With its remit of expanding HE provision and appeal to non-traditional students, polytechnic teaching was often more politicised, aiming to supplement practical training with a critical awareness. Hence UK media teaching was receptive to developments in Marxist and Western Marxist theory, foregrounding the media's ideological functioning. By the 1970s a political economy approach was common; the Frankfurt School's work was available in translation; Althusser's Structuralist critique was widely read and the Glasgow University Media Group were developing their critique of mainstream news coverage that would be published as *Bad News* (1976) and *More Bad News* (1980).

US communication studies had remained dominated by empirical research until the late 1970s when the European interest in political economy and critical theory began to make its influence felt. Todd Gitlin's powerful 1978 *Theory and Society* article, 'Media Sociology: The Dominant Paradigm', represented an early attempt to turn this critical tradition upon functionalist communications research. Here Gitlin offered an extended assault upon the dominance of behavioural empiricism, systematically attacking the methodology and findings of Lazarsfeld's *Personal Influence* as well as the intellectual origins of the paradigm and its administrative and marketing orientation and corporate service. His opening question – why at a time of increasingly concentrated media ownership, centralised operations, national reach and ever more pervasive presence, 'has the sociological study of media been dominated by the theme of the relative powerlessness of the broadcasters' – implicated the entire field as providing an ideological justification for 'the existing system of mass media ownership, control and purpose' (see Gitlin, 1978).

By 1983 the European critical tradition had inspired a special issue of the US *Journal of Communication*, edited by George Gerbner. Entitled 'Ferment in the Field', it included a collection of responses by US scholars to the critical tradition. Whilst only partially successful in challenging the empirical dominance of the field it did represent a movement towards a socio-cultural dimension that would grow in importance in US communication and media departments, especially after the rise of the Culturalist perspective.

The development of Culturalism was perhaps the most important development in 1970s UK media studies. With its roots in earlier cultural debates by Matthew Arnold and F. R. Leavis, it came to the fore in the post-war period with the publication of Richard Hoggart's *Uses of Literacy* (1957) and Raymond Williams' *Culture and Society* (1958) and *The Long Revolution* (1961). Their reflections on historical changes in culture led them to promote the analysis of contemporary media and cultural forms. In 1964 Hoggart established the Centre for Contemporary Cultural Studies at Birmingham University with Stuart Hall as his deputy until 1968, then as director until 1979. The prolific publications of the centre's scholars and postgraduates led to the identification of a 'Birmingham School' of analysis.

Hall's most important contributions to media were his much-revised 1973 paper 'Encoding/Decoding' and his 1975 book (edited with Tony Jefferson) *Resistance Through Rituals*. In fusing a semiological analysis of media messages with a Gramscian vision of the hegemonic struggle for their meaning his emphasis upon reception and reading as the key moment in the communication process in his 1973 paper provided the theoretical justification for the rise of modern audience studies. But Hall also contributed towards methodology. Barthes' 1957 book *Mythologies* was translated in 1972 and the use of semiology by Hall, and later by Dick Hebdige in his *Subculture: The Meaning of Style* (1979), did much to popularise it as a method for visual 'texts'. *Resistance Through Rituals* was also important. Its emphasis upon research into sub-cultural groups and their behaviour inspired much later work on media audiences, shifting attention towards specific groups such as fans, whilst its use of ethnographic research paved the way for this to become one of the dominant empirical methods in media.

Hall's 'Encoding/Decoding' essay inspired David Morley's classic studies of the magazine news programme *Nationwide* in *Everyday Television: The Nationwide Study* (with Charlotte Brunsdon, 1978) and *The Nationwide Audience* (1980) and also influenced the rise of 'television studies'. Raymond Williams' rejection of McLuhanism in his 1974 *Television: Technology and Cultural Form* had opened the path for a culturalist analysis of television and in 1978 John Hartley and John Fiske published *Reading Television*, which followed Hall in emphasising reception and in applying semiological reading strategies to television content. Fiske's later work, *Television Culture* (1987), *Reading the Popular* (1989) and *Understanding Popular Culture* (1989) took the 'active audience' approach further in its explicit celebration of all audience behaviour as positive and progressive.

As James Curran argues in his 2013 lecture 'Defending Media Studies', this UK model of media studies has been 'globally influential'. In contrast to the 'effects-oriented communication studies' and journalism studies that dominated in America, the UK drew from a humanities tradition that 'gave extensive attention to the study of popular culture'. In doing so it reinvented communication studies as a culturally focused, critical media studies that 'helped to reshape the field internationally'.

Another post-war development was the emergence of 'film studies'. The study of film had been central to pre-war mass communication research, though its focus there was on the effects of the medium. Kracauer's *From Caligari to Hitler* (1947) helped change this. Funded by the Museum of Modern Art as well as the Rockefeller Foundation, it argued that German inter-war films revealed the psychological dispositions in Germany that aided Hitler's rise to power. Later studies adopted a similar cultural critique of content and texts such as Wolfenstein and Leites' *Movies: A Psychological Study* (1950) continued the application of psychological or psychoanalytic approaches to film. Film studies took off in universities through the 1960s–70s (often developing out of literary studies). The new discipline viewed cinema as standing apart from other media and as requiring its own critical language and methodology, drawing upon a range of perspectives including literary theory, linguistics, psychoanalysis, semiology and gender studies. Through the 1970s especially it developed a strongly critical emphasis, as epitomised by the influential journal *Screen* which combined Althusserian Marxist and psychoanalytic theory to consider how audiences were ideologically positioned as subjects by film.

Gradually, however, the interpretation of film as an *art-form* came to dominate and film studies came to focus upon cinema as an elite form and aesthetic category: one constructed by an artist, whose content was received and interpreted by a privileged, aesthetically trained critic. Even when, with the take-off of media studies, film found itself taught alongside media it retained its separate identity and approaches and its elitist perspective. Whilst it increasingly embraced selected, high-quality drama television programmes in the 1990s and began to merge with television studies by the new millennium, its aesthetic bias meant it retained a hostility to popular television and forms.

The 1970s also saw the rise of a feminist approach to media. 'Second-wave' authors such as Germaine Greer, in *The Female Eunuch* (1970), had attacked literary culture and now modern media became a target for criticism. The ideological analyses of the *Screen* school were most-famously articulated in Laura Mulvey's feminist critique of the 'male gaze', whilst the Birmingham School's approach also encouraged a feminist literature, as seen in Angela McRobbie's studies of girls' comics and women's magazines, which fused a semiological analysis of content with ethnographic studies of domestic reception. Other seminal feminist media analyses included Dorothy Hobson's *Crossroads* (1982), Janice Radway's *Reading the Romance* (1984), and Ien Ang's *Watching Dallas* (1985), all of which investigated women's reception of popular culture. Their 'active audience' emphasis on the viewer's power to create their own meaning, however, existed in tension with a critique of patriarchal ideology that implied a stronger structuring influence.

From the mid-1980s successive waves of French theory began to have an impact upon sociology and cultural studies, prompting new debates around the ideas of 'postmodernism' and 'post-structuralism'. With UK media studies dominated by empirical audience research and television and film content analysis, these theories had only a limited impact – mostly within courses and areas closer to cultural studies. The take-up of thinkers was selective. Semiology was already established and Foucault's theory of surveillance and power proved popular but other authors such as Deleuze and Guattari, Lyotard, Derrida and Virilio were largely overlooked by mainstream textbooks and publications. Jean Baudrillard – arguably the most important media philosopher of the late 20th century – received a particularly poor response. Though widely taught, his work was usually overly simplified or wilfully misrepresented in the textbooks.

One of the few critical perspectives to gain traction in media studies through the 1990s was 'public sphere' theory, inspired by the translation in 1989 of Jurgen Habermas's 1962 book *The Structural Transformation of the Public Sphere*. His book explores the 18th-century 'bourgeois public sphere' and presents a communicative ideal of a space of free, rational debate, whilst tracing its decline and commercial and spectacular replacement through in 20th-century mass media. Though his interpretation of this sphere has been criticised, Habermas's ideas stimulated a considerable body of work within Marxist and Liberal media theory on the question of the democratic potential of media, including the issue of whether new media technologies are returning us to that ideal communicative space.

By the 1990s the topic of 'new media' began to attract attention. Developments in digital technology and media were included in debates around post-industrialism, the information society and postmodernism but the take-off of the World Wide Web from around 1995 propelled them to the centre of attention. Cultural studies was at the forefront of debates under the banner of 'cyberculture', though media studies was less interested in these developments. One reason for this was its disinterest in technology. Even the revival of McLuhanism from the mid-1990s (owing much to the success of computing and the take-off of the internet) had little influence upon a mainstream discipline that still guarded itself against any 'technological determinism'.

The result, as I've argued, was media and communication studies was late coming to digital media and when it did address them it ignored the existing scholarship, focusing its attention upon its own existing areas of concern. Hence the 'active audience' theory was seen as confirmed by the rise of inter-activity and user-generated content, despite the contradictions of applying broadcast-era concepts to an entirely different technology and tradition. Most of media studies, however, continued without any recognition of the need to address the digital. With its focus still upon reception and content, the changing form of media didn't seem relevant to many. Film and television studies especially carried on analysing their chosen texts with barely a thought for the underlying material revolution.

As well as the analysis of content, audience studies remained dominant in this era though in a different form than that which Hall had envisaged in his 'Encoding/Decoding' essay. Influenced by Gramsci, he'd imagined the emphasis would fall on oppositional strategies, anticipating media studies exploring and promoting the counter-hegemonic political activities of audiences. Instead, by the 1990s audience research had developed into a largely empirical data-gathering exercise, based upon ethnographic or quantitative analyses of selected audiences or fans, with a description of activity and valorisation of all behaviour and responses replacing the political critique Hall had hoped for. Not that this mattered. Together this content analysis and audience research formed the centre of the discipline.

Duck science takes off

Discussing communication studies' creation of its own historical narrative, Jefferson Pooley (2008) points out that what was most important was not its accuracy but its existence: 'Communication research, as a field, badly needs the glue of tradition, however invented.' With its vocational taint and 'messy and recently formed institutional trappings', Pooley says, 'the field has from the beginning endured a deficit in legitimacy'. Ferdinand Tonnies' 1930 comment as President of the German Sociological Association, questioning the need for a separate communication studies, highlighted the problem: 'Why would we need press research within sociology?', he asked, ' We don't need a chicken or a duck science within biology.'

The question of disciplinary legitimacy is complex, but we can see it involves both internal and external factors. Internal factors include the subject's institutional position, its academic activities, its acceptance within the politics of the academy, and its self-identity. External factors include its broader social status and value: its acceptance by government, by employers, by the public and by prospective students and their parents.

It is easy to see that in the post-war period first of all 'communication studies' and then later particular variants of this, usually called 'media studies' or 'media and communication studies', successfully achieved institutional success, possessing their own departments, chairs and degree-awarding powers, and developing and engaging in academic activities, such as awarding undergraduate and postgraduate degrees, hiring qualified staff, organising conferences, developing peer-reviewed specialist journals, publishing original research and creating professional and disciplinary bodies to oversee the teaching and research interests of the subject area. The contemporary expansion of student interest has ensured media and communication studies is economically important to universities, bringing with it some degree of acceptance within university hierarchies. This leaves the question of self-identity: the subject area's framing of its own corpus of accepted theories, knowledge and methods and its agreement upon these.

US 'communication studies' has found this hardest. As a truly interdisciplinary subject it has found it difficult to agree upon a central focus of ideas and approaches. In his influential 1999 paper 'Communication as a Field', Robert Craig summarised these accumulated problems, arguing that 'communication studies as an identifiable field of study does not exist yet', due to the 'lack of consensus' between different traditions which have had almost no contact with each other. Nevertheless, he argued, the subject had the potential to become a field if dialogue could be achieved through the seven key traditions he identified:

the rhetorical, semiotic, phenomenological, cybernetic, social-psychological, socio-cultural and critical perspectives. Though his classification-schema has been reproduced in most communication textbooks, later commentators such as Wolfgang Donsbach (in his 2006 paper 'The Identity of Communication Research', in the *Journal of Communication*) remain more sceptical, denying even a 'common object' of research among communication scholars and emphasising the continued divisions within this 'field', as well as the problems of its institutional position.

In contrast, media studies has been more successful at achieving an intellectual coherence, developing, by the end of the 20th century, a distinct disciplinary identity. This was primarily due to five factors: its more specific focus; its convergence around a core of concerns, approaches and methods; its academic expansion; the growth of the textbook market; and the homogenisation of its academic courses around its central core.

Whereas communication studies suffers from its broad coverage, media studies has benefitted from its more limited scope. It emerged out of its parent subject in the 1920s with the focus upon *mass communication* and this has given it a clearer identity and disciplinary basis. In fact media studies is even more focused than this suggests, with a clear disciplinary emphasis on just four broadcast media: newspapers, radio, television and cinema. Media studies is really *mass media studies*, developing as the historical product and reflection of the broadcast era.

Similarly whereas communication studies is highly interdisciplinary, media studies follows a broadly *socio-cultural perspective*. From sociology it takes social theory and speculation about the media, a concern with the social impact of media forms and the use of quantitative and qualitative methodologies to study these effects. From cultural studies it takes a range of theoretical perspectives, a concern with cultural texts and their content and representation, and a range of cultural methods of analysis. This combination of social and cultural emphases, straddling the social sciences and humanities, has enabled media studies to achieve a focused intellectual coherence whilst allowing it to build links with and operate alongside related fields such as film, journalism, creative industries, and politics, etc.

In addition, by the 1990s media studies was increasingly converging upon a central core of concerns, approaches and methods, privileging especially *content* and *reception*. As the product and reflection of the broadcast era, media studies has primarily been interested in what has been produced and how it has been received. As we've seen, the question of reception developed first and has formed a strong central spine to the discipline, from early 1920s debates about the effects of media and behaviourist investigations of media influence to contemporary culturalist studies of the 'active audience'. The question of content emerged later, with the post-war success of film and cultural studies, treating products as texts whose construction and meanings are significant. Hence media studies has devoted much time to developing theories of representation, methods and modes of analysis of media content and to studying adverts, photographs, newspapers, television and film.

With its focus upon broadcasting, media studies was also interested in issues surrounding media production, media organisations and power, and media policy and regulation. Though an important element of the discipline they have nevertheless remained secondary to debates around reception and content. This is due in part to the difficulties of studying production and decision-making. Problems of access and empirical research meant theoretical perspectives came to dominate, drawn largely from sociology, political economy, politics and cultural studies. Though foregrounded in student textbooks, the question of production attracted fewer active researchers than media audiences and content.

Instead of being treated as historically arising perspectives linked to specific forms, and as theoretical positions with inbuilt biases and limitations, reception and audience studies and textual content analysis attained a meta-theoretical disciplinary status, as seemingly natural and inevitable models of media analysis. PhD students were trained in these models; lecturers reaffirmed their validity; conferences repeated their assumptions; and journals based on their research proliferated. The marketisation of the university system through the 1990s and government and private funding also favoured 'useful' empirical research over more radical theoretical approaches and critical responses, helping to cement the central core of the discipline (and, once again, its ideological service of industry and power). In this way media studies disciplined and reproduced itself around its central concerns, marginalising alternative approaches and ideas.

These core areas of reception and content were based on a set of assumptions that naturalised their approaches. These included a linear, teleological model of media transmission from information source to receiver; a privileging of the receiver as the most important element in the communication process (either in their interpretation of content or their response to and use of it); a humanistic model of the individual as free to choose their response; an anti-deterministic, even a-social, conception of this individual, denying or downplaying any technological, social, cultural or economic influence; an empirical consensus privileging specific, favoured methodologies as providing the primary means of knowledge production and legitimation; and an administrative perspective that saw these empirical studies as having more value and practical use than other analytical and critical approaches.

The phenomenal growth of media studies also played an important part in its coalescence as a discipline in the 1990s. Although its external reputation was poor, with government, media and public criticism of 'Mickey Mouse degrees', prospective students and their parents were far more accepting. In the UK its success began in the 1980s with a GCSE in media studies being introduced in 1986 and an A level in 1988. By 2004 the AS level was being taught in 1271 centres with 30,876 candidates and the A2 was taught in 1211 centres with a further 22,961 candidates. This A Level growth fed into degree level with the number of students enrolling in media degrees taking-off in the 1990s and rising through the next decade. According to HESA statistics, for example, the number of undergraduates studying media rose from 13,600 in 2006 to 27,705 by the 2009/10 session.

The number of university courses expanded to take advantage of new market and older universities increasingly offered media courses. The Higher Education Policy Institute's 2012 report 'Institutional Diversity in UK Higher Education' found that the number of institutions offering media studies had tripled in the last decade, rising from 37 in 1996 to 111 in 2009. Today UCAS lists a bewildering range of courses across dozens of universities and HE colleges, encompassing media studies or media allied with communication studies, film studies, cultural studies, production or practice, the creative industries, television studies, journalism studies or screen studies. By force of numbers, therefore, media had become an accepted discipline by the early 21st century.

One effect of this success was the expansion of academic publication to serve this market. The 1990s massification of higher education and economic pressures upon academic publishing led to a demand for and publisher's emphasis upon student-friendly textbooks. Importantly they weren't only read by students. The expansion of media job opportunities led many to move into the subject from related areas such as English and the languages and lacking any background in the discipline they too turned to the textbooks for their modules. Hence textbooks played a major part in disciplining media studies, confirming, in their agreement, its accepted positions and scope.

If, years later, Julian Assange could refer to the broadcast behemoths as 'MSM' or 'mainstream media', we can identify here the development of a 'mainstream media studies'. This was a mass media studies focusing upon newspapers, cinema, radio and television. Its textbooks offered a standardised survey of content (of texts and their interpretation; representation; semiology; genre and narrative; ideology and discourse, etc.); of reception (of audiences, fans and their activities); of advertising and modes of content (such as news and journalism and contemporary phenomena such as celebrity culture and reality-TV); and of issues around production (such as media organisations, globalisation, regulation, policy and power). With their broadcast orientation and emphasis upon audience reception and textual content, these textbooks reflected and reinforced the homogenisation of the discipline.

Media courses aided this convergence with their own similar standardisation. Although we think of media studies as interdisciplinary, examples of this are rarer than we think and what characterises most media courses and modules is their similarity. Contemporary media courses centre upon a theoretical, socio-cultural academic core, often taught alongside related areas such as practice, film studies, cultural studies, journalism and journalism studies. This central theoretical spine centres upon core modules, usually offering general and more advanced introductions to media studies (often based on key textbooks), overviews of media theory (broadly defined and often focused upon audiences and content), and modules on media representation (studying 'texts' and the accepted theories of their analysis and interpretation).

Beyond this, most degrees include a range of module choices covering issues such as television; cinema; audiences and fan-culture; gender and sexuality; journalism and news; advertising; celebrity culture and aspects of popular media culture. Modules on media organisations, media policy, globalisation and political aspects of media may be added; media history is relatively rare; whilst related cultural studies options, such as on music or consumer society, are common. Modules on digital media are rarer and are predominantly options placed at higher levels rather than forming the basis of the entire degree.

Ironically developments in digital technology were one of the most important reasons for the success of media studies with students. As we've seen, by the mid-1990s the take-off of the internet, the rise of personal technologies such as the mobile phone and changes to mainstream media meant that every aspect of the media lives of students was revolutionised and their personal relationships and activities were re-orientated around digital technologies and experiences. This, more than anything else, drove them to the subject. Whereas an earlier generation turned to philosophy, sociology or politics to understand their world, now media studies took over that role: students turned to media as a fundamental means to understand their own lives, society and reality.

The problem was the media studies that they met when they arrived at university. At exactly that point when media studies was coalescing as a discipline in the 1990s, focused upon the study of broadcast mass media and its content and reception, that entire ecology was already shifting. As a result media studies became a discipline that no longer reflected the contemporary media reality.

7 The emperor's old clothes
Why media studies didn't work

From the vantage point of a new century and a new digital ecology we're now able to look back at the broadcast era of mass communication and the discipline it gave rise to. Media studies, as we've seen, developed out of the broader field of communication studies, coming to the fore in the 1920s with the rise of mass media as the specific study of mass communications. It developed out of a concern with its impact upon mass society and public opinion, in an era in which newspapers achieved mass circulations, becoming commercial enterprises central to political and public life and culture; in which cinema was consolidating its position as a major, international commercial entertainment industry; in which the success of radio broadcasting swept America and Europe; and in which early experiments with television were beginning to develop the medium that would dominate broadcasting in the second half of the 20th century.

'Media studies', therefore, was a historical product and response to a specific model of media production, distribution and consumption – that of broadcasting. This set the limits and concerns of the new discipline: it would study post-Gutenbergian mass communication, focusing upon a small number of dominant 20th-century forms and industries. Establishing roots in academic institutions it developed over the following decades a disciplinary core, categorising its approach to media along broadly agreed lines and standardising its own theories, assumptions, methodologies and issues. As I've argued, by the late 20th century the issues of audience reception and the interpretation of content had become the central spine of the discipline. The interest in audiences and effects dates back to the beginning of the discipline, running through to contemporary Culturalist and empirical research, whilst the post-war period saw the development and adoption of a range of approaches concerned with the analysis of visual media. A significant proportion of the discipline has become devoted, therefore, to the study of audiences and the analysis of broadcast products.

All of this was perfectly understandable. In an era in which only a minority had creative, productive, editorial, publishing and distributive power, then the most common experience of media was of the product and its consumption. The media academic was in no better position than the consumer and they too concentrated upon the experience of mass media: upon the product, its meaning and our use of it. Hence media studies was also a *reflection* of the broadcast era: its classification of its subject, emphases, topics, themes and approaches were all designed to study mass media production, content and consumption. Its classification appeared natural and inevitable, perfectly matching the system it aimed to study.

Clearly a change in this system requires a change in the discipline that studies it: a digital, post-broadcast era requires a digital, post-broadcast media studies. But the problems of media studies go deeper than this. With hindsight we can see that broadcast era media studies suffered from several limitations that affected its ability to really understand either the history of media or its own era. Following Marshall McLuhan's acerbic comment, 'I wouldn't have seen it if I hadn't believed it', I want to argue that broadcast era media studies saw only what it had already chosen to believe.

Media before media studies

'Media studies', as we've seen, emerged as the study of mass communications. Though it nominally claimed a lineage back to Gutenberg's invention of mechanical-type printing, in reality its overwhelming emphasis was upon the major contemporary broadcast forms: newspapers, cinema, radio and television. In the broadcast era this focus was understandable, allowing the discipline to attain a coherent purpose and identity within the academy, but it came at the cost of an epochal separation of these mass media from all earlier media forms.

This is clearly unacceptable. Most people would expect 'media studies', by definition, to cover all media, but the fact is that *media studies isn't the study of media*: it is the study of selected broadcast forms. To understand media, therefore, we need to reject this limited focus, re-orientating our conception of media away from mass communication towards the history of our material technologies: towards the process of our physical experience of the world and the re-transcription of that experience and our consciousness, understanding and meaning back upon the body of the world in the objects we create out of it and our relationship with and through them. To understand the failings of broadcast era media studies, therefore, we first need to understand its disinterest in the question of technology. We need to understand how a discipline claiming to be dedicated to the study of media has historically been antipathetic towards technology; intentionally marginalising discussion of it and inculcating this perspective so thoroughly that its omission is rarely noticed or challenged.

The most significant exception is the work of the Toronto School and the ideas especially of Marshall McLuhan whose 1964 book *Understanding Media* (see 1994) advanced a radical, physicalist conception of media. As we saw in Chapter 3, he explained technology as an 'extension', 'amputation' and 'amplification' of the human body, central nervous system and consciousness, a perspective that saw our entire artificial environment as a mode of mediation of our bodies and will. For the mainstream discipline this vision remains unthinkable: no media student receives a grounding in the history of technological forms, nor are they invited to consider media as part of a broader technological system or environment nor would they ever be expected to think about the philosophical dimension of our technological existence and its – and our – existence in the world.

Media and communication studies' rejection of technology has a longer history but its most famous statement came in Raymond Williams' book *Television: Technology and Cultural Form* (see 1992). His critique there of McLuhan's 'technological determinism' crystallised a core belief in the discipline, giving explicit permission for later media scholars not just to reject deterministic explanations but more broadly to marginalise the entire subject of technology. For many media lecturers 'technological determinism' became a word-of-power, used to dismiss any discussion of technology or interest in its role and impact. Whilst Williams retained an appreciation of social and cultural contexts the discipline has largely stripped this away, becoming dominated by an underlying humanism in which only humans and their will appear. In this story technology incarnates human values and relations, being employed by corporations and institutions who construct content transmitted to an audience at liberty to interpret it as they choose and employ it as they will. Here, therefore, one only encounters the human and to understand media one need only interrogate these undetermined human moments.

This is an attractive philosophy, flattering us in placing ourselves and our choices at the centre of the media, but it is fundamentally flawed. First, in its emphasis upon our appropriation of media it has gradually abstracted the individual from *any* determining force, including social, cultural and economic phenomena. More nuanced views may be found but their acceptance of environmental determinations is in tension with a prevailing disciplinary perspective that assumes the active capacities of the receiver. Second, and most importantly, this philosophy depends upon a separation of humanity and technology that is increasingly being challenged.

Contemporary archaeology, anthropology and the philosophy of technology are moving towards the idea that the 'human' only exists *because of* technology. Timothy Taylor's *The Artificial Ape* (2010) argues that the 'human' was a product of our technological development: 'Instead of our becoming intelligent enough to invent things, the things actually allowed us to evolve into intelligent human beings.' 'The objects, in the most crucial instances, came first', Taylor says, and 'our changing biological capacities, physical and mental, positive and negative, followed.' Hence there is no original, natural, non-technological 'human'. Ours is instead 'a symbiotic form of life' defined by its technological being: as he says, 'the technology evolved us'. Taylor's book provides numerous examples from the archaeological record, from the use of fire and stone tools that allowed us to develop bigger brains and create more technologies to the use of the sling that allowed the human infant to be born prematurely and to continue its development outside the womb, removing 'the pelvic limits to bipedal brain expansion' and allowing the development of the modern human.

From this perspective humanity cannot be separated from, or thought without reference to, technology. Interestingly, however, they never actually have been. As we've seen, David F. Channell in *The Vital Machine* (1991) shows how the history of western culture is marked by the entwining of the human and the technological: by the idea of the 'organic' and the 'mechanical'. Whilst we tend to see a clear separation between these categories Channell argues that their interrelationship is much more complex, with the 'tension' between the two obscuring deeper levels of affinity. Channell traces the roots of the mechanical perspective to Greek philosophy and astronomy, chronicling its emergence through Renaissance atomism and the work of Galileo, Descartes, Gassendi, Hobbes and Boyle, the Newtonian worldview, through mechanical theories of chemistry and heat, work on automata and new theories of the body and mind and physiology and medicine. What links mechanical thought is the conception of the world as a giant machine and living matter as similar systems built upon the motion of material bodies.

Channell argues that these ideas stood in contradiction to an organic worldview that emphasised a teleological purposiveness; a directive force or spirit that directed growth and development, seeing the world accordingly as operating like an organism or plant. Again, he suggests, this perspective has roots in Greek philosophy and mystical thought, developing through alchemical and astrological theory, Renaissance Hermetic thought, the animistic and vitalistic worldviews of many early scientists and proto-sciences and cultural movements such as Romanticism and 'Naturphilosophie' and a range of evolutionary theories and models of development and society. In this philosophy even technology has a close link with nature, as seen for example in the mystical origins of metallurgy and the close association of magic and technology.

These opposing philosophies led to related conclusions: in one life is mechanical and blurs with technology; in the other technology is organic and blurs with life. In each case the relationship is significant and neither technology nor humanity were thought apart. The contemporary humanist separation of the two in media studies represents, therefore, an a-historic and reductionist treatment of technology. For us, it appears, technology is not part of media, nor of media studies, and it is opposed to and secondary to humanity and their will.

The same reductionist approach is repeated in 'media theory' – the discipline's selection of the key theoretical texts and movements that define its history and approaches. With only a few exceptions (such as Benjamin, Heidegger and Toronto School thinkers) the most important critics and philosophers of technology are largely excluded from the textbooks and disciplinary research. The ideas of Marx, Butler, Kapp, Engelmeier, Dessauer, Veblen, Marinetti, Spengler, Junger, Mumford, Gasset, Giedion, Simondon, Ellul, De Chardin, Virilio, Latour, Kittler and Stiegler find little place in the discipline's vision of media.

This is no longer intellectually credible. As I've argued, we are left with a discipline that claims to study 'media' and that attempts to think the historical process of communication, mediation and connectivity, and the shared knowledge and experience they produce, with little or no reference to technology – to their material forms, history, historical conceptualisation, or their relationship to us and their role in the creation of ourselves and our experience. Even in the middle of a transformation in the material, ecological, cultural and personal bases of our media existence the discipline continues to refuse it any significant role in human life and society. Of course many excellent books on technology are available, but they are written not by media researchers but by technology journalists, IT specialists, science writers and specialist collectors and are found in a range of different sections of the bookstore. Though media lecturers may use these texts the mainstream discipline demonstrates little interest in them.

Contemporary developments mean that we urgently need a more historically informed and sophisticated debate around technology, recognising especially its metaphysical and epistemological implications as part of our shared mode of being-in-the-world. Ongoing transformations in electronic communication, personal technologies, digital simulations and modes of interface can only be understood with an emphasis upon technological relationships and their materiality and history. The way in which we receive and reshape the world and communicate, interact and bring the world to each other has a role to play in what we know, think and feel and the consequences of these. Whilst we only see a 'determinism' in this we'll never progress to a greater understanding of what media are.

This renewed emphasis upon the history of technology allows us to rediscover neglected pre-broadcast forms. Rather than the digital revolution propelling us to a rejection of the past it enables us to correct the bias of broadcast era media studies and develop an awareness of the real history of media forms, reclaiming them from the disciplines they have been historically situated within. Early image-making and use, for example, are found in archaeology and anthropology; language, speech and writing are covered in linguistics; early religious image-making is the province of theology; historical western ideas about images and mediation are covered in theology and philosophy; manuscript era culture is found in English and history and aesthetic images are located in art history and photographic studies. Though the reasons for this are understandable media studies' broadcast focus and disinterest in these forms is no longer beneficial or defensible.

In helping us to look beyond broadcast forms and to recognise this era as only one historical phase, digital developments open up the opportunity to develop a more complete analysis of media, disrupting the linear histories of individual forms that have marked the discipline to find new insight into older forms and trace their continuities. New ecological and archaeological analyses enable us to discover that Facebook has more in common with cartes-de-visite and portraiture than with television or newspapers and that *World of Warcraft* has more in common with the stereoscope, zograscope, panorama and peepshow than it does with radio or cinema.

Media studies' marginalisation of pre-broadcast forms can be seen in its treatment of early visual media. Western history, thought and culture has been permeated by an awareness of the role and power of images yet both this historical context and this efficacy have been resisted by the discipline. The anthropological literature has historically provided many examples of the central role of image-making (of artistic and behavioural mimesis) and of the belief in its power. Frazer's *The Golden Bough* (1890) describes many types of 'sympathetic magic' – of mimetic practices considered efficacious – though his conceptualisation of this as erroneous science missed the real point which was, as Taussig points out in *Mimesis and Alterity* (1993), 'The notion of the copy, in magical practice, affecting the original to such a degree that the representation shares in or acquires the properties of the represented.' In such a worldview the very distinction of original and copy is erased: the image is effective as the real, becoming the real, however temporarily or fleetingly.

The decisive moment for western religious and philosophical thought was the separation of sacred and profane worlds, breaking from tribal beliefs to desacralise the physical world as a mere copy or image of a transcendent, sacred reality. Now the passage of influence was one way: in Judeo-Christianity the phenomenal world was an image of the real but it was no longer efficacious. The metamorphic power of images had been reduced; fixed as a copy it would no longer threaten the original. Platonism repeats this hostility to the threat of images and the urgent need to domesticate their power. Plato's *Republic* includes a famous critique of the artist and their productions as standing 'at third remove from the throne of truth' – as images of an image of the real – whilst in the *Sophist* he separates the good 'eikastic' image that participates in its form from the 'phantastic': that demonic 'simulacrum' that contains the power to usurp and replace the real. Like the tribal mimetic image, the simulacrum names a force that refuses domestication and that asserts its own power to move us as the real.

Christianity similarly condemned the image, whether that of the world as a fallen copy or the worship of 'graven idols' and the Bible repeatedly takes an aniconic stance, explaining the image's attraction as possession by demons (Deuteronomy 32:17; 1 Corinthians 10:20). Both the Greek apologists and Fathers and the Latin Fathers also fulminated against 'simulacra' such that for Tertullian even women's make-up was a devil-inspired corruption of the god-made image. This perception of the image's efficacy led to periodic iconoclastic crises, such as in Byzantium in 726–87 and 815–43. These outbursts centred around a core philosophical dispute as to the nature of the icon – whether they were objects of 'relative veneration', with honours paid to the good copy passing to the divine or dangerous simulacra usurping the real. Though the Second Council of Nicea in 787 temporarily resolved the dispute, Christianity has been marked by recurrent iconoclastic episodes.

This was more than just a theological issue: the status of the image was central to western ideas and culture. The epistemological debates of the 17th and 18th centuries centred around the security and reality of the images of experience. Descartes' *Meditations* (1641) resurrected the demonic image – a simulacral deity creating illusions that only a true, perfect God, proven by the cogito, could dispel, but empirical attempts to found certain knowledge in the senses faced the same problem of grounding the image as a copy and domesticating its apparent reality. Bacon's *Novum Organum* (1620) admitted that sensory experience and interpretation was prey to the distortions of the 'idols' – the phantoms, or deceptive beliefs and images – of the mind and society, whilst, as

Berkeley pointed out, Locke's emphasis upon sensory experience in *An Essay Concerning Human Understanding* (1690) led to the implicitly idealist conclusion that all we could really know were the 'ideas' in our mind, hence Berkeley's appeal, again, to an all-seeing God to fix the image as a copy. Hume pushed this empiricism to its logical conclusion, removing all certain knowledge of any external real, leaving us with only the simulacral image – sensory 'impressions' and the 'ideas' derived from them that fill our minds as the real.

Beyond these theological and philosophical debates, however, there was the simple fact of the popular belief in and use of images – delegates at the Second Council of Nicea, for example, came armed with considerable testimony from ordinary people about their efficacy. David Freedberg's *The Power of Images* (1989) surveys anthropology, ancient and classical history and art history to explore the will to representation that crosses every time and culture and our common response to their reality:

> People are sexually aroused by pictures and sculptures; they break pictures and sculptures; they mutilate them, kiss them, cry before them, and go on journeys to them; they are claimed by them, stirred by them and incited to revolt. They give thanks by means of them, expect to be elevated by them, and are moved to the highest levels of empathy and fear. They have always responded in these ways; they still do. They do so in societies we call primitive and in modern societies; in East and West, in Africa, America, Asia and Europe.

Freedberg's examples range from the 14th- to 17th-century Italian tavoluccie; erotic art; the living presence of idols and icons; the rituals of image-making, consecration and consumption; statues, carvings and shaped forms; reliquaries; images as objects of pilgrimage, enshrinement and adornment; votive images; architectural forms; prayer cards, printed images and reproductions; effigies; waxworks; automata and animated images. What emerges, again and again, from his examples is the centrality of images in human lives and their power to act upon us, to evoke and produce consolation, adoration, arousal, hatred, hopes, memories, and the mobilisation of our senses and desires.

What is noticeable is how many of these traditions are absent from media studies. Despite the central role of the issue of 'representation' and the analysis of media content the discipline has shown little interest in the history of images, the philosophy of mediation and representation and the key commentators that have defined western responses. Its textbooks find no place for Plato, Plotinus, Porphyry, Iamblichus, Proclus, Tertullian, Origen, Eusebius, Dionysius Areopagita, John of Damascus or Theodore of Studion: Peirce, Saussure, Barthes, Mulvey and Hall are seen as sufficient to understand representation today.

What this lacks is any historical sense of how we have treated images and mediation and their potential continuity with present practices. What is also lost is any sense of the media as having an effect. The discipline's early empirical research established the complexity of reception and more recent

Culturalist work has emphasised the active capacities of the receiver but, like its treatment of technology, this has simply become an established orthodoxy in the discipline. Discussing Baudrillard's concept of the simulacrum at a recent conference with a newly appointed lecturer my explanation met with the sudden, incredulous response, 'you mean you believe in a passive audience?'. What struck me was the confusion evidenced at meeting a media lecturer who didn't accept the primacy of the receiver and their horror at the suggestion that the media actually have *any* influence at all.

This humanistic valorisation of the receiver and their freedom isn't a natural or inevitable position nor one based upon provable 'facts' about media consumption, rather it remains a constructed position – a theoretical position that has been chosen and reproduced through its favoured methodologies. It is one that runs counter, however, to the entire history of media productions and responses, separating contemporary media and our knowledge of them from all their historical antecedents. It is a denial of the power of our own technological creations to create our phenomenal environment and shape and provoke our experience, thoughts, knowledge, emotions and physiological responses. Media studies as it developed through the 20th century too often refused to consider this historical context for its subject and still fails to understand that its own approach has ironic historical echoes. A discipline emerging out of an age-old fear of the power of media has responded to that threat in traditional ways with its own demonisation of technology and its power as well as its own mode of domestication – that of the form itself before the human subject and their will.

Mass media studies

Whilst it may not be surprising that a media studies focused on the major broadcast forms overlooked pre-broadcast media, one would expect it at least to provide a detailed coverage of the broadcast era. This, however, isn't necessarily the case. Although media studies traces the origins of mass communication to Gutenberg, the discipline has shown relatively little interest in the following centuries of print media.

Whilst newspapers have attracted considerable attention in the discipline – see, for example, Curran and Seaton's *Power Without Responsibility* (1981/2010), Williams' *Get Me a Murder a Day! A History of Mass Communication in Britain* (1998) and *Read All About It! A History of the British Newspaper* (2009) – the broader print culture is usually overlooked. The rise of printed books and the world of popular texts, journals, pamphlets and printed sheets are seen as part of History rather than media studies. Media degrees rarely offer modules on print history, few media lecturers research them and textbooks offer only a cursory overview of print culture. Other elements such as novels and literary forms are completely overlooked, being seen instead as English literature. This placing is obviously justifiable, but it doesn't explain media studies' disinterest. Regardless of content, books are media and the cultural success of literature formed an important part of the broadcast ecology.

Music fares better, with a niche academic literature developing to consider its importance. It remains dominated, however, by a Culturalist and cultural studies perspective covering musical creativity, audiences, fans, popular music culture, genres, youth cultures and the meaning of musical texts, whilst production is covered in discussions of the music industry. The early history of the industry is again seen as the province of historians rather than media studies and the early technologies are covered by specialist collectors and their publications not media researchers.

Visual media are similarly treated, with early printed images and artworks covered by historians or specialist art historians rather than media studies. The discipline has shown little interest, for example, in the remarkable range of printed images and forms available to the 18th- and 19th-century consumer, from printed plates and pamphlets to caricatures, advertising images, *vues d'optique* perspective prints, anamorphic images, portable panoramas and dioramas and mass-produced images for optical toys and viewing devices such as the zoetrope, phenakistoscope and praxinoscope. One might also add a range of other visual entertainments to this list such as the public panoramas, dioramas and georamas. Though not mass reproduced and broadcast they nevertheless exploited the same urban mass audiences and often played an informative or even news function and, as Oetterman argues in *The Panorama: History of a Mass Medium* (1997) they served, therefore, as mass media forms.

Whilst the marginalisation of these media isn't surprising, the treatment of photography is. Photography largely appears in media studies in its broadcast form, as mass-produced advertising images and news photographs, being primarily treated as a 'text' for critical interpretation. It is rarely considered as a specific medium, its history, theory and practice aren't usually taught, and its theoretical sources are mostly overlooked in media theory. Media degrees rarely include photography modules and references in textbooks are usually focused on the issue of representation. Even historical broadcast photography is ignored. Despite their significance as major entertainment industries and perhaps the primary photographic experience of the world in the 19th century, the mass-produced and distributed magic lantern slides and stereographs rarely appear in media texts, remaining again the province of specialist collectors and their journals, presses, publications and websites.

Even the discipline's treatment of its favoured broadcast forms is problematic. One issue that is rarely questioned is the separate status accorded to cinema. The study of film dates back to the early years of the medium – in early reflections such as Munsterberg's *The Photoplay: A Psychological Study* (1916) and Lindsay's *The Art of the Moving Picture* (1916) – but modern film studies only developed as a distinct academic subject area in the 1960s–70s. It emerged out of arts rather than social-science traditions, most commonly out of English literature, the languages, and Liberal arts or cultural courses, before becoming closely linked with cultural studies and media studies. It drew on its own history of theory, importing concepts from literary studies, gender studies, psychoanalysis, semiotics, linguistics and Marxism and honed its own analytical methods and accepted disciplinary assumptions and knowledge.

The success of media studies, however, created a strange schism, with film being treated as a separate entity to 'media'. To some extent the two were complementary: media studies' increasing cultural emphasis and modes of analysis and interpretation meant that film studies found a sympathetic place within media departments. In other ways, however, film studies was more problematic. The treatment of film as a distinct medium was justifiable but the separation of it from other 'media' was ludicrous. Film scholars saw few problems here, however, as their discipline increasingly moved from its earlier critical approaches to an aesthetic perspective that treated film as different from media as a privileged art object produced by an individual artist and interpreted by trained aesthetic critics and commentators.

This approach promoted an elitist separatism. As the study of *an artform*, film studies looked down upon more mundane popular media forms. Having had to fight prejudice against its own field, the emergence of media studies enabled it to reposition itself as a more elite discipline, closer to English literature, concerned with higher questions of art. Hence film studies' refusal to con-textualise cinema within the broader category of media or the ideas, knowledge and approaches of that discipline.

The digital transformation of cinema and convergence of older media should have made this separatism obsolete but the opposite has happened. The success of high-quality serial television dramas in the 1990s such as *The X-Files* (1993–2002) and *Buffy the Vampire Slayer* (1997–2003) led a film studies that needed to court popularity with students to increasingly embrace television. Recognising the similarity of these forms film embraced television but it did so selectively, with low-brow shows, comedy, soaps, news and current affairs and children's programmes all noticeably being seen as failing to possess the required level of narrative or dramatic form or aesthetic quality to deserve study. This has led to the untenable situation whereby *some television* has now been separated off to be partitioned within a carefully selected and aesthetically treated 'film and television studies'.

Hence the establishment in 2011 of BAFTSS, the 'British Association for Film, Television and Screen Studies'. Whilst its mission statement claims that 'research into and critical analysis of screen-based media are central to under-standing the culture, society and economy of the new century', its separation of its favoured forms from other media and remarkable failure to understand that digital convergence that has rendered these forms obsolete highlights their retrogressive approach. In an important email to the Media, Communication and Cultural Studies Association (MECCSA) list in June 2011 Martin Barker criticises both the timing of the new organisation, during a period of change in Higher Education that demands instead 'a broad unifying organisation' to defend the discipline (such as MECCSA), and the reasons for its creation: 'what I am sensing in some of what is lying behind the creation of BAFTSS is a sense of separateness, indeed specialness, of film studies'. He's right. At a time when the specificities of these media have been lost and when there are urgent new issues for the discipline to confront, this separatism is backward, ignorant and erroneous.

Another problem of broadcast era media studies was its treatment of production. Though a central part of communication, it was largely eclipsed in the discipline by the study of content and reception. One reason for this was the discipline's own bias. Media studies originated out of a concern not with how or why media were produced but with the effects of media and this was intimately tied to the question of how this knowledge could be used. For Lippmann and Bernays the hope was to exploit it by 'manufacturing' public knowledge, whilst for later empirical researchers such as Lazarsfeld the aim was to serve the needs of commercial industry and government policymakers. Media studies, therefore, was on the side of the producers and there was no economic or intellectual incentive to turn their attention to their activities.

It took the development of Marxist critical theory to subject broadcast production to a theoretical critique but it wasn't until the post-war period that the mainstream discipline became interested in media production, with important articles on US journalism by David Manning White (1950) and Warren Breed (1955). Academic explorations of the journalistic profession, such as by Galtung and Ruge (1965), continued through the following decade but it was fieldwork sociology rather than communication studies that pioneered the empirical study of the newsroom. Through the 1970s–80s the ethnographic investigation of news production became popular in the UK, in Tunstall's *Journalists at Work* (1971), Cohen and Young's *The Manufacture of News* (1973), Tracey's *The Production of Political Television* (1977), Chibnall's *Law-and-Order News* (1977), Schlesinger's *Putting 'Reality' Together* (1978) and Golding and Elliott's *Making the News* (1979), and in the US, in Tuchman's *Making News* (1978), Gans' *Deciding What's News* (1979) and Fishman's *Manufacturing the News* (1980).

These empirical studies, however, were rare and represented an infinitely small sample in relation to the totality of broadcast era industry output. The empirical approach soon declined in favour of alternative approaches largely drawn from sociology, political economy and cultural studies. Now the theoretical analysis of the media sector and media work and ideological and cultural analysis of news came to dominate the study of media production and there have been few detailed empirical studies since. Unsurprisingly media industries have shown little interest in allowing media researchers into their studios, offices and meetings to follow the day-to-day production process and interview and observe staff.

This disciplinary estrangement from production is exacerbated by the fact that most non-practice media lecturers came from an academic rather than industry background, typically having no experience of the industries they were studying. Being in the same position as any other member of the public the average media researcher found it easier to research the only relationship they had: that of the receiver and consumer of content. The success of audience theory also reinforced this neglect. Culturalist audience and fan studies followed Hall's claim that reception was the key moment in communication, rejecting in advance any approach that called into question or distracted attention away from the freedom of the receiver. The interpretation of media and film content similarly downplayed the question of production in favour of the critical individual and what they took from the material. Though media production was given a prominent position in the student textbooks this didn't reflect the reality of its treatment by media researchers.

If production has been relatively marginalised by the discipline the discussion of technological operation, media distribution and transmission is almost entirely absent. As Sean Cubitt notes in his 2005 *Cultural Politics* article 'Distribution and Media Flows', issues of distribution have 'rarely been addressed in media studies terms other than regulation and control'. He attributes this to disciplinary perspectives that emphasise culture, power and economics, 'indeed anything but what is here taken as the central act of human action: communication in general and its materialisation as media in particular'. The emphasis upon content and reception and hostility towards technology and materiality means distribution is overlooked, a situation exacerbated by the arts and social science backgrounds of many media lecturers and their limited interest in or grasp of the scientific or engineering principles of media forms. What's noticeable is how few textbooks or courses spend any time analysing issues around technical construction, producing media students with little idea about the scientific and technical principles underlying media forms and their operation. Media students can graduate knowing little or nothing about how the media they study even work.

Even media studies' focus on media products and their content, meaning and reception wasn't without its problems. The first issue the discipline faced was the scale and volume of broadcast production. Over the 20th century printed material, recorded music, films, radio programmes and television shows flooded from the broadcast era informational and entertainment factories and the academic discipline could do little more than sample this flow, studying only a small amount of this content.

But researchers also faced the problem of accessing this material. Unless it was recorded, television and radio content disappeared on broadcast, with repeats being rare and access to archives difficult. Books often went out of print and much printed material (such as magazines, comics or small press publications) was rarely available in local libraries. Newspapers were harder to find after the day of publication and even libraries limited the range of titles they kept. Company archives existed but, again, posed their own problems of access and use. Before commercial video, films were harder to see, with viewers relying on TV repeats, re-issues, and film clubs, few of which were conducive to detailed academic study. Video tape made research easier but researchers were dependent on availability and the publisher's decisions as to what to release. Ironically, the broadcast era is easier to study in the digital era. The digitalisation of older media forms and the development of easy-to-access, often free and easily searchable archives has made research easier whilst more material is also available, legally or illegally, either on or through the internet.

Another problem with broadcast era media studies was its treatment of its own discipline and its history and theory. There are relatively few histories of the subject and not only are most students unaware of this history but so too are many lecturers. Those coming into the discipline in the last decade have no necessary knowledge of this history and even those with long careers in the subject have only a limited grasp of the whole. The most accessible histories are found in the media theory textbooks, though these are partial accounts with little reference to the institutional and disciplinary development of the subject area or even agreement as to what to include. Czitrom's *Media and the American Mind* (1982); Mattelart and Mattelart's *Theories of Communication* (see 1998); Stevenson's *Understanding Media Cultures* (1995); Katz, Durham Peters, Liebes and Orloff's (eds.) *Canonic Texts in Media Research* (2002); Williams' *Understanding Media Theory* (2003); Laughey's *Key Themes in Media Theory* (2007) and Scannell's *Media and Communication* (2007), for example, all begin from different points and differ as to which authors and movements they include. Contemporary thinkers are especially poorly served and many key figures of the last quarter century receive only a cursory mention.

The idea of 'media theory' here also excludes specific media. For the most part literary and photographic theory find little place in these texts whilst film theory is also excluded from surveys of media theory. As I've suggested, film theory is rarely considered in relation to other media or the broader field of media theory by either media or film studies. This separatism certainly aided a medium-specific analysis but it was also highly limiting and it has become obsolescent in a digital era.

What are also missing from these surveys of media theory are almost all western attempts to think about human communication, media, mediation and images prior to the late 19th century. Here communication theory is better served. John Durham Peters' *Speaking Into the Air: A History of the Idea of Communication* (1999), for example, offers an important survey of the concept of communication in Plato, Socrates, Jesus, Augustine, Locke, Spiritualism, Hegel, Marx and Kierkegaard. Media studies, however, not only separates broadcast media from all earlier media forms, it also separates its critical analysis and theorisation of them from all earlier traditions. As I've argued, centuries of epistemological debate as to our experience of the world, its mediation, the use and status of images and their effects are largely ignored by the discipline.

The poor treatment of theory is also seen at the pedagogical level. Whereas no student in a cognate discipline such as sociology would complete their degree without a grounding in the founding thinkers and modules tracing later theoretical developments, in media studies this is common. It isn't unknown for media degrees to lack any theoretical component and many programmes will only offer one general module, usually based on a selected textbook. In part this reflects the poor theoretical grounding of many lecturers. Few specialise in media theory or study specific thinkers in detail and most have only a selective and limited knowledge of the range of media theory. The founding texts of the discipline – books such as Lippmann's *Public Opinion* and *The Phantom Public*; Bernays' *Crystallizing Public Opinion* and *Propaganda*; Lasswell's *Propaganda Techniques in the World War*; Park's *The Immigrant Press and Its Control*;

Dewey's *The Public and Its Problems*; Blumer's *Movies and Conduct* and *Movies, Delinquency and Crime*; Lazarsfeld's *Radio and the Printed Page*; Lazarsfeld and Kendall's *Radio Listening in America*; Lazarsfeld, Berelson and Gaudet's *The People's Choice* and Lazarsfeld and Katz's *Personal Influence* – are today largely unknown and unread by most media lecturers and researchers.

One reason for this disinterest in theory is the dominance of empirical research within the discipline. The Chicago School and Lazarsfeld began this process, with their rejection of the earlier speculative commentary and new emphasis respectively upon qualitative and quantitative sociological research methods and this empirical model still dominates both sociological and cultural media research. Audience and fan studies, for example, employ a range of methodologies including ethnographic research, questionnaires, interviews and modes of content analysis whilst even the critical interpretation of media content, such as in film and television studies, employs a range of methods and formalised techniques with the aim of producing rigorous and defensible analyses and knowledge. Theory may be employed in this process, for example, in framing discussions of audience research through the work of Hall, Fiske and Jenkins, but the overwhelming disciplinary orientation remains towards empirical research.

In such a context theory is seen as less important. PhD students are encouraged to pursue empirical research; academic journals favour empirically based articles over theoretical ones; research and funding bodies prefer empirical studies which seem to offer practical information upon and insight into specific phenomena, and institutional recruitment and promotion panels are more impressed by those who have won such awards or who can demonstrate industry or policy impact. All this reinforces the primacy of empirical research with practical or saleable consequences and makes it possible for a student to pass from undergraduate, to postgraduate, to qualified and employed lecturer without gaining any significant knowledge of the discipline's own history and theory beyond that necessary for the performance of their methodology.

The problem with this position is that all empirical research is the expression of a theoretical position. The paradigms of content and audience studies remain theoretical perspectives that are not proven by their research methods but rather employ research methods to support their underlying position. Audience and fan studies, for example, are built upon a prior model of communication privileging the position, power and significance of the receiver resulting in the decision to focus research at that point, as well as a model of empirical reality and belief in the capacity of selected methods to objectively capture it and render it as valid quantitative or qualitative data. The disciplinary rejection of the history of theoretical reflections on media and mediation, and disinterest in a range of contemporary media perspectives, is due to the dominance of a small number of privileged positions whose own theoretical status and biases are obscured by their naturalisation within the discipline and by the privileging of the form of knowledge they are led to produce. Once again, a discipline that claims to analyse constructed representations and their biases fails to interrogate its own representations of the media and their underlying methodological assumptions.

This brings us to the question of ideology. As we've seen, media studies' academic institutionalisation and success from the 1930s was founded on empirical research funded by and aiming to be of service to the media industries and government. This was 'administrative research', aiding private companies, advertising industries and official policy-makers with the promise of knowledge as to how to exploit and control the audience by getting them to accept mass-produced messages. *The aim of media studies, therefore, was not to understand the media but to help control the public.* Whilst its research increasingly argued for the complexity of reception, and even appeared to deny direct influence, media's post-war research centres were funded by the US government for help with Cold War propaganda campaigns.

In addition to the implication that disciplinary claims as to the lack of direct influence were disingenuous there remained a suspicion that these claims served as a cover for the industries themselves. It was this explosive position that Todd Gitlin took in his 1978 critique of 'the dominant paradigm', pointing out that 'since the Second World War, as mass media in the United States have become more concentrated in ownership, more centralised in operations, more national in reach, more pervasive in presence, sociological study of the media has been dominated by the theme of the relative powerlessness of the broad-casters'. For Gitlin the explanation for 'such a strange conjunction of events' was simple: empirical research has 'had the effect of justifying the existing system of mass media ownership, control and purpose' (1978).

Though far removed theoretically from this social-scientific tradition, contemporary Culturalist audience studies arrived at the same limited-effects position. Hall's 'Encoding/Decoding' essay was motivated by a broadly Marxist spirit and his positioning of reception as the 'predominant' moment of the various 'determinant moments' of the communication process, together with his employment of semiology, successfully reframed media analysis around the individual critical interpretation of meaning and media use. Foregrounding Gramscian ideas, Hall constructed reception as the site of hegemonic contestation hoping to make people aware of the possibilities of resistance against mass media forms. Later research within the tradition, however, de-politicised this approach or simply valorised all audience activity as positive modes of individual resistance or activity. Reception may have been a site of contest but any suggestion that the individual lost this contest, exhibited any passivity, or was directly influenced was rare.

Though many audience researchers take a more sophisticated view, admitting elements of media power and influence, most retain a faith in the ultimate power of the receiver. Marie Gillespie's student text *Media Audiences* (2005) is representative of the disciplinary position, her authorial voice making it clear that the discipline accepts the final power of the receiver. 'Throughout this book', she writes, 'we have challenged the view that media power lies mainly or even exclusively in the hands of media producers and institutions, and that audiences are predictable or powerless'. Gillespie enumerates several views of power but ultimately favours 'the "*interpretative power*" of audiences', arriving at the Culturalist conclusion that, 'Audiences have the power to challenge and resist dominant meanings "encoded" in texts and to use media for a variety of empowering purposes.'

Personal empowerment, however, came at the price of any conception of media power so, a quarter of a century after Gitlin, media studies again reached the apparent consensus that the mass media were, in the last instance, powerless. Even if unwittingly now, the discipline again served as an ideological support for media industries whose own massive investment in programming, advertising revenue and cultural success suggested they held a very different view of the power of their production. This industry service was reinforced by the empirical emphasis of audience studies, with funding accepted from government and private agencies on the basis of the value of the insight into audiences that would result. The UK 'Research Excellence Framework', whose role it is to evaluate the worth of disciplinary research, now includes a concept of 'impact'. Whilst this has a potentially broad definition, one clear example is the practical value of research for companies and policy-makers. In an increasingly marketised university sector, therefore, 'administrative research' has become the expected standard.

All of this helps explain what media studies became. Disinterested in the history of technology; unable to draw any lessons from the history of media; unwilling to explore the technical basis of forms, dismissive of issues around distribution or sensory experience and limited in its ability to adequately study production, media, film and television studies foregrounded what was left to it: reception and content. Media studies was a historical response to and product of one historical phase in media – the broadcast era – but even its coverage of that era was limited. For once was can say, therefore, that it was the Emperor's *old clothes* that offered less coverage than was thought.

These disciplinary limitations also help explain media studies' treatment of digital media. 'New media' had been explored first in debates around art and photography before becoming a core concern of sociology and cultural studies in debates around the 'information society', globalisation and postmodernism from the mid-1980s to the early 1990s. By the mid-1990s a theoretically sophisticated and conceptually radical branch of cultural studies had developed called 'cyberculture', exploring cyberspace and online relations, but it took until the late 1990s for media studies to notice the impact of the internet. When it did, it largely ignored these existing debates and their literature, approaching them instead from their own broadcast era perspectives, focusing upon issues of audience activity and downplaying the technological dimension and its theorisation. Hence Henry Jenkins' *Convergence Culture* (2006) redefined 'convergence' as a cultural process of the passage of content between different forms; removing any discussion of technology to see a smooth transition from the active audiences of the broadcast era to the full flowering of digital fans. The fundamental implausibility of this removal of technology from the concept of convergence and the lack of discussion of digital technology in a book that foregrounds digital culture are rarely challenged by those who quote Jenkins' work.

Digital media, therefore, were treated as something that could be understood within existing broadcast-era categories and concepts and as an addition to the broadcast ecology rather than as a fundamental transformation of its material base and of its systems of production, distribution and consumption. The final limitation of broadcast era media studies, therefore, is its inability to understand and follow the digital changes happening around it. For many years it treated digital media as an optional specialism within the field, for lecturers as well as students, and when it appeared it was placed in higher levels of courses or as final chapters in textbooks, a position simulating contemporary relevance without any understanding of how the digital revolution had transformed everything students had been taught or read before it.

The digital, post-broadcast era, however, opens up a threefold opportunity. First, it allows us to reflect back upon the broadcast era and the discipline it gave rise to in order to understand its limitations. Second, it allows us to rediscover and re-theorise older, pre-broadcast forms and develop a more holistic understanding of the whole of media and our relationship with them and more sophisticated, inclusive histories of their elements and development. Third, it allows us to move beyond broadcast-era assumptions and develop a radically receptive media studies better able to follow, understand and respond to its own age. It allows us to realise that a broadcast era media studies barely able to study its own era has even less relevance in a post-broadcast era. It allows us to realise that what's needed is an upgraded discipline: media 2.0 require a 'media studies 2.0'.

8 Upgrading the discipline
Media Studies 2.0

In order to argue for the need to upgrade media studies for a digital era I first of all had to defend the idea that these changes were revolutionary. Hence I traced a series of transformations – in the material basis of media; in their ecological organisation; in the cultural mode of production, distribution and consumption; and in the relationship of the individual to media. Second, I had to defend the claim that the existing discipline was unable to deal with these changes. Hence I considered the history, development and form of media studies. I traced its roots to the 1920s in debates around the impact of mass media arguing that it developed as the product and reflection of the broadcast era and its dominant forms. Though it studied all aspects of this broadcast model I argued that the issues of reception – the effect of media upon the audience and their use of material – and content – the critical interpretation of media products and their meaning – came to form the discipline's core. Finally, I argued that this media studies failed to adequately deal with the pre-broadcast era of media and suffered from significant limitations even in its coverage of the broadcast era.

It was precisely these limitations, however, that ensured media studies' success. Its broadcast focus, broad socio-cultural approach and convergence upon a core of concerns, perspectives and methods gave it an internal coherence, distinct disciplinary identity and place within the academy. By the end of the 20th century they'd helped media studies become a highly successful discipline, with rising student applications, growing course and student numbers, an established research culture, a thriving textbook market and a homogenisation of provision around its central interests and perspectives. Despite negative pronouncements from Government ministers and tabloid attacks on the subject, students were interested in media: it filled their lives and imaginations and they wanted to learn about it or work in it.

By the mid-1990s this interest was exacerbated by the take-off of a range of digital forms and the increasing role of digital me-dia in their everyday lives. Students came to study the media world they lived in but those applying to the discipline didn't realise they wouldn't study media: they'd study media studies. Whereas in the broadcast era this fact was invisible as the discipline was in synch with the external media reality, the success of digital media led to an increasing separation between what students studied and the media worlds they experienced and used. The discipline's core focus, theories, assumptions and subject matter were often unwilling and unable to understand the extent of the digital revolution or its implications. In this chapter I want to explore the idea of upgrading the discipline. I want to suggest why the practical and theoretical discipline need to be reconfigured and the challenges digital media pose for any attempt to follow and understand them.

Installing updates ...

Media are changing and media studies has to adapt. If the digital post-broadcast era is the product of the meeting and merger of two trajectories – mass media and computing – then it is clear that media studies alone is not sufficient to understand the new situation. Following the merger of their subject matter, to some extent media studies must also meet and merge with computer science in order to grasp the present.

One immediate consequence is that media lecturers need a greater under-standing of digital media and its operation. With a background typically in the arts, humanities and social sciences, their knowledge and interest in technology is usually limited. Whilst this marginalisation of form and its operation appeared acceptable in the broadcast era (and, indeed, became central to the discipline's dominant approaches) this has become a significant hindrance to understanding contemporary media. Today's media lecturers need a detailed understanding of how digital technologies work, from the hardware level and its operation, to the process of software production and implementation, to the content layer and the applications that run on it, their interrelationships and the platforms accessed through it.

They also need a greater practical ability with digital technology. Ideally they would have a basic understanding of software and coding but at the very least we all need to develop a high level of computing competency to understand contemporary digital media. Like everyone else, lecturers have a range of com-puting competencies and create their own personal me-dia ecology of uses and modes of consumption, but most still have only a limited ability with their own work machine and other devices. For some, the problem of basic technological literacy is especially acute.

Beyond this, lecturers need an awareness of and competency with the entire digital ecology of technologies, sites, services, functions, platforms, uses and possibilities. Whereas the broadcast-era lecturer was confident that there would be few developments in film, television, newspapers or radio that they wouldn't hear about or be able to understand, today that's no longer true. In a complex digital ecology lecturers are not at the forefront of their topics and it's harder to hear about, follow, participate in and understand what is happening. The rapid evolution of technologies and practices, together with the rise of personally arranged me-dia worlds leads to what Chris Anderson in *The Long Tail* (2006) calls a fragmented, 'massively parallel culture' that is far more difficult for any researcher to grasp.

The challenge today, therefore, is to pursue, join in, embrace and move around this digital ecology, exploring its niches and ongoing developments, following the cultures, habits, interests and experiences of digital users and integrating them into our own lives. The longer we've been in the discipline the harder this is. Professors with international reputations based upon a lifetime's work on the broadcast industries are more at risk of being out of touch with the media realities around them and the lives of their students. But even younger lecturers struggle here, often having built early careers upon the specialised study of one media form, one TV show, one genre, one director, or one cult audience and fan group.

Media personalisation helps academics remain specialised. If they choose to, lecturers can continue within their broadcast bubble, convinced of the continuing significance of their approaches and methods, hosting conferences for themselves and publishing papers for each other to read, without any necessary engagement with the broader digital ecology and its transformations. Unless, however, we can keep up with the changing forms and practices and unless they become as central in our lives as they are to our students then we'll lose the ability and right to teach them. In an era in which we watched television we had the right to teach it; in the future unless we share our students' me-dia lives and activities we'll have little to say to them and no authority with which to say it. Our students may not know the texts, the history, the arguments and the ideas of our discipline but our knowledge of these is devalued if they don't reflect the world they live.

The meeting and merger of media studies and computing also needs to happen in our courses and modules. In particular we need a revised conception of media practice, to include within it the teaching of computer science and digital production. Media practice is a significant part of institutional media studies, whether in practice-based, professionally accredited courses offering recognised qualifications for entry into the industry or, more commonly, in courses that mix practical and theoretical elements. The majority of media degrees include 'taster' modules in practice to demonstrate the skills required and roles available in the industry; to increase student employability with practical experience and to open up the option of more in-depth training after graduation. Historically these courses and modules have been oriented towards work in the main broadcast industries of print, journalism, film, radio and television.

The position of practice, however, needs rethinking. One might question its value in a world where professional technologies with industry-standard effects are becoming cheaper to acquire and easier to use. If my 10-year-old son is already making and posting YouTube videos it's unlikely that, in eight years' time, he'll have much use for a final year video production module with caps on entry and one camera shared amongst a group of students. In the future we can expect many students to arrive with self- and peer-taught skills that will expose the paucity of much university provision. Google searches and YouTube tutorials already provide enough to learn how to create. One might also query the training for broadcast industries that are in the process of significant change or even possible extinction. I teach students with an interest in entering journalism who don't read it, don't pay for information and who want to join an industry their own media practices are strangling.

But the real issue with media practice teaching is that today's media are increasingly digital objects and actual media production is digital production. If we want to train our students to compete in the current and future marketplace then they need to know more than how to use a camera or edit video. To be truly capable and employable students need to know how to create digitally: they need computing science.

The question of computer education rose up the political agenda in 2011 with the growing recognition of the failures of UK ICT teaching and the poor standard of computer science students. In the Edinburgh MacTaggart lecture in August that year, Google Chairman Eric Schmidt criticised the UK's failure to build on its record of innovation, saying it was 'throwing away' its 'great computer heritage' by not teaching programming. 'I was flabbergasted to learn today computer science isn't even taught as standard in UK schools ... Your IT curriculum focuses on teaching how to use software but gives no insight into how it's made.'

The February 2011 independent review of the skills needs of the video game and visual effects industries, *Next Gen*, reached the same conclusion and the government was forced to agree that teaching how to use wordprocessing was inadequate. The *Observer* took up the call for coding skills, with John Naughton arguing that whereas kids in the 1980s bought computers and learned how to program them, today that direct engagement has been replaced by interfaces turning them into 'passive consumers of information appliances and services created by giant foreign corporations'. Hence his support for the 'Raspberry pi': the late 2011 launch of a cheap, programmable computer that would grant children again a 'license to tinker'.

These arguments also apply to media students. If media production is digital then our students need to understand computing and coding. This requires a revolution in media practice teaching, with departments hiring computer scientists or merging their programs so students can learn digital skills. Media departments haven't even begun to realise this. Our students trust a discipline that had decided that using a camera, recording a radio programme and reading the news in a pretend studio are sufficient training for the digital ecology. But that broadcast world is changing and the number of newsreaders and presenters it needs is very limited. Today's media students would benefit more from being able to produce software, apps, web pages and businesses than a 10-minute group video. As my son demonstrates, that isn't a rare skill any longer.

All this foregrounds the question of 'media literacy'. As Douglas Rushkoff argues in *Program or Be Programmed* (2010), real literacy involves learning 'not just how to read but how to write'. Hence, he says, 'As we move into an increasingly digital reality, we must learn not just how to use programs but how to *make* them.' The choice is simple: 'Program or be programmed.'

'Choose the former,' he says, 'and you gain access to the control panel of civilisation':

> Computers and networks finally offer us the ability to write. And we do write with them on our websites, blogs and social networks. But the underlying capability of the computer era is actually programming – which almost none of us knows how to do. We simply use the programs that have been made for us, and enter out text in the appropriate box on the screen. We teach kids how to use software to write, but not how to write software. This means they have access to the capabilities given to them by others, but not the power to determine the value-creating capabilities of these technologies for themselves.

For Rushkoff: 'The less involved and aware we are of the way our technologies are programmed and program themselves, the more narrow our choices will become; the less we will be able to envision alternatives to the pathways described by our programs; and the more our lives and experiences will be dictated by their biases.'

As we've seen, broadcast era media studies was a reflection of the system it studied. Just as there was a separation between the minority of mass media producers and the mass of consumers, so there was clear disciplinary division between practical modules teaching students how to write – how to produce broadcast industry products – and theoretical modules teaching students how to read – how to understand media industries, media products and their effects. This division was naturally competitive. Whilst one part of the discipline taught students how to *serve* industry, the other taught students how to *protect* against its products. If media practitioners saw the relationship between practice and theory as like that between artist and critic – those who can, do, whilst those who can't, criticise – many media theorists saw it instead as more like the relationship between drug dealer and police – one pushed pernicious products at the public and the other alerted them to it. Hence the difficult position of practice and its often strained relationship with the academy. Whilst practical modules emphasised saleable skills for the workplace, many theoretical lecturers saw the discipline as involving more than the functional reproduction of the media workforce, pushing for a critical understanding that was often missing from industry-orientated teaching.

Where broadcast era media studies, therefore, offered two competing conceptions of 'media literacy', the post-broadcast era offers a more holistic and empowered concept, uniting practical skills and critical understanding in our need to be able to both read and write digitally. I'll develop this point in the next chapter, but here we can say that both the practical skills our students require and the theoretical understanding that needs to accompany these all revolve now around digital production. The broadcast discipline's theoretical focus on consumption skills – on understanding reception and content – is now obsolete and these skills need to be supplemented, and even supplanted, today by a focus on the digital producer, their activities and the new threats to their use. Once again, we find the existing discipline isn't sufficient to understand the contemporary media world. What we need instead is a 'media studies 2.0'.

If media studies was a product of the broadcast era and reflection of its time and dominant forms and processes then media studies 2.0 is a reflection of a changed media environment, exploring the post-broadcast digital era and its implications. This is a media studies for the 21st century: one radically receptive to the contemporary age, following and deciphering the media worlds our students live in. Media studies 2.0 is a call for every part of media studies to recognise and open itself up to the changes caused by digital media and to broaden and update its knowledge and references.

The idea of 'media studies 2.0' first came to public attention through the work of David Gauntlett, and the success of the idea owed much to his high profile in the field. He independently developed the idea in early 2007, posting a short essay about it on his website. Having Googled the term to see if it was in use he found my original blog and linked to it in the article. We subsequently discussed our ideas together, co-developed the concept and helped provoke a broader discussion in the discipline about its form and future in the digital age. Gauntlett's starting point was the concept of 'Web 2.0' which led him to wonder if a similar development in the discipline – 'a media studies 2.0' – was necessary to capture this age. He contrasted this new orientation with 'the still-popular traditional model' of media studies – or 'media studies 1.0' – which was marked, he argued, by its fetishisation of experts, its celebration of particular popular key media texts and theorists, its vision of particular modes of pedagogy, its privileging of western media, its limited critical stance, its poor treatment of digital media (in primarily seeing it as an 'add-on' to traditional modules and textbooks), and a preference for particular research methods with their built-in biases.

Against this Gauntlett (2007) proposed a different approach focused upon 'the everyday meanings produced by the diverse array of audience members accompanied by an interest in new qualitative research techniques'. This media studies would also foreground the range of amateur and peer production across the internet and contemporary personal technologies, the international dimension of media production and consumption, the digital transformation of *all* media forms, a recognition of the intelligent reading strategies of audiences and our students, new research methods that reject 'outmoded notions of "receiver" audiences and elite "producers"', and new conceptions of media power in an era of empowered public creativity. The aim, Gauntlett says, is not to 'throw away all previous perspectives and research' but to 'rework them to fit a changing environment'.

Gauntlett provides a brief history of the changing disciplinary mood, noting how in recent years he and a number of others had begun to consider how digital media were leading to a reconsideration not just of the content of media studies but of what it was and how it worked. Interestingly Gauntlett and I approached the issue from very different backgrounds. Gauntlett has published extensively on mainstream disciplinary concerns such as media effects, television culture, audiences and gender and identity whereas my own background is in issues around media theory, philosophy, media history and technology and especially more marginal, radical and controversial figures such as Baudrillard and McLuhan. What's significant is that despite these different backgrounds and some differences in our formulations of 'media studies 2.0' we arrived at a similar evaluation of the current discipline and similar ideas about the impact of digital technology. Others working on issues around digital media and its impact were also unhappy with contemporary approaches so the idea of a media studies 2.0 was well timed, capturing a range of questions that were already in the air, crystallising these concerns and enabling a rare debate within the discipline about what it was and what it should be.

These debates were carried out online and across a range of journals (such as *Interactions* and the *Media Education Research Journal*) as the idea attracted considerable interest and considerable hostility too. This was to be expected. Whereas most media research speaks only to a small number of interested researchers, discussions of the discipline itself affect all those who teach and study it and everyone has their own opinion, based upon their own reading, research and experience. If the discipline is to continue to develop, however, it won't follow the agenda of one person. Any defender of 'media studies 2.0', or any other concept, can't write that future discipline by themselves: a discipline is a collective project and its direction and concerns emerge out of the collectivity and its discussions and activities. This book, therefore, is merely an attempt to intervene in those discussions to change our activities. It is a critique, a provocation and a manifesto designed to make visible the limitations of the discipline and prompt the collective of researchers, lecturers and students to think more radically about what is happening and the response that is needed. As I explained in the introduction, this specific formulation of media studies 2.0 is my own and I don't claim to speak for others such as Gauntlett who've written on the topic. However I am certain that, whatever our differences, what Gauntlett and I share is an awareness of ongoing changes and the need for the discipline to remain relevant in the light of these. This, I would suggest, requires two things.

First, it requires rethinking the content, categories and concepts of broadcast era media studies, dispensing with those elements that no longer function, leaving behind outdated paradigms and testing assumptions, methods, arguments and ideas against the contemporary world. It requires a systematic revision and updating of the discipline in the light of changing media technologies, worlds, social uses and experiences. These changes are widely recognised by our students, the broader public and media professionals but the academic discipline has been slow in recognising the extent of the changes or their significance for digital users. As I've argued, the products of me-dia – their own IMs, PMs, status updates, comments, 'likes', tweets, postings and repostings, are more important to most people than any of the hit films and television shows, the newspapers or news coverage the discipline privileges.

Second, the discipline needs to foreground new forms of media, new aspects of media use and experience and develop new concepts, categories and ideas to study them. This requires embracing elements seen as outside the discipline. We need to turn to philosophy to rethink our relationship with technology and to computer science to follow innovations in computing technology; we need to rethink our media histories, developing new archaeologies of our technologies and practices; we need to return to sociology, politics and economics to think through the changes of digital society and to law to follow its implications for creativity, ownership and personal me-dia production; we need to follow – and critique – the explanations offered by neuroscience, psychology, natural science, economics and business studies for the processes of online life and the activities of the networked individual; we need to immerse ourselves in information studies to understand our historical relationship with data and its classification, storage and collection; and we need to understand science and engineering to trace the hardware and infrastructure underlying the digital world.

This requires far more of the researcher. In a fluid world where forms are in a perpetual beta state, undergoing constant testing, upgrading and improvement in the marketplace, and where intercommunication between devices means that developments in one area send waves through and remake the entire ecology, the individual must be more responsive to changes, taking a more holistic view of media and their interrelationships. The media researcher can no longer specialise: understanding contemporary forms requires the tracing of the ecological connections that surround each form and practice. It requires a continuous overhauling of one's modules and lecture notes; it requires a bridging of the gap between the discipline and reality through following actual developments in media rather than the developments in the disciplinary literature.

Perhaps the best way to think about this is through Thomas Kuhn's idea of 'paradigm' shifts. Although his 1962 book *The Structure of Scientific Revolutions* dealt with the physical not the social sciences, the argument remains relevant. Both progress not through the accumulation of facts and knowledge but through periods of upheaval in which older paradigms and frameworks are challenged by new ways of looking at the subject. As Kuhn says:

> Scientific revolutions are inaugurated by a growing sense ... often restricted to a narrow subdivision of the scientific community, that an existing paradigm has ceased to function adequately in the exploration of an aspect of nature to which that paradigm had previously led the way.

The result is a polarisation into camps and arguments over each paradigm, though what is ultimately decisive is the number of 'anomalies' that the older paradigm fails to incorporate and the gradual movement to the newer perspective until it attains 'the assent of the community'.

It is this disciplinary paradigm shift that we're dealing with today. Developments in digital media aren't an 'add-on' to be studied in optional modules and the post-broadcast ecology can't be adequately explained or followed using broadcast-era concepts, knowledge and assumptions. It requires a remaking of the discipline and the way we approach research and teaching. The established paradigms, however, have an institutional and ideological investment in their own status quo and are hostile to any threat to their position. This, of course, isn't new – the computer pioneer Howard H. Aiken warned, 'Don't worry about people stealing an idea. If it's original you'll have to ram it down their throats' (Frauenfelder, 2005), whilst McLuhan had the measure of academia in his definition of a sociologist as someone who 'permits himself to see only what is acceptable to his colleagues'.

The idea of media studies 2.0 has attracted similar resistance. I've already addressed opposition to the idea that digital media are revolutionary and that media studies 2.0 is a-historical. The emphasis on digitality seems to suggest a simple periodisation of 'old' and 'new' that breaks down when we realise that many 'new' forms have histories that predate modern broadcast media but, as I've argued, one can identify both a historical evolution of mass media and computing and a revolutionary change: a tipping point of popular digital take-up following their meeting and merger and the subsequent transformation of the media ecology, culture and individual experience. I've also shown that it is actually the existing media studies whose historical basis is weak, in its separation of broadcast media from all earlier media forms and even its selective treatment of broadcasting.

A lot depends on how we use media history. Used negatively it can be a conservative force, historicising contemporary developments to re-immerse them in the everyday passage of time, thereby suggesting that nothing new occurs and that the present is not deserving of special attention. Except that discontinuities definitely exist. As Schivelbusch's *The Railway Journey* (1979) and Standage's *The Victorian Internet* (1998) demonstrate, the railway and telegraph can historically inform our understanding of the internet and its cultural impact but we also have to recognise that the internet is different: no prior medium offered its real-time, personalised, interactive, multi-media experiences and possibilities.

A more positive media history recognises that historical processes extend into the present and thus intertwine with digital media. Interested in the layers of continuity and discontinuity, it tries to understand both the way in which the past reappears in the present and the way in which changes in the present require us to create new histories. It urges us to explore new aspects of the past, allowing us to develop new insights into the history of forms and practices. A media studies 2.0, therefore, rejects simplistic linear histories that privilege single forms (such as television, newspapers, cinema, etc.), recognising the broadcast era as one phase in the history of media, but it applies its archaeological methods to digital media as well, emphasising the discontinuities that constitute its revolution whilst simultaneously exploring the continuities of older forms and of unwritten and neglected forms and practices. It remakes media history in the light of the appearance of digital media and the new modes of life that surround it.

This is a more complex position than its critics might imagine. Media studies 2.0 might be assumed to be a simple rejection of older media forms in favour of the new, but it is more interested in the way in which print, radio, cinema and television have been transformed in their material basis, ecological position and relationships, cultural production, distribution and consumption and their individual use. Each medium has had to realign itself to meet the demands of a different era and different market conditions, changing their economic models, content creation, modes of distribution, relationship with other forms and even their own idea of what they are doing and how their forms will be used. Media studies 2.0, therefore, doesn't propose a separation of a 'new media' studies from the older media studies as this implies that those older forms have survived unchanged and that the discipline that studied them can survive without any consideration of the digital revolution. Neither of these is true.

Importantly, whilst media studies 2.0 privileges digital media as a revolutionary force in consuming older forms and practices and creating new modes of media experience, it isn't an uncritical celebration of these forms or these modes. McLuhan commented how 'many people seem to think that if you talk about something recent, you're in favour of it' and discussions of digital media attract the same reaction. A media studies 2.0, however, assumes no particular critical position: its starting point is merely the necessity of exploring the digital revolution. In fact, as I'll argue in the next chapter, the new centrality of productive power has direct and significant implications for an individual who was far safer as a consumer of broadcast, manufactured product. A media studies 2.0 is needed precisely because of the urgency of understanding the dangers of the digital era.

Updates failed?

Although the idea of media studies 2.0 argues that the current discipline isn't adequate to deal with contemporary digital changes, the question remains as to whether *any* discipline can adequately follow and survey the digital ecology. Just as mainstream media studies has tended to see the digital world as requiring few disciplinary changes – the study of content and reception continues as before – so too it has seen no reason to question the continuing value of its existing methodologies. If, however, as I suggested in the last chapter, broadcast era media studies struggled with the volume of broadcast product one might question how it will cope with the much more complex digital ecology.

With its background in the social sciences and humanities, media and film studies employs a range of favoured empirical methodologies. Images are subjected to semiotic analysis, texts are analysed using content analysis and discourse analysis, whilst audiences are studied using both qualitative and quantitative methods, from ethnographic observation, open questionnaires and interviews to more formal, structured questionnaires and interviews. The success of these methods depends on an uncomplicated relationship between the researcher and their object but it is precisely this relationship that is changing. Studying the digital ecology requires us to understand key limitations in our knowledge and its collection and legitimation and in the theorisation of contemporary developments.

The first problem is one of volume. We know the broadcast era was marked by the industrial, factory line, identical, serial mass production of information, messages and products and their distribution by road, rail, wires or airwaves to encompass and culturally cement together entire populations. Decades of broadcast production led to a huge, accumulated volume of media output. In the post-broadcast era we have all that plus our own horizontal, personally produced me-dia output and user-generated content. Add up the almost-continuous one-to-one, one-to-many and many-to-many messages, updates, comments and responses and we are left with a cumulative production whose effect is vast. Speaking at the Techonomy conference at Lake Tahoe on 4 August 2010, Google CEO Eric Schmidt made a remarkable claim: that every two days we now create as much information as we did from the dawn of civilisation up until 2003 – about five exabytes of data – with the real driver being user-generated content, especially pictures, messages and tweets. As I've argued, critics of the value of this 'information' miss the greater personal meaning and significance this me-dia has above broadcast product.

It's hard to even map the scale of informational production today. According to mobile phone statistics, from 2007 to 2010 the number of SMS sent globally rose from 1.8 to 6.1 trillion. According to Portia research 7.8 trillion SMS were sent in 2011, a figure they expected to reach 9.6 trillion in 2012, and to these figures we could add all the MMS, IMs and OTT messages also produced. YouTube provides another example. As already noted, by July 2012 YouTube was already reporting 72 hours of video being uploaded every minute, with 'more video uploaded to YouTube in one month than the three major US networks created in 60 years'. By 2012 Facebook's newsroom was reporting its 901 million monthly active users were uploading over 300 million photos every day, producing over 3.2 billion likes and comments. By early 2012, *every 20 minutes* 1 million links were being shared on Facebook, 1.5 million event invites were sent, 1.8 million status updates were posted, 2 million friend requests were accepted, 2.7 million photos were uploaded, 2.7 million messages were sent and 10.2 million comments were made. By 2012 it was claimed there were 175 million Tweets being sent and 1 million new Twitter accounts being created every day.

In March 2013 Intel released a study claiming that in one minute on the internet there were 1300 new mobile users, 320 new Twitter accounts created, over 2 million Google search enquiries logged, 3,000 photos uploaded, 100,000 new tweets posted, 20 million photographs viewed, 277,000 Facebook log-ins, 6 million Facebook pages viewed, 1.3 million YouTube videos watched and 204 million emails sent and, in all, 639,800 GB of global IP data transferred. The number of networked devices already equalled the global population, they said, and by 2015 there would be twice as many devices as people on the planet. By then it would take five years, Intel claimed, to watch all the video crossing IP networks in a second.

All these statistics will be hopelessly outdated by the time they're published but the general point – and trend – is clear: add up all our user activities and creations, our use of personal messaging services, profile-based services, web pages, forums and blogs, etc. and the overall picture is almost unthinkable. If broadcasting overwhelmed the researcher, the post broadcast era eclipses them. Moreover whilst broadcast production was predictable enough to be sampled (in genres such as rom-coms, sci-fi and action movies or categories such as tabloid and broadsheet), the complexity of our digital production resists this. We can't keep up with me-dia and nor can we even research its scale. Importantly, the media researcher cannot even access the data as it is produced, recorded and owned by the private companies that dominate the digital ecology.

The second problem is that of dispersal. Broadcasting was dominated by mainstream, well-known, widely publicised publishers and distribution channels. The 'publisher' of the material had an official, public point of contact and made their products available through expected channels – bookshops, newsagents, cinemas, radio frequencies, etc. In contrast much of today's digital production is atomistic and decentralised. It happens wherever people are and whenever there is a connection. Even if the technological channels are identifiable – the mobile network, broadband, Wi-Fi – the dispersal of its availability and place of publication makes it difficult to find and follow. Produced for another's phone, or profile page, or for a specific webpage, we have no conceivable way of mapping all the places me-dia are available. This is the age of *thin* media: of media spread over every digital outlet, hidden by the number of possible media experiences and places.

A third problem is ephemerality. Digital media have a particular relationship with time. In some ways digital forms are resilient – electronic trails, records, messages and archives are retained by ISPs, websites and hosting companies; our posts survive on pages long after we've forgotten them; back-up services store copies and information is physically hard to erase or destroy off hard-drives – but in important ways they are also ephemeral. Digital technologies are physically fragile (the broken screen), easily lost (the phone left in a taxi) and information kept on them is left behind with every upgrade (the photos of my children on my old desktop and last mobile). They are ephemeral in their use and attention (our messages and photos are seen, consumed, shared, replied to, deleted and immediately forgotten) and in their relevance and meaning (relating to present concerns and plans and personal issues of the moment), and they are ephemeral in their personal and public availability (messages and posts are rapidly buried, sites and pages are left for dead, comments and contents become harder to rediscover and our productions are easily deleted by ourselves, by administrators, or by automatic software). All of this has significant implications for the media researcher.

The fourth problem is one of access. Broadcast products were designed to be public, open and accessible to the majority of the population: they were made to be seen, were made available through popular channels and were widely advertised to maximise audiences and revenue. In contrast an individual's IMs,

PMs, social-networking pages, messages, comments, updates, activities and photos are inaccessible without permission and much of it is specifically made *not* to be public. This is problematic for a discipline that depends upon the ability to recognise, see and analyse media production and consumption. Embedded in private relationships and networks, with highly personal meanings and content and with individuals reluctant to open these spheres for greater scrutiny, a significant part of our media productions is unavailable to the researcher. Even if they gain access there is no way of determining how representative the information is and only a miniscule amount could ever be sampled. Information about individual use does, of course exist, but it is held by the private companies who control the platforms and whose business models depend upon its exploitation. Meta data about informational activities is as inaccessible for the media researcher as the use itself.

The fifth problem is that of discovery. In the broadcast era discovery was simpler, thanks to public information channels, listings magazines and advertising pushing the products at the population and reviews and word-of-mouth picking up what one missed. The post-broadcast era, however, is marked by a fractal splitting of media interests and attention into entirely personalised and optional worlds of specific cultural forms. Each individual samples very little: our personal interests ensure that we miss what others are interested in with entire media worlds, habits, debates, developments, fads, memes, jokes, knowledge and expertise passing silently by us. Media lecturers have no privileged position from which to trace and study these worlds and their specialised research into particular phenomena misses the diversity of the digital ecology. We have a range of personal search and discovery tools, from search engines, our own interests and hobbies, link-sharing amongst peers, recommendations, reviews and lists, filter sites such as Digg and mass media reporting of net 'hits' but these are imperfect methods that will miss the majority of digital phenomena.

A sixth problem is that of significance. Traditional media studies studied broadcast content produced for mass, public consumption; being created for specific reasons; being designed for mass comprehensibility and meaning and possessing prestige and potential cultural significance as an expression of a major productive outlet and its creative staff. Media researchers studied such content because it had some degree of cultural meaning, affecting the lives of many people and reflecting the ideas and values of the society that produced it. With the rise of cultural studies even popular culture and niche cultures were accorded value. What happens, however, in a culture where mass-produced product constitutes a far smaller proportion of information? – where the fractal dispersal of attention and interests into personal ecologies means that most of this product is overlooked by most of the people, with mass-unifying products becoming far rarer; and in which the personal and peer-produced content has more personal meaning and significance than anything produced by the broadcast industries? One may still study television and film but one can no longer claim the same level of cultural significance or individual meaning broadcast products once possessed.

Though personal and peer-produced media are significant there are problems with how to study its mode of significance. Intended for private, limited and highly specific consumption, it has different modes of meaning, comprehensibility, reference and relevance. It is material with personal or peer significance with no necessary claims to cultural or mass significance or impact and this is a challenge for media researchers. How do you study the ordinariness, incomprehensibility, private jokiness, banality or offensiveness of personal me-dia production: how do you study and what meaning do we derive from 'LOL', 'You suck' and 'Where RU?'

A seventh problem involves the ethical issues of studying individual and peer media production, given the personal nature of the communications, the fact that much will involve young people (or the age cannot be easily determined) and much will also involve illegal or sensitive activities. Studying media activities that will include copying and sharing of material, pornography, libel and abuse and other potentially criminal or offensive forms of behaviour is difficult but studying media consumption and activity *without* including these will result in a skewed representation of personal media use and production.

The eighth problem is that of production. Broadcast producers were public and locatable whereas me-dia producers may not even be found or identified. Who precisely is the user name on sharing sites or forums? How do you establish with any certainty the origins and reality of the me-dia content you study? How do you study anonymous, inaccessible producers? How do you study the vaster ecology of producers and the producers of the technologies and platforms behind them to allow them to create and distribute their thoughts and work? In the post-broadcast era the nature of producers has changed and much remains personal, private and hidden.

The ninth, related problem is that of the audience. The concept needs reconsidering in the digital post-broadcast world but even on its own terms we face the problem of how to study audiences today: how we know about them, identify them, follow their activities and sample and study them. Media studies increasingly treated the audience as the truth of media – as the teleological end-point of the communication process and hence as the final moment and ultimate determinant of the message's meaning. The 'reality' of media was discoverable by studying individuals and audience groups and asking them about their activities and its meaning for them. This is no longer so simple. Who are the audience of a specific YouTube video; who is the audience for social networking and how are they studied; who looks at what web pages; who receives group messages, IMs and PMs, or views public content such as blogs? Who diggs, tags, shares, and reposts? Today's audience can't be easily identified, located, claimed as representative, or known and questioned with certainty.

The tenth problem is that of generalisability. A central assumption of natural, empirical science was that results obtained and confirmed by observation were spatially and temporally generalisable: phenomena recorded in one space and time would also be recorded at any other. The emerging 19th-century 'social sciences' were influenced by positivist ideas, taking the practical success of science in that era as the model for their own methods of knowledge production and legitimation. Though they could not produce absolutely generalisable 'laws', they saw themselves as producing similar observations that built up into objective knowledge about the processes of broadcast consumption that broadly applied across a population.

This faith in a broad generalisability falters in a digital era. The rise of me-dia means that patterns of use, habits and behaviours increasingly vary. What I do with my own media – the sites I look at, my own range of interests, my specific searches, the apps I've got and play with, and my personal ecology of technology, practices and habits – are different from everyone else's. The personalisation and optionalisation of media worlds make it difficult to assume that any information or practices are as generalisable as they were in the broadcast era. But the real problem here is temporal generalisation. The perpetual upgrading and hybridisation of digital media technologies, capacities and uses and the variety and ongoing transformation of user behaviours and pleasures mean that any knowledge we acquire dates very rapidly.

The more focused and detailed the empirical case study the less it stands for anything other than its own moment and place of capture. Such studies tell us what has happened, but not necessarily about the present. Looking for material recently for a module on digital media I found a surfeit of articles based on empirical studies of new technologies and practices but their overly specific focus and the timescales of journal publication meant little if any was still relevant, usable or even interesting. Developments in the digital ecology and personal use of me-dia make the glacial publications of the discipline look increasingly irrelevant.

Given the scale, volume and speed of production today it is impossible to empirically capture a generalisable model of the real. One hundred hours of video uploaded every minute onto YouTube would require an army of researchers to track and analyse, and no matter how great the sample one took it would be devalued every second by the appearance of new material. The scientific ideal of detaching the object to reduce it to elements that can be dissected and analysed at length and in comfort is impossible in the digital world of permanent accretion and flux.

This brings us to the final problems of specialisation and accumulation. The Liberal model of science was based upon an undirected, freely chosen scientific inquiry that would, it was believed, accumulate into a greater whole, leading (as in the market model) to the most efficient system of knowledge. Media research has followed a similar pattern of individually chosen and highly specialised research projects which collectively coalesce into disciplinary knowledge. Today, however, digital convergence and hybridisation makes every media form, content, culture and practice intimately connected with other technologies, levels and practices, with media intertwining in a way that demands a holistic perspective and ecological analysis.

Moreover, individual research cannot accumulate into a coherent whole the way we once expected. No amount of researchers can cope with the production and flux of the digital mediascape. Whilst broadcast media, with its more formulaic production could be sampled through the study of genres and categories or assumed demographics, groups and markets, post-broadcast production doesn't follow these market-led conventions and it's harder to classify and categorise and hence to sample and generalise from. Constituting a smaller and smaller proportion of an expanding ecology, any subject or sample one chooses tells us little of the whole. This is like trying to study the sea through a cup of water.

One solution being developed by digital media researchers is to turn to computational tools and methods. If media studies needs to meet and merge with computer science then this obviously suggests the discipline also needs to incorporate computing's techniques and processes into its own research methodologies. In the era of 'big data' we need computational techniques that enable us to capture and analyse this vast informational landscape. Unless media studies can work on this macro scale then it will never really understand the new digital ecology as ethnographic observation and questionnaires are useless at capturing the system-level phenomena and relationships that we need to be tracking and analysing today. Hence today's media researchers urgently need to update their skills or form strategic alliances with computing researchers.

Lev Manovich already argued in *The Language of New Media* (2001) that 'new media calls for a new stage in media theory', suggesting that 'to understand the logic of new media, we need to turn to computer science. It is there that we may expect to find the new terms, categories and operations that characterise media that became programmable.' Though anticipating the central arguments of this book, his vision of a future 'software studies' or 'software theory' is more specialised than my concept of a broader disciplinary merger. He is correct, however, that computing can serve as a key research tool for the digital environment, with data visualisation software allowing the analysis of large collections of information.

In his 2002 article 'The Anti-Sublime Ideal in Data Art', Manovich argues that 'dynamic data visualisation' constitutes 'one of the genuinely new cultural forms enabled by computing'. In particular he picks up on their ability to deal with the complexity and scale of contemporary digital products: 'They carry the promise of rendering the phenomena that are beyond the scale of human senses into something that is within our reach, something visible and tangible.' In contrast to the Romantic ideal of the 'sublime' – of the unrepresentable – 'data visualisation artists aim at precisely the opposite: to map such phenomena into a representation whose scale is comparable to the scales of human perception and cognition'. 'The challenge of data art', however:

> is *not* about how to map some abstract and impersonal data into something meaningful and beautiful – economists, graphic designers and scientists are already doing this quite well. The more interesting and at the end maybe more important challenge is how to represent the personal subjective experience of a person living in a data society.

Manovich's 2010 paper 'What is Visualization?' expands on this, explaining the value of data visualisation in allowing us 'to discover the structure of a (typically large) data set' and 'to reveal patterns and structures' in data objects.

His examples come from his own 'Software Studies Initiative Lab' which has been working on 'techniques and software to allow interactive exploration of large sets of visual cultural data' such as the display of every cover of *Time* from 1923–2009 or 1074790 manga pages organised by their stylistic properties. Such 'direct data visualization' methods, he concludes, 'will be particularly important for humanities, media studies and cultural institutions' which now are just beginning to discover the use of visualisation but which eventually 'may adopt it as a basic tool' for research, teaching and the exhibition of cultural artefacts.

Computing techniques, therefore, provide one response to the problems of informational complexity, in managing large-scale data and re-presenting it in a way that the human mind can access with the aim of discovering patterns and meanings. But this doesn't solve all the problems I've identified and all meth-odologies remain modes of simulation, modelling their object and our knowledge of it. Another response, therefore, might be to turn from empiricism towards the critical theorisation of the digital ecology. Perhaps the best way to grasp it holistically is not through specialised researches but through the vision of media theory.

McLuhan provides the model here. He famously said that he didn't try to predict the future as anyone could do that: he tried instead to tackle 'the really tough one' – he tried to 'predict the present'. One reason why we don't see the present, he says, is the sensory closure that accepts our dominant environment, placing it beyond perception – as McLuhan gnomically commented, 'Although we don't know who first discovered water it was almost certainly not a fish.' In another metaphor McLuhan describes us as living in 'the rearview mirror' – like being in a car, travelling forward whilst looking backwards, interpreting what we see according to older experiences and categories that we think still fit. Hence 'what we ordinarily think of as present is really the past'. As McLuhan says: 'People never want to look at the present; people live in the rear-view mirror because it's safer, they've been there before, they feel comfort. Anybody who looks at the present is a threat.'

What McLuhan advocated was a *radical presentology*: an ongoing real-time confrontation with the present as it unfolds. He was fond of quoting Edgar Allan Poe's mariner in 'A Descent into the Maelstrom' who survived a whirlpool by following its currents and reading its patterns, arguing that 'his insight offers a possible stratagem for understanding our predicament, our electronically configured whirl'. The only way to cope with our own rapidly changing electronic whirlpool, therefore, is through a similar process of real-time interpretation: 'Faced with information overload,' he argues, 'we have no alternative but pattern recognition.'

The discovery and exploration of patterns, therefore, isn't simply something computer software can help us to do: it becomes the central method for following and understanding the ongoing digital revolution. Media studies 2.0 is a call to recognise that highly specialised empirical studies and analytical readings aren't adequate for grasping a vast, interconnected and rapidly changing digital ecology: what's needed instead is a broader, greater vision and ambition. It is a call to rediscover the essential value of media theory, the role of critical reflection and theoretical analysis as key media research tools, giving us the power to respond in real time to new developments, to comprehend their ecological position and relationships and to trace their political, economic, social and cultural implications. In forcing us to confront ongoing developments in media it frees us from merely following the discipline to following the actual media worlds that exist.

Above all this is a call for a *faster* media studies; a media studies that is more responsive to the world its students inhabit; a media studies confident in its deployment of the ideas of numerous disciplines and historical examples and that pushes at phenomena to capture their radicality. Declaring himself willing 'to junk any statement' he had ever made, McLuhan (1969) laid claim only to a single method – 'the probe'. He saw himself like a safe-cracker, using speculation and experimentation to test ideas and see what worked, playing with ideas and concepts to push things further and break through to new insights. Whilst his critics simply denied anything was happening – 'For all their lamentations,' he said, 'the revolution has already taken place' – McLuhan rejected this 'ostrichlike' denial of the electronic world, advocating instead a more robust, critical approach, urging us 'to charge straight ahead and kick them in the electrodes'. If it wants to grasp the contemporary media world, it is a lesson media studies needs to learn.

9 The 21st-century discipline
User studies and the productive turn

The aim of this chapter is to ask what a media studies 2.0 would look like. What new developments are central to a 21st-century discipline? What should it include and what are the aims of its teaching and research? Any simple list of topics risks becoming rapidly outdated in the digital age but our analysis of the digital revolution and the transformation in media use enables us to identify a broad approach that serves as the basis for understanding ongoing developments in digital media. This approach focuses upon the question of production.

As we've seen, the primary interest of media studies historically has been in consumption. By this I mean the experience of a distributed product: the audience's reception; the effect it has on them and their behaviour; their use of content and their interpretation of its meaning. As I've argued, together these areas of reception and content formed the core of the discipline. Media studies developed out of a concern with the effects of mass media, developing a focus upon sponsored empirical research into audiences. The post-war period continued this tradition, supported by a growing interest in analysing media content with the rise of film studies, ideological and semiological analyses and the take-off of Culturalist perspectives.

This focus on consumption was entirely understandable. The primary experience of informational production and distribution in the broadcast era was *as a receiver* and media studies developed both as a response to and reflection of that system, in its organisation and concerns. Whilst media practice taught production skills, the academic discipline privileged consumption – investigating the habits of consumers for industry and government or teaching students the skills needed as a consumer, such as understanding the complexity of effects, the construction of meaning and the critical interpretation of its codes.

The key skills needed in the digital age, however, are very different from those required in the broadcast age. No one ever went to prison, lost their job or faced extradition to the USA for misunderstanding the active audience, misunderstanding the colour symbolism of Hitchcock's *Vertigo* or failing to grasp the representation of gender in *Desperate Housewives*, yet these are real possibilities with digital media. Consumption skills remain essential, and indeed are central to real democratic participation, but they are only a small part of the skills required today.

This is because, as we've seen, the digital era is marked by the *productive turn*. This is the passage from a world broadly bifurcated between a small number of product or content producers and a mass of consumers, to one where individuals are increasingly empowered as producers of signals, responses, objects, messages and content and where they become the centre of their own personal media ecologies, managing their own equipment, connections, storage, data flows, inputs and outputs and the selection of information, entertainment and communication. Very simply, today, everyone is a producer. So, today, this user, their capacities and their skills have become central to the discipline. Where media studies 1.0 was orientated around consumption and its skills, a media studies 2.0 is orientated around production and one's productive skills. At the centre of this productivity is 'the user' and to understand what a media studies 2.0 entails we need to first understand this user and what skills they need today.

The birth of user studies

Although, as I've argued, the study of media production has been largely eclipsed by the investigation of consumption, there was at least a shared disciplinary conception of what 'production' actually was. Media studies employed a linear, teleological model of communication tracing the creation, distribution, reception and interpretation of a message and valorising the latter as the privileged end point and ultimate meaning of this process. As such it saw production (1) as an isolatable element of communication; (2) as a largely professional practice, involving the creation of a message within major broadcast industries; (3) as a unilateral process, with a top-down distribution to a mass audience; and (4) as secondary to the process of reception, as the success of a message could only be judged by the audience's consumption.

One immediate problem with this model is that it no longer applies to the digital era. Today production isn't isolatable, but rather extends through a population who are engaged in an ongoing process of continuous communication and response, and as such it has become more socially and culturally important than reception. But the main reason why this conception is inadequate is that it defined production simply as *the creation of content*. What digital developments allow us to recognise is a broader process of production that includes the production of the technologies, of the systems that exploit them and, most importantly, of the users themselves. To understand this we need to understand what 'the user' is and why they are different from the 'audience'.

The 'audience' was the key category of the broadcast era, representing the collective entity that products were produced for, with individual consumers of mass-produced content together forming that broader, abstract unit. This audience was determined in many ways – by their economic position and culture and also by a media content that was carefully designed to appeal to key demographics or produce specific emotions or behaviour. Mainstream media studies downplayed such determinisms, emphasising instead the audience's empowered position as the critical receiver of content. Digital media were quickly incorporated as an extension of existing media and their practices. Hence the new digital interactivity and empowerment of the individual was seen as confirming everything the discipline thought about the audience. 'The user', therefore, was claimed as a logical development and realisation of the 'active audience'. The key figure allowing this connection was 'the fan' and the key author promoting this view was Henry Jenkins.

Jenkins' *Textual Poachers* (1992) was a central text in the rise of fan studies. Directly inspired by the Birmingham School, it offered an ethnographic account of pre-digital, mass media fan activity including fan fiction and videos, aiming to counter received ideas about fans and promote the Culturalist position that media consumers were 'active, critically engaged and creative'. By 2006's *Convergence Culture* Jenkins says this idea of the active audience has now become widely accepted, a development he attributes to the rise of 'new technologies' which 'are enabling average consumers to archive, annotate, appropriate and re-circulate media content'. Jenkins here redefines 'convergence' as the flow of content across multiple media channels, enabling him to downplay technology and privilege the appropriation and use of material by fans. Thanks to digital media, he says, fan culture has become mainstream: 'The web has brought these consumers from the margins of the media industry into the spotlight', collapsing the distinction of consumers and producers to leave us as 'participants' in a 'participatory culture'.

This idea of a passage from active audiences, through fans, to digital users has become popular in the discipline, being taken as proof of the centrality of the audience and re-energising research into their activities. Hence the 'audience' and 'user' have become synonymous in the discipline with 'audience studies' and 'user studies' referring to the same research and being hosted in the same academic conferences. The two concepts, however, are not synonymous and indeed are diametrically opposed, emerging from different traditions and possessing important implications for the kind of media studies that results.

The concept of the 'audience' is intimately tied to broadcast modes of consumption. With its Latin roots in 'audire' (to 'hear'), the term developed from its use for a legal hearing to come to refer to congregations for public speakers, then theatre-goers and print readerships before becoming associated with mass media in the early 20th century with the success of cinema and radio. In contrast the term 'user' has a different history. It first became popular in the 1930s to refer to drug takers but the broader idea was associated with the concept of tool use. Benjamin Franklin's 1778 claim that 'man is a tool-making animal' challenged traditional emphases on the mind and rationality and helped spark 19th century palaeoanthropological debates about tool use and evolution. Though naturalists and archaeologists have disproven the idea that humanity is definable by tool use, tools have become seen instead as central to the process of 'hominisation'. The modern concept of the 'user' is traceable to these debates but it emerges out of the use of one particular type of tool: the computer.

Much has been written about the invention of the personal computer but what is overlooked is *the simultaneous invention of the user*. One of the earliest appearances of the term in computing is in Vannevar Bush's 1945 essay 'As We May Think', which presents a remarkable image of a future recorder-producer and 'user' of the 'Memex' – a hypothetical device many see as anticipating the internet, which they controlled, manipulated, read from, recorded to, linked within, added to, copied and shared. At the same time Norbert Wiener was developing his philosophy of 'cybernetics' (1948), which offered a vision of the symbiotic conjoining of humanity with an active technological partner in a hybrid system, not only receiving signals from their environment but sending messages of control and changing in relation to new inputs.

Wiener's philosophy would have a huge influence on J. C. R. Licklider's 'Man-Computer Symbiosis' (1960) and his prediction in 'The Computer as Communication Device' (1968) of the potential of networked computer 'users' to create their own informational environment and produce and share their own content. Along with McLuhanism, cybernetics would also influence Stewart Brand who would become a key figure, introducing into computing circles counter-cultural ideals of the free, creative use of small-scale, self-sufficient tools for individual transformation and mental expression: ideas that – echoed through Schumacher, Illich and Nelson – would influence the personal computer pioneers.

Licklider funded the work of Douglas Engelbart at SRI, though Engelbart's vision of 'human augmentation' owed more to Bush's human-centred approach than Licklider's cybernetics. Engelbart's research led to the famous 1968 demonstration of the modern graphic user interface, mouse, icons, interactive text, hypertext, electronic mail and real-time collaborative text editing. If Engelbart invented modern personal computing he didn't solely invent usability – that owed as much to the Xerox Parc team who produced the Alto, the working model of his ideas, and to Alan Kay who conceived of computing as a medium that should be usable by everyone. Kay embraced the educational theories of Papert, promoting modes of computing that children could use and produce with. All these ideas about the user would be incarnated in the personal computers that would emerge from the hobbyist community in the late 1970s.

This is a different lineage from the audience and it has three important implications. First, unlike the audience, the user cannot be treated apart from technology. Whether thought in terms of symbiosis or augmentation, the technology is actively and intimately connected to the user and their desires, abilities, productions and effects. A real 'user studies' is a study of this relationship and as such is opposed to much contemporary audience studies.

Second, whereas the audience was about consumption, the user is about production. The dominant broadcast technologies limited the technological relationship to functional manipulation (tuning in the radio, or changing the channel) and reception. The idea of the active audience merely valorised behaviours that were local and responsive and which had few means of significant feedback due to the unilateral nature of broadcasting. In contrast the digital user is defined by their bilateral signals of communication and control: by their ability to communicate back, to steer the technology and make it do what they want and to produce and share their own signals.

This certainly involves spectatorship – we still watch digital content for example – but this does not make us an 'audience' as the defining element of the experience is the ability to control consumption, to organise the signals and to produce one's own response in turn. We naturally recognise this control in our use of other technologies. Hence although driving involves watching the road we still refer to ourselves as 'car drivers' not 'road audiences' and the same principle applies to our use of digital tools. The user is always active, always controlling and directing their experience and always producing and changing in response – even when watching TV or a film they will be checking their phone, tweeting about the programme, responding to a friend, or commenting upon and sharing something. What distinguishes the user from the audience is this real time, ongoing, operative control, direction and feedback, the new signals that are continually created and the changes in the user and environment caused by their production.

This is what Jenkins misses. The pre-digital fans stopped being audiences at the moment they became users of other tools – video cameras and tape, typewriters, photocopiers – and turned existing content into their own productions. The development of networked digital tools allowed the full flowering of their productive and distributive capacities and hence their realisation as users rather than audiences. Jenkins admits this, in moving to the term 'participants' but he retains a limited Culturalist perspective ignoring both the technological relationship and the production of the user themselves.

Because this is the third and most important aspect of the user: *they are always produced*. The digital empowerment of the user appears to prove the Culturalist idea that the creative individual and their activities are the most important part of the communication process, with the rise of me-dia seeming to reinforce the humanist position underpinning this view. But an understanding of the user's lineage demonstrates not only that they cannot be separated from the technological relationship but that they are the *product* of this relationship. The user has always been conceived of, planned and designed alongside and into the technology, being determined by the process of its production with their needs, desires, capacities and communicative and productive potential decided and implemented for them. This isn't a perfect determinism – one may choose what to write with a wordprocessor, and uses such as SMS were unanticipated by the phone industry – but what the user does is always in response to and is either determined, constrained or guided by what has been designed into the form.

Production, therefore, involves more than the creation of content: to understand production we first need to understand the production of the user and their capacities. This design of the user has become central to many companies' business models. Jonathan Zittrain's *The Future of the Internet* (2008) explores this, tracing the movement from open 'generative' systems such as the PC and early internet that could be added onto by their user to the closure of user possibilities by companies who increasingly produce 'sterile *appliances* tethered to a network of control'. Zittrain's example is the iPhone which he contrasts with Apple's PC revolution: whereas the Apple II encouraged user programming the iPhone comes 'preprogrammed' with all innovation for it coming from or through Apple.

Apple carefully produce their own users. Steve Jobs refused to give people 'what they want' arguing, 'our job is to figure out what they're going to want before they do ... People don't know what they want until you show it to them. That's why I never rely on market research' (Isaacson, 2012). Apple's aim, therefore, was not simply to produce a designed and controlled product, but to design and produce its user and monitor, direct and control their ongoing interactions with their devices and experience of the products. Their user moves within a closed ecology of Apple technologies and services, locked together by their iTunes and iCloud accounts, with payment details stored for the seamless purchasing and downloading of authorised, tightly controlled content, with their needs and capacities all decided in advance. Whilst jail-breaking the iPhone or transferring music back off your iPod is possible, these possibilities exist in tension with the smooth running of the pre-programmed experience and require some degree of expertise to accomplish. These productive tensions between the user design and user skills are central to understanding production.

The production of the user is linked, therefore, to the production of the technologies and the ecology of devices that we use. Hence the need for an analysis of the process of technology's creation, the agents, engineers, designers and marketers responsible for it and the social values implicated in these designs. This also involves an understanding of the deep materiality of the medium: the 'layers' Lessig describes, their constituent elements and inter-relationships and the architectural 'constraints' upon our use. For the invisible elements of technology are as significant as the visible.

These invisible elements include the key role of computer software in today's media experiences. Manovich introduced the idea of 'software studies' in *The Language of New Media* (2001), and this term has been taken up and developed in the work of critics such as Matthew Fuller, Noah Wardrip-Fruin, Wendy Hui Kyong Chun, Alexander R. Galloway, David Berry and Adrian Mackenzie. Software studies is an emerging field, combining humanities and computational perspectives to explore the significance of software to all areas of contemporary industry, cultural production and media consumption, linking with other emerging fields such as 'platform studies' (which considers the relationship of hardware and software) and 'critical code studies' (which is concerned with the interpretation of source code) to form an essential element of today's media analysis.

The materiality of our networked systems and informational experiences is also part of this analysis. Our media world includes the underlying infra-structure that links it together – the cables, wires, connections, exchanges and transmitters that provide the basis of our seamless experiences and the organisation and operation of the companies that manage the exchanges and servers. The January 2008 breaking of an undersea cable that cut off internet access for 75 million people in the Middle East and India highlighted the material reality beneath our ethereal connections.

This leads to the question of how we manage this materiality. The physical management of electronic data has attracted increasing attention within information and library studies. As David Weinberger's *Everything is Miscellaneous* (2007) and Alex Wright's *Glut* (2008) demonstrate, how we classify, organise, store and retrieve information, the meta-data we attach to it and how we extract meaning and value from it have become central issues with the digitalisation of older forms and content, ongoing developments in digital media and the take-off of digital archives. New practices force us to examine historical models of organisation and their impact to understand contemporary processes better. Today search has become central to our personal media ecologies. How we manage the digital flow and the mechanisms of sorting, classification, discovery, recommendation, tagging, sharing, reposting, linking, liking, and retweeting need more disciplinary attention, as does the way in which these possibilities are produced: the software that enables them, the design of user capacities and needs, the platforms and services we use and the companies that underlie them.

The study of media materiality also involves the study of its failure. Virilio argues each new technology invents its own accidents – 'to invent the sailing ship or steamer is to invent the shipwreck'. Hence the need for a *digital accidentology*, encompassing the precariousness of our technologies and connections; hardware and software failures; ISP outages and traffic management; broken, failing, slow and obsolete equipment; web crashes, lags and error notices; our continual management of our own connectivity, use and informational experience; the reliance on electricity, chargers and batteries; the problem of data loss, superseded storage forms and file formats; the decay of data and the physical destruction and wear of our devices. Neglected in the broadcast era, these highlight again the centrality of the user and their activities and experience.

So too do developments in 'natural user interfaces'. Traditional media studies paid little attention to these, due to the over-familiarity of broadcast interfaces and the discipline's disinterest in technology, whilst computing interfaces have remained stable since the invention of the GUI/WIMP paradigm. The year 2002's *Minority Report* famously gave us a vision of future multi-touch and gestural computing but what was remarkable was the speed of its realisation and commercial exploitation. The iPhone (2007) popularised touchscreens, developing a series of finger gestures producing a new bodily choreography of the user. The iPad (2010) developed these further and most smart phones and tablets and laptops and desktop mouse pads now employ touch.

Gestural computing, based upon sensors in gloves and equipment tracked by a computer, has also taken off. Oblong industries provided the system in *Minority Report* and their G-speak spatial operating environment illustrates its possibilities, but it was the Nintendo Wii (2006) that made gesture an everyday technology. Motion capture became popular with the Xbox 360 Kinect (2010) and in September 2012 Microsoft were awarded a patent for an immersive motion capture game system including image projection onto the room's walls. 3D has also been commercially revived with digital television, cinema and the Nintendo 3DS (2011), whilst 'augmented reality' (AR) systems, overlaying digital data onto images of the real world, are being used by everyday services such as the 'Nearest Tube' app and experimental devices such as Microsoft's 'MirageTable'. In 2012 Google unveiled 'Google Glass', an AR wearable computing system, whilst Apple's 'Siri' voice-command application was released in 2011.

Perhaps the most remarkable developments have been in 'brain–computer interfaces' (BCI). Emotiv demonstrated the 'Epoc' EEG headset game controller in 2008 enabling video-game control by brainwaves but other experiments in direct neural interfaces using brain-implanted electrodes have also shown results, enabling first monkeys and later humans to control robotic arms by thought alone. Though at an early stage, it suggests a path of development towards intimate, internal, symbiotic interfaces biologically uniting technology and humanity and rendering the very concept of 'media' – as a mediation – obsolete.

Whilst media studies still privileges film, television, radio and print, the last few years have seen remarkable developments in digital media use. These include a movement from the static, single desktop placed in a study and shared by all to a new mobile, individualised, always-on experience. Smart phones began this process but the rise of home Wi-Fi, cheaper laptops and netbooks and the tablet form liberated the internet within the home, allowing more users, increased mobility, a greater penetration of digital entertainment and a realignment of domestic media attention. Where Gibson's 'cyberspace' was a Gnostic realm apart – an informational space separate from the lower, phenomenal world of 'meat' – requiring special access, today's informational space implodes with everyday life, interpenetrating and layering onto real-world relations in a single, augmented world.

The rise of apps is another example of this change. Few media texts have caught up with them but since the opening of Apple's 'App Store' in July 2008 they've become an important part of the digital ecology, changing the production and consumption of software, increasing the personalisation of devices and experiences and altering our patterns of informational access, use and production. Apple's store passed its 25 billionth download in March 2012 and just over a year later it had doubled this, reaching its 50 billionth download in May 2013. In May 2012 Rovio announced their *Angry Birds* app franchise alone had had over 1 billion global downloads. By September 2013 that too had doubled to 2 billion, bringing in US$199m in game and merchandise sales in the previous year. Apps, therefore, have become an important economic sector. Mobile app store downloads were expected to have increased from 64 billion in 2012 to 102 billion by the end of 2013 with total app store revenues increasing in the same period from US$18bn to US$26bn. Apple's app store revenue alone has risen from US$769m in 2009 to US$3.6bn in 2011 to an expected US$9bn in 2013 and a projected US$22.4bn by 2016.

This move to a 'post-PC paradigm' is reinforced by the rise of cloud computing: the accessing of computing services and information from a network rather than local storage. What began as a business service took off with Web 2.0, as people increasingly moved their personal information online, whilst the success of mobile devices with limited storage aided the success of cloud streaming and storage services such as those offered by Amazon, Google and Apple in 2011. Today much content is accessed through the cloud, with automatic synchronisation across our personal devices, and this trend has significant implications for our ownership of our own information; for its security and privacy; for our guaranteed access to data and content; for the existence and stability of information; and for our control over our informational experiences. As Amazon's withdrawal of cloud services from WikiLeaks in December 2010 demonstrates, there are political implications here with the storage and distribution of information constituting an important future source of power.

The user experience, therefore, is continually interwoven with the issue of who designs the user and provides, designs and controls the technologies and services. A media studies 2.0 demands a renewed attention to the political economy of media and the ecology of companies. Technology companies such as Apple, Microsoft, Google, Intel, Vodafone and China Mobil have joined energy, banking and transport giants as among the most successful in the world whilst other nascent companies such as Amazon and Facebook have become central to our everyday media experience. Though discussion of their business models, patent wars, innovations, competition and ecology of products and services is common online and in newspapers and magazines, media studies texts pay them far less attention. It is significant that Charles Arthur's analysis of the operations of Apple, Microsoft and Google, *Digital Wars* (2012), was written by a technology journalist not a media lecturer.

What needs to be understood is the role of the user for these companies with the convergence of business models around the individual. Businesses that began with different services – Google's search and advertising; Amazon's book sales; Facebook's social networking – now compete across a range of technologies, products and services. At the heart of this competition is the attempt to capture, control and fence the individual within the company's own ecology, promote their free and paid services and harvest their information in a mode of vertical integration that goes far further than anything the broadcast industries managed. This harvesting is continuous and near-invisible, giving rise to companies such as Flurry Analytics whose business is gathering individual data. Flurry is used by over 7,5000 companies, placing its products into over 200,000 apps where it is used to measure a range of aspects of their use. Without the user's knowledge it takes in 1.5TB of data a day from over 1.4 billion app sessions on 574 million devices, recording all aspects of the user's relationship with their own apps.

The question of the user also includes the issue of the digital self. Early cybercultural studies such as Rheingold's *Virtual Community* (1993) and Turkle's *Life on the Screen* (1995) explored the expression of this self on BBSs and MUDs but the rise of Web 2.0 has pushed this to the fore. Contemporary media studies is paying more attention now to digital self-presentation but its description and analysis isn't sufficient. The online self isn't simply a voluntary performance but is produced through and in response to the technologies, sites, services and platforms created for its inhabitation. As such, as we've seen, it cannot be understood apart from its technological relationships and the companies and business models exploiting its appearance. Hence the importance of analyses of 'digital labour' such as Terranova's *Network Culture* (2004) and Scholz's collection *Digital Labor* (2012). The online self is central to our me-dia experiences but it also represents a convergence of individual and technology and of personal expression, play, everyday life and pleasure with the sphere of political economy, labour and exploitation.

A media studies 2.0 begins, therefore, from the digital revolution and the productive turn. It involves the study of the user and their activities as both modes of empowered expression (producing their own response to the world and making their own ecology), and as designed, produced, controlled, guided and monitored modes of being. The user's behaviour is a product of the tensions between their design and their own designs; between their production and their own productions; between their controls and their own control of their use. The user is important not only as a positive avenue of liberated expression, creativity and connection but also for their technological insertion, use and relationships and the ecology of businesses, services and platforms that produce and exploit their possibilities.

Understanding production

As we've seen, the digital revolution and the rise of me-dia are central to the democratisation of production. This revolution has seen the take-off of personal technologies, messaging options and platforms, mobile cameras and videos with easy uploading and sharing options, user-generated content, sharing sites, social media and networking systems, specialised publishing platforms, options to respond or comment, forums and boards and online gaming and community relationships, all of which have made production ubiquitous. One of the most important consequences of this reorientation of the informational ecology is a shift in values as me-dia productions become more important to us than commercial content.

As an example, I spent the night of the opening ceremony of the 2012 Olympic Games on Facebook, along with many friends, following, commenting upon and critiquing the event. The entire spectacular event was secondary to our own activities: it was just a background to the real meaning of the evening for us which was what *we* were doing. The athletes felt the same. Close-ups of the parade showed they were filming the event with their own cameras. Their own personal experience was more important than their allotted role as a spectacle for the audience: for them too the mass media coverage was far less important than their own need to capture their moment, to save it for themselves and their family and friends. Their recording of the event was more important than the official recording.

This shift in values is confusing and even terrifying for media professionals as me-dia disrupt and remake the broadcast ecology. Individuals who, historically, have had little ability to communicate with each other or respond to messages find digital networks suddenly allow the unleashing of the full range of their private and public everyday behaviours, thoughts, desires, emotions and interests. Commentators approach this ecological disruption from particular political perspectives: liberal texts such as Benkler's *The Wealth of Networks* (2006), Shirky's *Here Comes Everybody* (2008) and Leadbetter's *We Think* (2008) all champion the positive contributions of the creative, enlightened individual, whilst conservative texts such as Keen's *The Cult of the Amateur* (2008) and *Digital Vertigo* (2012) have attacked the rise of the ignorant, destructive, talentless mob.

But the digital public adhere to no simple political philosophy. What they realise is not a political but an *aesthetic* idea of participation; one whose lineage is traceable to the Futurists and their evening soirees where they presented their ideas and poems to a boisterous public who bought fruit to throw from sellers who pitched their stalls outside the theatre. There had been audience participation before, most notably in the theatre and music hall, but the 19th century had seen a systematic disciplining of the spectator under the demands of capitalist business and Victorian morality, leading to the installation of seats, timed performances, reduced audience interaction and the removal of alcohol. Public participation, therefore, was part of the experience but it wasn't yet the centre – and the point – of the experience. That came one day in 1910 when the audience turned up to find the Futurists had double-booked the seats, leading to arguments and fights throughout the theatre whilst the Futurists watched from the stage. This was the moment when public participation became not just part of the event but *the event itself*.

The Dadaists extended this provocation and solicitation of audience participation in their own performances but it was the German Dadaists that took this to the streets. Their launch of the journal *Jedermann Sein Eigner Fussball* on 15 February 1919 was accompanied by crowds of people as the copies were distributed. The journal's title was important: there has rarely been a better expression of playful, chaotic participation than 'everyman his own football' with its image of a crowded pitch with 22 balls, breaking all the rules of the game. There was, therefore, an avant garde idea of participation in the early 20th century that was very different from the prevailing mode of the elite, hierarchical representation of the people, whether in democratic politics (with organised parties controlling participation and voters represented by politicians) or the mass media (where wealthy newspaper barons or institutions such as the BBC laid claim to be the 'voice' of the people).

The aesthetic idea re-emerged in 1956–57 in Allan Kaprow's idea of 'the happening' – a largely improvised public performance in which all public participation was part of the art event – and in the 1960s counterculture where 'the happening' became a description for any be-in where being there and doing your own thing was all. 'Participation' became a buzzword in art and popular culture and McLuhan leapt upon the term to explain why electronic media were more participative than older forms. This participation, however, remained limited to an extended experience and empathy and when McLuhan wanted to laud the productive powers of the individual he had few technologies other than the photocopier to point to. Digital media, however, realised this aesthetic ideal of participation, creating a space where all are invited and all behaviours form the event, regardless of the political ideals, expectations, values, rules or laws of those who oversee or comment upon it. In the Web 2.0 world 'everyman his own football' is replaced with everyman their own printing press, camera and video camera.

This mode and its behaviours clash with existing systems, destabilising existing models of media production, distribution and consumption; eroding business models and overthrowing stable ideas of what the 'public' is, what it wants and what it does. It annoys, confuses and exasperates media professionals, broadcast companies and everyone using broadcast techniques to influence the public. Governments, authorities, institutions, organisations, private companies, advertising agencies, public relations firms, and all those whose modes of address, assumptions, operation, power or business have been built around broadcasting, have had to adjust to a changing ecology of media use and power.

Established content providers such as the music and film industries, for example, have been caught out by bottom-up developments in digital use such as breaking DRM, ripping and copying content, the development and take-up of file-sharing systems and software, the circumvention of legal and technological attempts to clamp-down on these behaviours and the sharing of tips and links as to how to acquire content. Where once the industries easily produced and controlled their consumers through a limited range of technologies and user possibilities, they now face a bewildering diversity of user needs, desires and preferred modes of consumption; differing levels of familiarity and capability with technologies and a differing willingness to use illegal avenues or share expertise and content.

The same ecological shifts are seen in the news content industry, with the rise of 'citizen' or 'participatory' journalism and the broader culture of free access, online user-generated content and informational sharing having complex effects upon journalism. It has impacted upon its business models by taking its readers and advertisers and threatening the status and jobs of professional journalists, though it has also been profitably incorporated as a cheap source of authentic user-submitted content and stories and as a means of reinforcing audience identification and loyalty. Professional producers haven't always welcomed these shifts, as seen in Joel Stein's 2007 *LA Times* column, 'Dear Reader, Please Don't Email Me', with its critique of interactivity and hostility to non-professionals ('I don't want to talk with you; I want to talk at you'), and also *That Mitchell and Webb Show*'s 2008 satire of the news' invitation of comments: 'What possible reason could there be for you not to email us. Certainly ignorance shouldn't be a bar. You may not know anything about the issue but I bet you *reckon* something. So why not tell us what you *reckon* ... '.

This ecological disruption should be at the heart of contemporary media studies. The major broadcast media of television, cinema, radio and print remain key modes of informational experience dominated by powerful firms who produce content, control their copyright and manage the international exploitation of their products. A media studies 2.0 foregrounds their transformation and their attempts to reconfigure their services for a post-broadcast era, considering how they have tried to continue with their existing business models whilst adapting to new modes of production, distribution and consumption and changing markets. It explores how the industries have included or become digital technologies and their ongoing deployment of new technologies to improve their services or market position, pursuing an analysis of the rapidly shifting ecology of big digital media and their ecological manoeuvres.

This includes the consideration of the competitive responses of businesses to these changes, especially those aimed at the empowered user. The music industry is typical here in its legal response with lawsuits against individuals; attempts to sabotage and monitor file-sharing systems; legal action against claimed copyright infringement (from legal University file-sharing systems to P2P services such as Morpheus, Grockster and Limewire and digital locker services such as Megaupload); and lobbying governments to influence law and policy-making (such as in campaigns to extend copyright terms). This lobbying encompasses both national campaigns (such as the stalled 2011 US SOPA and PIPA acts) and international ones (such as ACTA, the 2011–12 proposed multinational agreement against copyright infringement). Such activities are, again attempts by an industry to define and determine the digital user and dictate and control their activities.

As well as corporate attempts to control the user, governments and other authorities have also become increasingly intrusive. John Perry Barlow's 1996 'Declaration of the Independence of Cyberspace' proved naïve in its vision of a separate, transcendental, unregulatable sphere and governments have developed both a close interest in the online world and the means to impose their will through the control of the infrastructure and DNS, control of ISPs, search engines and companies operating within their jurisdiction and the arrest of individuals and seizure of equipment. China has most famously developed an effective system of censorship based upon directive-led editing and filtering, official surveillance, public monitoring, attempts at licensing and real-name registration, and arrests and imprisonment, whilst censorship is common in countries such as Iran, Burma, Pakistan, Cuba and Saudi Arabia.

These attempts at control are once again in tension with users who may attempt to circumnavigate both legal and technological limitations on their actions and share tips and expertise with others. During the Iranian election protests of 2009–10, for example, protestors used YouTube and other sites to globally highlight the death of Neda Agha-Soltan at the hands of government militia; used social media to swap lists of proxy servers and employed anti-censorship software such as Freegate and Haystack (though concerns over the latter's security later came to light). Western democracies also try to control and censor the internet, usually for legal reasons, though it may have explicitly political overtones, such as the US action against WikiLeaks, or be in the explicit service of major content industries, such as requests to take down copyrighted material under the US DMCA (1998) or requests for the IP addresses of copyright infringing individuals under the UK Digital Economy Act (2010).

Beyond explicit censorship there is also the problem of surveillance for the user. Every level the user interfaces with – their phone provider, their hardware manufacturer, their ISP, the platforms they use, the apps they install, the companies they interact with or purchase from and the websites they move across or use – and every digital click and action produces informational value for someone. Governments are also interested in monitoring user activities and even democratic countries are pushing to extend real-time surveillance and informational data collection and mining.

This was confirmed from June 2013 when newspapers began publishing a range of revelations about the US and UK government's activities based on information supplied by the whistleblower Edward Snowden. This included information about 'Prism', a code name for a US 'Signals Intelligence Address' – a mass-electronic surveillance data-mining programme in use since 2007. This was a set of technologies and operations allowing it to collect information from a range of leading US companies including Google, Apple, Facebook, Microsoft. Though these companies denied any 'back-door access' and published the numbers of government requests they'd received, others leaked information suggesting government access was routine and relatively simple. There was also the suggestion that the UK intelligence hub GCHQ could bypass legal procedures in the UK to access information about suspects' use of US-based services via Prism, though this was officially denied.

Information also materialised about the US 'Boundless Informant' programme, an NSA tool for collecting records of communication (or 'metadata'), categorising it and making it available for analysis via an interactive map indicating its source. Leaks show that in March 2013 the NSA collected 97 billion pieces of intelligence as part of this programme from worldwide computer networks. The UK's GCHQ was revealed to have its own 'Mastering the Internet' programme, later named 'Project Tempora', which involved plugging into the cables connecting the UK to the broader internet, filtering a proportion of the incoming and outgoing traffic and storing metadata for up to 30 days. This required the cooperation of the cable companies and access to the information was granted to the NSA.

Add on stories of the NSA and GCHQ's successful cracking of the basic encryption technologies used to secure our personal accounts and transactions and keep our activities private, and the NSA's attempts to track TOR ('the onion router') private communications, and a picture builds-up of huge, heavily funded, secret, state-based surveillance systems with little democratic oversight, able to access records of (and sometimes the content of) email, video and voice chat, videos, photos, voice-over-internet chats, file transfers and social networking data, as well as the everyday use of a range of company services for their entire population, as well as for many others globally accessing services or communicating with that country. In such a situation everyone is guilty:

everyone's information is meaningful and can be used against them as part of a system of 'pattern of life' profiling. Even innocent actions can now count against you, as shown by the case of one New York family in August 2013. Their house was surrounded by Joint Terrorism Task Force Officers who searched the premises and questioned the family based on information received about their online search enquiries. The mother had an interest in pressure cookers; the father was looking how to buy back-packs and the 'news junkie' son was Googling information about the April 2013 Boston bombings and this had been sufficient to alert the authorities.

The user, therefore, is *not* the audience. Whereas the latter are safe from the media companies and authorities, unreachable except by audience research testing and simulations and dissolved into a hypothetical mass with their real opinions, activities and use of the content largely unseen and unrecorded, the user is individually visible, informationally important, identifiable, trackable and traceable. All of this has significant implications for what media studies itself should be.

In the last chapter I argued that broadcast era media studies emphasised two competing forms of literacy – production skills to serve the media industries and consumption skills to aid the critical interpretation of industry products. In the digital, post-broadcast era this competitive division is obsolete. With every individual empowered as a producer, the discipline needs to confront and teach the new practical and theoretical skills needed by this digital user. I've already suggested that media practice needs to focus on computing skills and digital production but whilst this better prepares the student for 21st-century media employment (and fulfils the 'employability' needs of an increasingly marketised Higher Education sector), this is only a minor part of the changes required. The digital user doesn't simply need to learn how to serve the industry or produce for profit but, as media theoreticians have always understood, they need to learn how to defend themselves in the digital world.

Hence the theoretical skills taught by the discipline need to be updated. Broadcast-era consumption skills based around interpreting content and understanding reception are no longer sufficient. Today students need a theoretical understanding of the issues around their own digital production and use. They need to understand their production and management of their self, their own media ecology, communications and responses and the electronic footprint created.

This includes an understanding of the law. Activities that are possible and legal in respect to older forms may well be illegal with digital technologies – whereas you have the right to sell on your analogue music, for example, you cannot legally sell on purchased digital music files. Users need an understanding of the laws of copyright, digital property and IP in their interactions with information and their posting, downloading, sharing, mixing, publication and republication of content. So too do they need an understanding of the laws of communication and the appropriate legislation on the freedom of speech and its limits within each territory. If we all become media producers we need to know how that production may be used against us.

Social media use, for example, increasingly impacts upon employment: in October 2011 a Manchester housing worker took legal action after being demoted for expressing critical comments about gay marriage on Facebook; in November 2008 Virgin Atlantic sacked 13 cabin crew after they posted negative Facebook messages about their passengers and jokes about faulty engines; in February 2009 a 16-year-old girl in Essex was fired when colleagues reported she'd described her office job as 'boring' on Facebook, and in March 2009 a sandwich bar worker was fired after a video appeared on YouTube showing him stuffing lettuce leaves up his nose then replacing them in their trays.

More seriously social networking can also lead to arrest and imprisonment. In August 2011 two men were sentenced at Chester crown court to four years' imprisonment for inciting disorder after posting about the riots on Facebook, even though no violence occurred, whilst in December two Dundee teenagers were sentenced to three years each for breach of the peace after setting up a Facebook page called 'Riot in the Toon'. In August 2009 a teenage girl became the first person jailed for bullying on Facebook, receiving three months in a Young Offenders Institution for harassment. In June 2011 a juror was prosecuted for contempt of court after their Facebook contact with a defendant led to the collapse of a multi-million pound drugs trial. In September 2011 a 'troll' was jailed for 18 weeks for posting videos and messages mocking the deaths of teenagers on Facebook and YouTube, whilst in September 2012 a teenager was found guilty of sending a grossly offensive communication – 'all soldiers should die and go to hell' – after the deaths of 6 UK servicemen in Afghanistan.

Twitter's more public stage makes a legal response more likely. Paul Chambers was famously convicted in May 2010 under the 2003 Communications Act after his joke tweet suggesting he'd blow up an airport after delays to his flight and it took a second High Court appeal to have this overturned in July 2012. Twitter made headlines again in 2012 as a series of cases sparked a debate about 'trolls' and the freedom of speech. In March a 21-year-old student was jailed for 56 days for posting offensive and racist comments on Twitter following the collapse of the footballer Fabrice Muamba and in July a man was arrested for sending racist tweets to the footballer Danny Simpson. That same month a 17-year-old was arrested in Weymouth after sending offensive messages on Twitter to the Olympic diver Tom Daley. Though new legal guidelines in 2012 attempt to take a more pragmatic view, arrests will continue.

The user differs from the audience, therefore, in being personally responsible. Whereas professional journalists and broadcasters have editors and legal teams, the individual is alone with their own judgments, hence their need for greater digital skills and legal knowledge. Even perfectly legal actions can have significant consequences: texts and Facebook posts are regularly used in divorce courts, whilst others have suffered from their postings, such as the woman murdered by her estranged husband in March 2009 after she changed her Facebook status to 'single'. In January 2012 a judge ruled that UK student Richard O'Dwyer could be extradited to the US for running a website hosting links to pirated TV shows and films. He faced 10 years in a US prison for actions that were not illegal in the UK (in only hosting links), did not take place in the US or use US computers or servers, with the UK government supporting the extradition process, before his case was dropped in December.

Hence digital empowerment is accompanied by accountability: the fact that the user can be identified, monitored, traced and held accountable, with their own records being used against them, makes *every action* potentially significant. This significance has no time limit – our actions and posts survive on the network and on company databases long after we've forgotten them. The jokes we make or photos we post may one day return to embarrass us. Most Facebook users have only a few years of use behind them, leading to the question of how younger users might fare in decades to come when *all* of their youthful activity is retrievable in their adult life. Every aspect of our everyday use and management of technologies is important in potentially implicating us.

This has an added political importance as we cannot predict the future. We have no certain knowledge about what kind of government, laws, or policing may exist in the future and how the history of our activities may one day be used against us. Imagine what one of the 20th century's dictatorships could have done with access to decades worth of information about the personal thoughts, contacts, opinions and behaviour of each of its citizens. We need, therefore, a greater understanding of the political implications of our productions, and of debates around democracy, governmental transparency, informational freedom, and digital civil liberties and rights.

We also need to understand how the services we use work. We need to understand their privacy policies, their data collection and retention activities, the security of these sites, the extent to which they own, control or can access our information or stored data, their use of our data, and how they process it, store it and delete it. A media studies that analysed these processes and the operations of the major digital informational providers and services would be of vastly more relevance and value than one that continued to privilege reception and content. Given the volume of media we consume consumption skills remain valuable, but they are less important today than skills around production. We need to promote a holistic understanding of the media ecologies we create and use, the layers we navigate, the traces we create, the use of this information, the way we present ourselves, the information we volunteer, and the legal, political, economic, social and cultural implications of this creation and its afterlife.

The practical skills taught by media studies, therefore, also need to be updated. Firstly we need to know how to act as a digital user – what technologies, software, platforms and services are available or emerging and how to use them, as well as what open-source alternatives exist. We need to know how best to access information, how to download, stream, tag, store, recover and use information, and how best to produce and share it. And if what we need isn't available then we need the digital skills to code and create it and make it available for others. We need a competency with the entire shifting ecology of products, technologies and services in order to retain and expand our productive capacities.

But we also need defensive digital skills. An understanding of privacy needs to go hand in hand with the practical ability to delete and obscure our traces, to anonymise our activities, to use privacy technologies and software and disrupt our digital pattern and outlines. With no security about the future use of our information then advanced hacker skills and precautions need to become basic everyday skills. We need to maximise our control over the information we produce about ourselves and our activities: we need to learn how to hide our identities and scramble our information; how to secure our connections, communications and behaviour; and how to delete older traces. We need to learn practical security techniques to avoid any form of intrusion into our activities, whether from companies, cybercriminals or states.

Because we cannot trust the future, the greatest need today is for each of us to learn more about digital protection, following every development in social platforms and productivity software, new ways to route around censorship or disrupt surveillance, new techniques to enhance one's privacy and new ways to control one's environment and security. And we need to do this regardless of whether authorities consider these activities legal or illegal as this status is not absolute but rather varies between territories, reflecting political, economic or cultural decisions, and is liable to reversal. On 26 January 2013, for example, it suddenly became illegal under the Digital Millennium Copyright Act for Americans to unlock their own smartphone without the permission of the carrier that locked it. We cannot predict what personal capacities may become illegal or why and this cannot determine what skills we need to know.

This is an explicitly political project. It is founded on the idea that practice should no longer primarily be directed towards serving industry but instead should serve the individual: aiding not only their ability to create media and find employment but also their ability to navigate, use and defend themselves in this digital world against present and future threats. This might be the most important skill-set for the 21st century and this is a contribution media studies can make. The shifts in media ecology that empower each individual have led to a backlash from professionals, companies, elites and authorities and media studies should aim to balance this relationship. Instead of valorising the fiction of an empowered media consumer it should create the reality of an empowered media producer.

This is a completely different vision of the theoretical and practical skills to be taught than that found in most contemporary media or communication studies departments. But this only highlights the inadequacy of current provision. Today's students need staff who can teach these digital skills far more than they need lecturers who can teach them to be a TV presenter or how to watch a DVD and follow a film. They need the skills that will allow them to produce digitally and defend themselves digitally. Consumption skills still have a place but they are significantly less important and urgent than improving practical and theoretical digital productivity skills.

Media studies doesn't understand this yet. On the day I write this I've just seen an advert for a newly launched MA in Film and Television, promising both an insight into how to read these media and a way into broadcast industry employment. Students will apply because it is what's familiar to them, but it's a 20th-century vision of what they need and what they should be doing. It ignores the digital transformation of these forms, assuming that their study is the most urgent task today; it offers little that relates to the actual processes of digital production, whether by individuals or companies; it tempts students instead with the remote chance of employment in an industry that no longer exists as it assumes and it fails to see that its students already are, or could be, active producers of their own content. Marshall McLuhan's claim that we 'live in the rear-view mirror', travelling forwards but looking behind us, turns out to be too optimistic. Media studies reaches for the reverse gear.

10 Open sourcing knowledge
Towards a university 2.0

Reflecting upon education at the height of the 1960s Marshall McLuhan, as usual, took few prisoners and made fewer friends:

> Education, which should be helping youth to understand and adapt to their revolutionary new environments, is instead being used merely as an instrument of cultural aggression, imposing upon retribalised youth the obsolescent visual values of the dying literate age. Our entire educational system is reactionary, orientated to past values and past technologies, and will likely continue so until the old generation relinquishes power. The generation gap is actually a chasm, separating not two age groups but two vastly divergent cultures. I can understand the ferment in our schools because our educational system is totally rear-view mirror. It's a dying and outdated system founded on literate values and fragmented and classified data totally unsuited to the needs of the first television generation.
>
> Marshall McLuhan (1969)

For him the situation was simple. Education was a literate institution and product, designed to teach not only literacy and the book-based knowledge of the centuries but an entire mode of being: that of modern, civilised, literate man. Outside the universities, however, a new world had arisen. With the flowering of television and electronic media the entire educational system was anachronistic, McLuhan claimed. New media exploded older educational approaches.

McLuhan was wrong, but in an important way. Bringing television into the classroom didn't explode the educational system, it reinforced it. Few lecturers haven't felt a sense of relief after successfully inserting a DVD at the beginning of the hour. McLuhan was correct that the electronic world clashed with the literate educational system but he overlooked the cultural deployment of technologies and the fact that a broadcast medium that lectured its audience actually fitted well with an educational system that functioned the same way.

Historically the links between education and broadcasting are strong. If the dominance of the broadcast model has come to an end then this has important implications for education. In this book I've argued that changing media technologies demand a corresponding change in the discipline that studies them, but in this chapter I want to argue that they also demand a change in the institution that contains that discipline. Building on a comparison between the university and broadcasting I want to consider how digital technologies transform the university's internal relationship with its own students and external relationships with the public. In conclusion I want to return to a theme discussed in the introduction – the need for open-source models of informational production if we want our disciplines and educational ideals to survive.

The university as a broadcast system

As we've seen, broadcasting is a cultural process, not a purely technological one – many broadcast media could have been deployed differently whilst some non-broadcast forms have had a minor broadcast application. I've already suggested that broadcasting preceded the printing press and that the medieval church might be seen as a broadcast form in distributing its messages for mass consumption. As a centralised, hierarchical institution it produced and crafted a finished message which it disseminated through available technologies such as ships, manuscripts, monasteries, churches and pulpits to become one of the central sources of acceptable knowledge.

Universities developed as part of this system. The European university has a complex history but broadly we can say that it has a religious origin, emerging out of cathedral schools and monasteries. The first European universities were formed in the 11th to 12th centuries, with Oxford and Cambridge tracing their roots to the early 13th century. It is possible to argue that if the church was the dominant informational medium then these universities were the first media studies: training this informational class for productive service within the broadcast institution. University study developed key theological, critical skills, providing instruction in theory and practice to reproduce the informational class and form.

In predating printing, McLuhan sees early universities as part of oral, manuscript culture. He ties their rise to the success of scholastic methods, emphasising the oral nature of their techniques of disputation and defence and tracing the decline of these to the rise of print culture. This, he argues, intensified the literate character of education, making individual textual acquisition and knowledge more important, transforming the student into 'the passive role of consumer of uniformly packaged learning'.

McLuhan's explanation of this passage from orality to literacy is over-simplified – for a long time university instruction retained both oral and literate elements and this mixture is retained to this day in different modes of teaching delivery and assessment – but the broad point is correct. The take-off of printing increased popular literacy and literate culture. It challenged the church's informational privilege and gave easier access to worlds of knowledge outside its doctrine and beyond its control. Over time the universities would replace the monasteries as the centre of intellectual life and their curricula and character would be increasingly stamped by that broader secular culture and its knowledge.

As important as the university's literate character, however, was its broadcast organisation. This has two elements: its internal relationships with its students and its external relationship with the broader public through published research. Internally, universities developed as centralised, bureaucratic, hierarchical institutions, employing the expert voice to decide the value of information; developing closed, elitist, professional employment structures that limited who could give instruction; and employing a top-down, one-to-many dissemination of this information to their students. Their modes of feedback, interaction and assessment similarly evolved into more controlled forms, soliciting and producing those responses desired by the dominant structure. The university, therefore, employed broadcast principles, although for a long time its distribution was limited to a minority of the population.

The rise of mass education was closely tied with the rise of mass media. As we've seen, the newspaper industry underwent rapid industrialisation in the last decades of the 19th century, paving the way for the emergence of mass-produced, mass-circulation dailies by the turn of the 20th century. Over the next two decades cinema and music would develop as major commercial entertainment industries and organised radio broadcasting would take off. The same era saw developments in mass education. In the UK the 1870 Elementary Education Act introduced compulsory universal education for those aged up to 13 and subsequent acts in 1880, 1902 and 1918 refined its requirements until, by 1921, schooling was compulsory until 14. University education also expanded. Six 'redbrick' universities were created from 1900–1909, joining Oxford, Cambridge and Durham, leading to an increase in 20–24-year-olds in higher education by 1910. The post-war period saw the extension of both mass media and mass education. The success of television established the dominance of the major broadcast forms whilst the 1944 Education Act created a largely standardised mass-education system.

Higher education remained an elite experience until the 1960s. The 1963 Robins Report led to the creation of 'Plate Glass' universities (such as UEA, Essex, Kent, Lancaster, Sussex, Warwick and York), and through the 1960s numerous other institutions attained full university status. In 1964 Labour created a system of 'polytechnics' emphasising vocational, professional and industry-based qualifications and these would eventually be reclassified with the 1992 Further and Higher Education Act leading to the creation of 65 'new universities'. By 2000 the Greenaway Report noted that a third of 18–19-year-olds were in full-time higher education and although Labour's 2001 pledge to increase participation to 50 per cent wasn't fulfilled by 2010 the figure was 43 per cent. The post-2008 economic crash impacted on this as a government committed to spending cuts introduced higher fees and changed university recruitment policies. This led to a contraction in entrants but didn't change the nature of higher education as a mass-education system.

This was the mass, broadcast system that was in place when I first began lecturing in higher education in 1996. Within a highly centralised bureaucratic structure I, the expert, crafted communications that were delivered in one-to-many lectures, with seminars similarly increasing in size to become broadcast experiences. In my first full-time post, for example, my Mondays consisted of a one-hour lecture to a theatre full of students, followed by five seminars with up to 30 students in each. As a research-active academic, however, I was also expected to produce and distribute articles and monographs for an external 'public'.

Universities were already publishing academic journals and texts by the 18th century and by the 19th century the 'French' and 'German' university models had become established. Whilst the French model focused on the internal university control of the educational experience, the German model, established by Wilhelm Von Humboldt, focused on research. In 1810 he convinced the King of Prussia to build a university in Berlin based upon the liberal ideas of Friedrich Schleiermacher in which the student would take a more active role. As Humboldt explains: 'Just as primary instruction makes the teacher possible, so he renders himself dispensable through schooling at the secondary level. The university teacher is thus no longer a teacher and the student is no longer a pupil. Instead the student conducts research on his own behalf and the professor supervises his research and supports him in it' (see Clark 2007). The point of universities was to promote education through research, to allow students to gain knowledge by the same process that their lecturers had. In time lecturers would be expected to continue this process and disseminate their own research, hence the modern research university developed as a space for original enquiry whose results would be publicly available.

This was aided by developments in industrialisation. As Marx suggested in *The German Ideology* the division of labour 'manifests itself also in the ruling class as the division of mental and material labour' and within this class 'one part appears as the thinkers of the class (its active, conceptive ideologists, who make the perfecting of the illusion of the class about itself their chief source of livelihood)'. Hence the complex division of labour enabled the development of a specialised profession devoted to the production, legitimation and distribution of social knowledge within specialised academic disciplines. From the late 19th century, under the influence of a positivistic framework, the human and social 'sciences' were created, their traditions and methods clarified and their content 'disciplined'. Whilst this class didn't have the monopoly on informational production they nevertheless formed a leading centre of its creation, disseminating their work through peer-reviewed journals and books. Though this was in principle public, in practice its audience was small and a specialised academic publishing industry developed to serve both research and student markets.

Thus higher education was a broadcast form, mass producing information for consumption by a mass of students within a centralised, hierarchical hub-and-spoke structure whilst its lecturers formed a professional class of knowledge producers whose research was publicly distributed through external broadcast channels. Universities matured in an age of informational scarcity when, culturally, the production and legitimation of knowledge was expected to be the province of specialised experts, and when this expert class had to be geographically concentrated in institutions for the most effective organisation and distribution of their production. The question is, therefore, what happens when these conditions and expectations change? In this book I've traced the material, ecological, cultural and personal revolutions in digital media but we need to consider how these have impacted upon the broadcast form of mass education. How have they changed the university's internal relationship with its own students and external relationships with the broader public?

The university in a Web 2.0 age

Digital technology has been widely adopted within universities though it has primarily been used to reinforce its existing broadcast structure and relationships. University websites, for example, are closely controlled, corporate, promotional spaces, advertising their wares. They are typically non-interactive, poorly designed, difficult to navigate, slowly updated and centrally controlled. Despite the possibility of globally publishing staff research, draft papers, think-pieces and new arguments, most staff pages offer little more than a dull, static biography and publication list.

Beyond this there is a walled garden available to paying students, giving access to proprietal materials stored on a Virtual Learning Environment (VLE). These have become common technologies across every educational provider over the last decade. My university uses 'Blackboard', a site requiring multiple log-ins, whose ugly design, poor navigation and painful speeds create a depressing, outdated user experience. VLEs do offer Web 2.0 experiences through their inclusion of blog and wiki tools and discussion groups for example but these are controlled, poor simulations and students only participate if they are assessed. The primary value of VLEs is twofold: serving for the university as a standardised and controlled repository of their worker's intellectual property and for the students as a broadcast medium, pushing announcements, module information, handbooks, links and classroom material at them.

Digital technologies have also played a central role in the expansion of university administration. As noted by Benjamin Ginsberg in his 2011 book *The Fall of Faculty* and in a widely reported 2012 *Wall Street Journal* article on university 'administrative bloat', this is one of the most significant contemporary developments in HE. UK Higher Education Statistics Agency figures demonstrate the same expansion here, with administrative staff increasing by 33 per cent from 2005–10, compared to a 10 per cent and 9 per cent rise in academic staff and students respectively. This rise of administration is a response to the Neo-Liberal marketisation of education, with a new class of administrators being tasked with improving university competitiveness through organising larger intakes, improving student communications, aiding student recruitment, course promotion, developing initiatives to support their experience and employability, promoting the university and its activities nationally and internationally, and helping develop government and business links, monetise IP and research and increase profitability. Digital technologies obviously enable or support many of these activities.

The result for lecturers has been a digital proletarianisation. Squeezed between the demands of the centre and their students, an increasing proportion of their time is spent on electronic administration and service. From above they face an increasing control from an administration intent on centralising, regulating and collecting information on every aspect of student service, academic management and professional development, whilst from below they face an increasing student demand for information and service. This digital labour isn't optional: students *expect* lecture notes, PowerPoints, class readings and essay advice to be available (often as a substitute for attendance). My own institution's 'Blackboard site minimum content' policy makes it clear the VLE exists primarily for staff to serve students – there is no equivalent 'minimum student engagement' policy. Thus the VLE isn't a Web 2.0 space of equal access, decision-making power and creative interaction but an extension of the one-to-many communication of the lecture, unilaterally distributing information to the student.

Except, as I've suggested, the receiver of this broadcast product is in a strong position here, empowered by both this marketisation – by competition for their custom, their status as fee-paying consumers and university fears of their complaints or poor reviews – as well as by changes in technology such as student email. Hence the rise of a lecturer–student service relationship characterised by the lecturer's real-time management of the student's needs and the provision, on demand, of personally tailored advice. Increasingly what this student wants isn't more contact hours or content but *me*: my time, attention and response. Most importantly they want it *when they want it*, not at hours I schedule; and they want it for as long as they need it, whether a minute's query over referencing or an afternoon's dissertation advice. As in media, therefore, education is re-orientating around the individual, but here consumer pressure isn't for increased participation but rather for a more personalised flow of information and service downwards.

This university marketisation is manifested in numerous ways. Customer satisfaction now becomes paramount – student complaints and module feedback impact upon staff whilst UK National Student Survey results impact upon departments – whilst staff also become responsible for their student's success. At one UK institution, for example, 'key performance indicators' have been introduced by the HR department for annual lecturing staff reviews, based upon a range of statistics including the percentage of module completions and failures and the number of students achieving marks over 60. By implication, failure in these indicators is the lecturer's not the student's failure. The result has been a reluctance by lecturers to give marks below 60 per cent and a significant overall inflation in the student grades, all of which serves the university's interests by improving its results and its league-table position. Most importantly, market-isation has led to the idea that the purpose of universities is to serve the economy and industry and that the aim of education isn't knowledge but employment. This has increased student instrumentalism, as they reserve their efforts for assessed work and treat VLEs and staff time as a unilateral service to help them maximise their grades.

There have been attempts to genuinely employ Web 2.0 technologies in universities, especially in assessment, where new modes such as individual or group blogs, wiki creation or editing and forms of social media production enable institutions to address and incorporate contemporary developments. One of the best examples I've seen is a media theory module by Marcus Leaning at Winchester where students are asked to respond to set readings by making a YouTube video for seminar discussion. There are obvious benefits here, from increasing student engagement, testing different skills and producing different and richer modes of learning, but this integration is necessarily limited. The main problem is participation: real engagement is voluntary and students are only engaging in these activities because they are assessed. Add to this the unilateral student–assessor power relationship and literate education's valorisation of individual achievement (even group work has an individual component) and it's clear that the character of Web 2.0 experiences is changed when it is used in assessment.

This is because Web 2.0 just doesn't fit in a broadcast system. Contrary to what McLuhan believed, television was easy to integrate in a literate system, both at the level of form, as a surrogate lecturer, and at the level of content, as media production skills and media courses served and contributed to the post-1963 massification of HE. Digital technologies can be used as a broadcast form in education but they can't be integrated in the way they exist outside: in the way our students are using and experiencing them and in their cultural application as part of the post-broadcast me-dia world.

Knowledge within universities has been constructed, reviewed, filtered, disputed and accepted over a long period by experts, being made available to each enrolling mass through the one-way media of books and lectures. It is individually researched, held and evaluated; it is selectively chosen, accumulated, quoted and referenced and evaluated once again by experts who determine how well its corpus has been understood and it exists in bounded disciplines whose limits are patrolled and whose assumptions are imposed. Outside, however, knowledge and content is produced by anyone; created with limited or cheap tools; personally distributed among networks or globally disseminated; critiqued and discussed after publication; shared and linked to; collectively created and owned; pulled by individuals according to their own decisions and interests; existing in a personal ecology of content and experiences, and is permanently unfinished and added to by anyone else. It can't be marked and individual credit can't be given. Two different cultures of knowledge therefore exist inside and outside of the university system and the latter can only be accepted and integrated if it is first controlled and changed into a form that ultimately fits within the system's broadcast principles.

These new knowledge practices have often been seen as a threat. Many institutions rewrote their unfair practice policies to condemn social networking and there were early cases of punitive action. In November 2005 Kansas State University investigated over 100 students who'd used a Facebook group message board to share class information without the professor's authorisation, whilst in March 2008 a chemistry virtual study group set up by a Ryerson University student led to him being charged with 147 counts of academic misconduct as he and 146 other students shared tips on credit-bearing homework questions, even though such activities weren't illegal in real-world study groups. Today many lecturers would be pleased by any sign of online engagement and participation but there remains a tension between the individualised knowledge forms the university valorises and the collective modes of knowledge online.

Perhaps the most important attempt by universities to employ digital technologies in teaching is the emergence of MOOCs – of 'massive open online courses'. These are globally available courses, usually free, without entry requirements, taught by short online videos, supported by etextbooks and a variety of discussion and networking forms across the web. As most courses are science-technology-engineering-maths-based marking is automatic, though humanities and social sciences are experimenting with forms of crowd-sourced peer-marking. They are not yet credit-bearing (so as not to clash with high fee-paying students) but a certificate is sent upon successful completion.

These ideas aren't new. Correspondence courses developed from the 1890s and radio, cinema and television have all been used for teaching courses and giving lectures. In the UK the Open University, opened in 1969, became the leading media-based distance-learning educational institution also pioneering open entry policies. From 2007 'iTunes U' began offering university lectures and content for free and by October 2011 the Open University and Stanford had both had over 40 million downloads of their lectures, though these recordings didn't involve any registration or coursework. Modern MOOCs originate from about 2008, emerging out of various forms of virtual learning, especially those of the Open Educational Resource movement (OER) and Connectivist educational philosophies. Their take-off, however, dates from 2011.

In October 2011 Sebastian Thrun and Peter Norvig of Stanford University opened their 'Introduction to A.I.' course up as a MOOC, attracting 160,000 students, 23,000 of whom graduated with a certificate. In February 2013 Thrun co-launched 'Udacity', an online educational provider that offered 24 courses by April 2013. MIT meanwhile had launched their 'MITx' scheme in February 2012 offering an electronics course attracting 155,000 users from 160 countries. This was more students than the entire number of living students who had graduated from the university and close to the entire number who had studied there since the 19th century. By June 2012 MIT and Harvard formed a US$60m alliance to launch 'Edx', an online service, being joined by UC Berkeley and the University of Texas. 'Coursera' also developed out of Stanford University, launched in April 2012, attracting 70 partner universities and 3.2 million registered users by April 2013. The University of London reported one of its Coursera courses attracted 9,000 students in its first 24 hours. Other online providers include 'Udemy', launched in May 2010 and 'the Khan Academy', established in September 2006 by Salmon Khan, initially to teach maths. Its YouTube channel has over 1 million subscribers and a total of 268 million views to date.

The MOOC business model is still being developed. Free courses may work as a promotion, pushing students to fee-paying degrees; charges may be made for courses, for certificates, for real-world exam invigilation and marking; whilst recruitment is also a possible funding stream, selling contact deals of top students to companies. In time courses may become credit-bearing and they may develop in numerous, hybrid ways, mixing credits from universities, or real and virtual world learning experiences and periods of study in ways that transform the traditional modes of education. Universities, at least, are taking these possibilities seriously and venture capitalism is funding many of the private platforms.

In many ways MOOCs successfully chime with broader developments in digital culture and knowledge. They fit in with a world of free, open, easily accessible information as a social good, with their immediate access and democratised participation, and a world where individuals arrange their own ecology of interests and activities, as they can mix and match courses, schedule their own classes, work at their own pace on their own portable devices and control the lecturer, repeating information until they grasp it. Users also appear more participative than in real-world study, with detailed course discussions and groups spontaneously forming across the internet, sharing information, advice and help outside of university control. Thrun and Norvig report, for example, that their 2011 course spawned a Facebook group, discussions across numerous forums and volunteers who translated the videos into 44 languages for other students.

Ultimately, however, the MOOC represents the consolidation of traditional university practices. It marks a new era in the massification of education as the global, competitive extension of the university's broadcast form; employing the internet to distribute its one-to-many expert messages to a potentially huge audience and to overcome the physical limitations of campus study and teaching and tap the global long tail of demand for higher education. The potential economic benefits of this for successful institutions are huge. The monetisation of a global audience would constitute a significant income stream, whilst profitability is also helped by the remarkable staff–student ratios, the need for fewer staff, and by the spontaneously emerging online discussions that effectively crowd-source seminar classes and obviate the need to employ tutors. Although Web 2.0 technologies and platforms are an essential element of the MOOC's success, they remain secondary to and designed to serve the broadcast educational system.

We needn't be entirely pessimistic about the take-up of Web 2.0 technologies within universities, however, as they were actually successfully introduced a long time ago by students themselves. Phones and tablets are easily carried and used by bored students whilst laptops and netbooks have the added advantage of shielding activity and making it look like the student is working instead of on Facebook. Perhaps they are indeed working, researching lines of enquiry from class, but it's as likely that they're also playing, searching, looking for entertainment, messaging or social networking, often with people in the same room. And why not? Perhaps the tutor or lecture is dull; perhaps expecting interest in a subject not chosen by the student and at an hour outside of their control isn't the best approach; perhaps an hour is too long to listen; perhaps they're uninterested in a PowerPoint that's available anyway on the VLE; or perhaps multitasking is now the norm. Few of us can hold a conversation or watch television without reaching for our phones so why expect students to?

Or perhaps they're using these technologies against their lecturers. The digitally empowered individual has the tools to criticise or challenge any authority and lecturers are increasingly under student scrutiny, especially on sites like Rate-myprofessor.com or Facebook pages devoted to the university or even to individuals. Students are also filming their lecturers and their activities. In November 2010 three lecturers made headlines after videos were posted to YouTube – one showed a Cornell University lecturer getting angry at yawning students; another a Louisiana State professor attacking students for their views on global warming; and another showed a Central Florida lecturer criticising a class he believed to be full of cheaters. The lecture hall as a privileged space of open discussion and exploration of often controversial ideas and themes is threatened by the evidential threat of video and the institution's fear of controversy. This monitoring and recording of staff and their activities and the reviewing or exposure of university services is at an early stage but it will almost certainly develop into a significant phenomenon impacting upon lecturers and the university's future public relations management.

In conclusion, therefore, attempts by universities to integrate digital technologies have had a limited success, hindered by their need to retain control, by consumer demands for a one-way service and by the fundamental clash between the broadcast system universities are built upon and the broader digital post-broadcast culture that has emerged outside. But the university has not only had to rethink how it responds internally to these digital developments, it has also had to consider how its external relationships with the public are affected by changing modes of knowledge and its dissemination, and here too its response has been lacking.

'All the world's a sage'

As we've seen, the most common way universities relate to the external world is through academic publishing broadcasting its research to the wider public. There are, however, problems with this model of dissemination. First, within it not all broadcast forms are equal. Academics have internalised the values of literate modernity, subscribing to a hierarchy of expression that places print publishing above dissemination through other media such as radio, film and television. Within print itself there is a hierarchy of prestige, at the top of which are peer-reviewed journals and single-authored monographs, whilst there is also a complex series of judgements as to which particular journals or publishers have the best academic reputation, with a resulting pressure to publish there. Second, publication opportunities are limited. As well as making judgements on quality, academic publishing, as a physical, broadcast form, has limitations on the number of titles that can be produced and the page count of books and journals. With the need for profit as well as prestige, academic publishers make careful editorial decisions about the books they commission and their potential markets, and researchers, editors and readers spend a long time crafting proposals and submissions to ensure not just quality but market appeal.

Third, the expansion of higher education through the 1990s and its increasing marketisation impacted upon academic publishing. The primary market of research academics and students became skewed as student intakes increased and publishers increasingly focused on the booming textbook market, either through producing primers or reworking and packaging academic texts as student friendly. Academics realised that if they wanted to get their research published their proposals needed to demonstrate a broad market appeal; they needed to identify national or international courses that taught the book's subject or that it would appeal to; ideally they needed to be able to claim it would be adopted as a 'core book' rather than as specialised reading, and it would also fare better with the commissioning editors if it could include 'boxes' containing summaries, seminar questions or exercises and suggestions for further reading.

The result of these problems has been a restricted conception of academic dissemination, and a series of gate-keeping restrictions on what is published and the form it takes. The drive for textbooks results in less original research becoming available, fewer monographs published and a difficulty in placing anything that doesn't repeat the existing field in a way that guarantees its use for pre-specified courses. This has led to a predictability and conservativism in publisher catalogues, the loss of reputations built on the variety and originality of titles, and a promotional inflation of ordinary texts as new and revolutionary to simulate the innovation lacking in the commissioning process. This conservativism feeds back into the teaching and research of staff, affecting what they will study and try to publish, as well as their conception of the discipline. As media courses boomed through the 1990s, for example, many staff found employment there from a variety of other disciplines and often the proliferating textbooks provided their primary orientation into the field.

Academic journals have their own problems. Their business model has increasingly come under attack in the last few years by academics, institutions and politicians. Academic journals get their content and much of their productive labour for free: academics provide articles, work for free or for very little as editors and administrators, and referee submissions without a fee. This academic research is publicly funded (by student fees, government grants and funds and research councils) but it isn't publicly available: publishers sell it back to university libraries who have to pay significant fees to subscribe to the journal, or even purchase subscription bundles to get the journals they want whilst individuals wanting to access articles must either have access to a subscribing library or pay for individual copies of articles. Researchers wanting to follow back a path of footnotes face significant costs, and universities are locked into purchasing journals as academics need up-to-date research. Academics can't publish their work in more than one place and are unable to disseminate it themselves as journals retain copyright of the articles.

At a time of cuts in funding, libraries are increasingly complaining of journal subscriptions taking a rising proportion of budgets. In the UK, for example, 65 per cent of university library spending goes on journals. For the larger publishers this is a highly profitable model: in 2010 Elsevier made £724m on revenues of £2bn with an operating profit margin of 36 per cent. Although many journals, especially in the humanities and social sciences, are cheaper, the broad model holds across the sector, prompting complaints. In April 2012, for example, the Wellcome Fund, one of the largest non-governmental funders of UK medical research promoted a move to open online journals, announcing it would launch a scientific journal called *e-Life* to compete with *Nature* and *Science*, whilst the same month Harvard University, exasperated by its 'fiscally unsustainable' US $3.5m journal bill, encouraged its staff to publish in open access journals and resign from 'academically restrictive' journals that retained pay-walls. By June 2013, 'The Cost of Knowledge' website had over 13,718 academic signatures for a boycott of journals that restrict the free sharing of research in a move that was being described as an 'academic spring'.

The UK government entered these debates in July 2012 when it announced plans to make publicly funded scientific research immediately available for anyone to read online for free by 2014. This was a response to 'The Finch Report' in June, which explored how best to transition to an open access publication model whilst retaining high-quality peer review and supporting the publishing industry. The report favoured the 'Gold Model' where the costs are transferred to the researchers rather than the readers, with academics paying an 'article processing charge' (APC) and journals making research immediately available on the web for free. The cost would be met by reduced library spending though until the rest of the world followed suit journal spending would have to be retained or the UK would lose access to international research. Some critics favour a 'Green' model where, once it is accepted, researchers would make their work available in institutional disciplinary repositories.

Academics themselves have long recognised the limitations of traditional publishing and have begun exploring the opportunities offered by digital technology. Sites such as the 'Public Library of Science', 'arXiv' and 'ResearchGate' all give free access to material, whilst online e-journals, such as *CTheory* and *Culture Machine* publish material for free. Books are also increasingly published under 'Creative Commons Licenses' allowing a range of user relationships with the text – 'CC-BY' for example, allows others to 'copy, distribute, display and perform the work and make derivative works based on it' provided 'they give the author or licensor the credits in the manner specified by these' – whilst new publishing ventures such as the Open Humanities Press make books and journals available online for free. The result is an increasing movement online by academics whose main desire is for their work to be published and to be noticed.

These developments are obviously welcome but most don't go far enough. Discussions of open access have become concentrated around the moral case of making publicly funded research publicly available; the economic case of free access against perceived profiteering; and the technological case of the internet being superior to print as a distributive medium, but these are only part of the problem. In particular they don't address certain important issues.

First, the current models of publication aren't working. The UK research assessment exercise has increased the volume of research produced and journals have proliferated and increased their frequency to provide an outlet for it but the vast majority of humanities and social science articles are almost completely unread. Academics can't keep up with the quantity of articles published, read far fewer articles than they'd admit to, and tend to focus their reading on their specific field of interest, hence most articles achieve, at best, only a small number of highly specialised readers. Few articles reappear in reading lists, and many have little interest or application even for researchers. Their value primarily lies in the academic prestige of their publication rather than in the meaning or significance of their content and its impact upon the field. Ironically, a research exercise that increasingly emphasises 'impact' forces academics to publish in journals that few can access, even fewer read and that consequently have little impact. Most research isn't even being read by academics, let alone the broader public.

Second, academics collude in the system of prestige that valorises particular media above others. Media lecturers might be expected to challenge this but progress is slow – online publications aren't seen as having the same prestige or high-impact factor of print publications, forcing lecturers to continue to publish in traditional locations and forms. This book provides an excellent example. My idea of 'media studies 2.0' began in a series of blog posts in 2006, culminating in an expanded essay posted online in 2008. It is unlikely that its polemic would have been accepted by a refereed journal but in sparking a debate it was significant enough, after the fact, to be included in a special issue of the journal *Interactions* in 2009. That article had more value for my CV, my promotion chances and for the research exercise than the identical blog post. For the most part the blog post would not have been an acceptable publication for the research exercise. Ideally, if I wanted to maximise the disciplinary prestige and professional benefits of my ideas on media studies 2.0 I'd have to develop them into a single-authored monograph with a recognised prestigious publisher (such as Routledge). The same chapters posted for free on a blog, however, would bring few professional benefits.

Third, most academics still hold to a belief in an 'expert culture' of referees. Peer review of research claims is considered the basis of ensuring academic quality, functioning as a check upon error, misinterpretation and false conclusions. In many scientific disciplines these checks are obviously essential – the revelation in October 2013 of a fake scientific paper written by science journalist John Bohannon being accepted by hundreds of open access journals reinforces the need for quality controls in those fields – but in most humanities and social science disciplines the consequences of error or weak research are far less serious and rarely life threatening. Indeed, here peer-review may not even be as beneficial as is assumed. Contemporary arguments about the 'long tail' of knowledge (Chris Anderson), 'collective intelligence' (Pierre Levy) and 'the wisdom of crowds' (James Surowiecki), suggest that these gate-keepers are no longer needed. In a world in which the physical limits of publication have been overcome and cheap global publication is possible then we could let the audience decide for itself the value of ideas placed in the public sphere.

Many academics will be outraged by this idea: the transformation of publication may be defensible but the abolition of pre-production filters seems to strike at the heart of academia and its belief in expertly validated knowledge. Without it *anyone* would make judgements about what constituted valid knowledge. But every academic knows that this refereeing process is flawed. Each academic has horror stories concerning dubious referee comments and decisions and the disproportionate weight given them by editorial boards and publishers. The expertise of chosen referees varies considerably; the suitability of their selection may be questioned and many use their position to further their own agendas, their own work and their own interpretation of the field or to control what will be allowed to be read. As Chris Anderson points out, pre-production filters lead to a limitation of what is available and its manipulation into pre-existing successful forms and patterns and this analysis applies to academic publishing. To be fit for publication for other academics research must fit into the approach of particular journals, must fulfil particular criteria for knowledge production and validation and must conform to accepted disciplinary paradigms and assumptions. The end result is a conservativism at the heart of research and the exclusion of more radical, different or new ideas.

The biggest problem with academic publishing, however, is that it is always obsolete. Long turn-around times impede research. It takes time to research and write an article or book but add to that the time it takes to pass through a series of readers, referees, proofreaders and editors and the time it takes to fit into publisher schedules and for them to prepare the marketing and to print and ship it to the shops. Then add the time it takes to be noticed, read, reviewed and quoted in the field and it's obvious that traditional publishing models can't keep up with contemporary media. By the time a book's published it's out of date. That may always have been true, but accelerating and interlinked developments impacting across entire media ecosystems make this one of the most important problems for contemporary media studies. Our published research is always massively behind the student's experiences. It took years after the rise of Facebook and YouTube, for example, for the first articles and texts to begin to make their way onto the bookshelves. This is clearly unacceptable.

What is needed is a more radical conception of the academic's role in a digital post-broadcast era. Current conceptions of openness focus on access – on opening up publications and allowing the broader public *into* the academic world and academic debates – but we need to think about this the other way around, about how academic knowledge and ideas *can take part in the public's world and debates*. This isn't about research 'impact' – about congratulating ourselves for our effect on the outside world – it's about actually joining that world: it's about recognising a cultural change in the place and form of knowledge in society and taking part in this changed informational and knowledge ecology.

We've dreamed for a long time that computers might transform education and learning. Indeed, the development of modern computing owed much to this hope. Vannevar Bush explored how technology could change how 'we may think', directly inspiring Douglas Engelbart's theory of human 'augmentation' and his contribution to computer interfaces. In 1960 J. C. R. Licklider proposed a theory of 'man–computer symbiosis' that would couple human brains and machines in a partnership that would 'think as no human brain has ever thought and process data in a way not approached by the information-handling machines we know today'. By 1968 he'd developed a vision of 'creative interactive communication' through computers where instead of just receiving information we would be able to 'interact with the richness of living information', as active participants in an ongoing process, feeding back, connecting with others and forming 'online interactive communities' to collaboratively model new ideas. Licklider helped fund both Engelbart's research and the development of the ARPAnet – that network of computers whose initial purpose was for academic researchers to freely share information and ideas.

Licklider thought computers could change education. His 1965 report 'Libraries of the Future' looked towards the digitalisation and instant computer availability of all texts, whilst his 1967 article 'Televistas' criticised broadcast educational methods and pointed towards the potential of computers and 'a comprehensive, flexible, interactive, multi-purpose information network that includes large collections of information and advanced facilities for storing, processing, transmitting and displaying it'. Others had similar ideas. Alan Kay's 1972 idea for a 'dynabook' was designed for children and their playful, creative learning, whilst Ted Nelson's 1974 *Computer Lib/Dream Machines* emphasised the liberatory possibilities of these 'thinkertoys' for learning and creating.

By the late 1960s McLuhan was arguing that real education went on outside the classroom in the experience of the electronic mass media, with the literate world of schools and universities constituting a limited and limiting sphere increasingly out of touch with contemporary children's electronic culture. The city is 'a classroom', McLuhan says – a 'classroom without walls' – and education needed to change to reflect these shifts. Older ideas of fragmented data and specialised disciplines need to give way to a more holistic vision of the inter-relationship of information, one aiming at 'pattern recognition' and 'total field awareness', and memory-based 'answer-learning' needs to be replaced by a more participative, exploratory mode of learning, based on the 'deep involvement' of the individual with the learning environment and collaborative relations with others. As McLuhan argued in his 1971 Convocation Adress at the University of Alberta:

The university and school of the future must be a means of total community participation, not in the consumption of available knowledge, but in the creation of completely unavailable insights. The overwhelming obstacle to such community participation in problem solving and research at the top levels, is the reluctance to admit, and to describe, in detail their difficulties and their ignorance. There is no kind of problem that baffles one or a dozen experts that cannot be solved at once by a million minds that are given a chance simultaneously to tackle a problem. The satisfaction of individual prestige, which we formerly derived from the possession of expertise, must now yield to the much greater satisfactions of dialogue and group discovery. The task yields to the task force.

Here there is already a different vision of the collective production and sharing of knowledge. As he so wittily put it (anticipating later discussions of collective intelligence): 'all the world's a sage'.

Perhaps the best known contemporary critique of education was Ivan Illich's *Deschooling Society* (originally published in 1971). Much of this is an attack on existing institutional educational forms but there has been an increasing attention paid to his alternative model of education – informal peer-to-peer-based learning. As he explains: 'The current search for educational *funnels* must be reversed into the search for their institutional inverse: educational *webs* which heighten the opportunity for each one to transform each moment of his living into one of learning, sharing, and caring.' He even suggests computers could aid the development of these 'learning webs': 'The operation of a peer-matching network would be simple. The user would identify himself by name and address and describe the activity for which he sought a peer. A computer would send him back the names and addresses of all those who had inserted the same description. It is amazing that such a simple utility has never been used on a broad scale for publicly valued activity.'

Others were even more forceful about the revolutionary possibilities of new technology. Educational and computer theorist Seymour Papert famously argued in a 1984 *Popular Computing* article: 'The computer will blow up the school. That is, the school defined as something where there are classes, teachers running exams, people structured in groups by age, following a curriculum – all of that. The whole system is based on a set of structural concepts that are incompatible with the presence of a computer.' Such ideas, however, have been easy for educationalists to dismiss – clearly educational institutions aren't going to disappear and most serve other purposes than simply education. Physical universities, for example, include the benefits of their social experience and staff contact; their qualification-awarding powers ensure they play a significant social role in the reproduction of privilege; and the institutions themselves are major economic and cultural centres, functioning to disseminate and exploit their own research advances and profit from their tuition. Given these established roles, counter-cultural visions of the end of traditional education are premature.

And yet something *has* changed: the digital, post-broadcast era does actually realise many of these counter-cultural ideals. For Illich a good educational system should have three purposes: 'It should provide all who want to learn with access to available resources at any time in their lives; empower all who want to share what they know to find those who want to learn it from them; and, finally, furnish all who want to present an issue to the public with the opportunity to make their challenge known.' Digital technologies achieve precisely this: they make resources and information easily accessible; enable individuals to connect with others in specific networks and communities, and empower them to produce and broadcast their ideas, opinions and creations with anyone interested. Hence, outside of the universities and across the span of daily life digital media have been remaking social knowledge and its production. We have moved from a world in which only a limited, mostly professional, elite created, framed and debated knowledge to one in which each individual is a productive force, able to craft and share opinions and ideas, and this has led to an explosion of contributions and debate across the entire media ecology. Where once media academics and professional media commentators dominated debates around media (in academic texts and articles and journalistic products) today anyone can publish their thoughts about its operation and effects.

So this is where we arrive at the end of this book: with a call for a radical disciplinary openness. This has several levels. In the introduction I explained the need for an open-source discipline – for one that didn't just explain what media studies *thought*, but which exposed *what it was* and opened its own background and assumptions to scrutiny and critique so that each student could move forward with the possibility of improving and adding to the discipline. This is a call for a conversation with students about their own worlds and knowledge rather than a one-way, top-down transmission of research and ideas which often have more to do with the researcher's own worlds and experience and the safely agreed assumptions of their colleagues.

That's part of the openness we need but it isn't enough. We also need another openness: not one that rests on the assumption that the public is free to follow disciplinary debates if it wants to, but one that acknowledges that debate about media is no longer located in universities or even limited to our discipline but is happening everywhere, at all times, and that the discipline needs to be out there, in among these debates, taking our ideas to the broader public as part of their conversations. Conferences based around our favourite themes and buzz-words and journal special issues that speak to the current interests of their own editorial board and friendship networks are no longer adequate.

One way to begin this is by embracing open web publication. Unconstrained by the physical limits of traditional publication, the internet offers an unparalleled opportunity to control one's own production; to publish as much as you want; to vary the form of production – from books, to articles, to shorter pieces – and the chance to take ideas out of the academy to a broader public. In the humanities, arts and social sciences checks on work are less important and often no longer necessary. We should trust the academic and public community more and leave it to our readers to judge the lasting value of our contributions. Why hold onto a small group of often poorly selected referees when we could have a global system of referees? Web publishing without filters will help open up the discipline, giving rise to and helping us enter into conversations about media and its role and future and allowing comments, feedback, arguments, discussion and revision. This is barely possible in the present system where responses take as long to see print. Today, for the first time, our academic research and criticism could exist as a living phenomenon, developing in the moment in response to others and with others, partaking in and taking advantage of a collective process of knowledge production.

And in the process we could publish more and better – more relevant and more original – work. Instead of most of a year spent writing and rewriting an article we could respond in near real time to a real-time media world; we could develop and try out new ideas and concepts; we could push back at a media ecology that we have hitherto remained too separate from; we could create new and exciting interpretations of media instead of the secondary texts and barely disguised textbooks we usually publish; we could critique and develop our own discipline instead of trying to fit into it; we could push the boundaries of its assumptions rather than satisfying the communities and experts that patrol them.

Cheap, instant and global, web publishing allows for faster, updateable commentary, freer expression, more debate, and the possibility of a rapid response and an ongoing critical dialogue. It may not yet replace print publications but it enables us to throw out faster responses to the world, to engage with it as it changes. As media lecturers and students the least we can do is reflect upon the disciplinary medium of our knowledge and the media we use to disseminate it. That requires us to think much more about how our knowledge is created, disseminated and added to. Without that reflection – without a continual process of upgrading, radically confronting the present and the new ecological forms and processes reshaping around us – the discipline will make itself obsolete. The call for a media studies 2.0 is ultimately not a critique of the discipline but its best defence.

11 Conclusion

'Shit just got real'

In March 2012, 21-year-old Liam Stacey was sentenced to 56 days in prison for inciting racial hatred after posting a series of offensive comments on Twitter about the Bolton Wanderers footballer Fabrice Muamba who had suffered a cardiac arrest during a match. Reflecting upon this later, Stacey said:

> What I struggle to get my head around was the week or two before I was just a normal kid getting on with my work in university, getting on with life, playing rugby with all my mates, then a week or two later I was just going to prison, everything had been turned upside down.

By then arrests and even jail sentences for social media postings were happening regularly but this one stood out for me because the news said he was a student at Swansea University where I taught. When I heard this I immediately checked my student lists to see if he was one of my media students, but he wasn't. I've used his case since in my lectures on digital media law and I've often thought that if he'd chosen to study media here instead of biology, and if he'd taken my modules, he might have stepped away from the keyboard in time.

Either way what these high-profile sentences really brought home to me was that this was important for media studies. Though arrests for media use were possible before (for piracy or obscene materials for example), realistically they were rare and few people were under threat. This was something new: from now on everyone's everyday media use could potentially land them in prison. In the words of the internet meme, 'shit just got real'. It meant media studies needed to drop what it was doing and pay more attention because in a world where our students could miss tomorrow's class because they were in court then teaching *Buffy the Vampire Slayer* or *Breaking Bad* just wasn't going to cut it any more.

When I first described the idea of media studies 2.0 in 2006 it proved to be a controversial concept, attracting considerable debate and criticism. This was intentional as my aim was polemical. Inspired by thinkers such as Marshall McLuhan and Jean Baudrillard who chose provocation as their method, combining a malicious pleasure in intellectual trolling with insights that often surpassed the conservative claims of their contemporaries, my hope was similarly to provoke the discipline and promote a debate as to what it was, how it worked, and what it should be doing. I wanted to simultaneously take aim at its deficiencies and complacent assumptions whilst offering a new vision of its 21st-century role and value. Every lecturer has a different experience of the subject and it soon became clear that there were almost as many media studies as there were academics working in the discipline. Despite these differences, however, two things struck me about the disciplinary response.

Whilst most lecturers had an opinion as to what media studies currently was, few had any detailed knowledge or understanding of the theoretical and institutional history of the subject. Its pre-history, origins and disciplinary development were under-researched and taught, and few lecturers knew much beyond the bare outline available in textbooks or had an in-depth knowledge of earlier media analysis. Indeed, the majority of the founding texts from the late 19th century through to the early 1960s were almost entirely unread and untaught by staff in the discipline. There was also a concomitant lack of reflection as to the built-in biases of the discipline and its textbooks and research with few books showing any interest in discussing the discipline itself or considering its fundamental assumptions. It seemed ironic that a discipline that devotes so much time to critiquing constructed representations fails to question the medium that carries it and its own textual representations. The discipline that many were quick to defend, therefore, wasn't as well understood as might have been supposed.

In addition I was surprised by how many media lecturers seemed to think that the digital transformation wasn't that revolutionary or impacted upon their work. With the hyper-specialisation of academic research, intellectual frameworks derived from another era and the support network of colleagues and of a discipline similarly inured to ongoing changes, it has been easy to downplay the impact of digital technologies. In many ways, however, the situation is getting worse. The academic discipline is becoming increasingly unmoored from real media experiences and practices and its response to the digital me-dia world has been too slow, too cautious and theoretically inadequate. Lecturers unconvinced by this need only print out a list of their own department's module offerings and compare them to their student's daily use and experience of media. In all likelihood there is a chasm between the two.

Indeed, few current programmes could survive this kind of scrutiny: where are the modules on digitality and technology; coding and digital production; algorithms; software studies; data journalism; data visualisation and analysis; social media; digital skills and hacking skills; privacy and surveillance; digital media law; participatory journalism; digital peer production; digital companies, business models and practices; digital regulation, censorship and control; the post-PC paradigm, apps, clouds, mobiles and tablets; digital politics and digital warfare; information search, storage and management; digital leaking, hacking and the fight for informational freedom; digital video and photography; online advertising; pornography and digital sexuality; digital theory, ecology and archaeology, etc.? Further Education suffers even more than Higher Education here as lecturers are forced to follow specified syllabi that remain focused upon broadcast media production and representation, foregrounding, for example, the study of television drama, national cinema or film genres, radio drama, broadcast advertising, the newspaper industry and film posters, etc. Even if contemporary media were included in the syllabus, teaching it could prove difficult: at one local Swansea college access to popular websites is blocked, even for lecturing staff.

Hence there is still a need for this book. Several years on from the initial debate the question of what media studies is, how it's confronting the changing digital ecology and what it should be in the future is more urgent than ever. This book is unusual in being aimed at both media students and lecturers. For students it provides an overview of the elements of the digital revolution and an introduction to the history of the discipline whilst giving them open access to issues and debates about what its limits are and what it should be focusing upon, enabling them to press for a more relevant discipline and contribute to it themselves. For lecturers it offers a critique of the existing discipline and suggestion of the way forward, supported by a detailed understanding of the digital transformation of older forms and of the history and nature of the broadcast-era discipline. Like every good polemic, of course, the concept of a 'media studies 2.0' is bound to fail. However, even if the term proves of fleeting interest the ideas it is based upon will not fade. We can barely anticipate what developments in media will happen over the next decade but they will have more in common with the ideas here than with those of the broadcast-era discipline. In particular, by way of a summary, I would suggest that the future form and direction of the discipline will build from and upon the following points.

First, what we call 'media studies' was a product and reflection of the broadcast era. It emerged out of the broader field of communication studies coming to the fore in the 1920s, with the rise of mass media, as the specific study of mass communications. It emerged out of concerns with the impact of mass media upon the public, public opinion and democracy, developing as an academic field committed to the empirical investigation of the impact of mass media upon audiences, typically in the service of government, private bodies and industry. It was a historical response to the broadcast model of mass production, distribution and consumption of information and mirrored that organisation in its linear model of the communication process, its classification of the subject and its themes, concepts and organisation of its research. Though it would develop an interest in broadcast production and regulation by the end of the 20th century the dominant emphases within the US–UK disciplines were the empirical and Culturalist study of media audiences and the analysis of visual, televisual and cinematic material. Reception and content were the primary focus.

Second, there has been a digital revolution whose nature, forms and impact we are still struggling to map. Though it has longer historical roots, at the end of the 20th century digital technologies met and merged with mass media, engulfing them within itself. This constitutes a material revolution in media with analogue media increasingly giving way to a digital, computational form, impacting significantly upon what our media are and what they can do. The specific nature and deployment of digital technology precipitated a series of related revolutions – in the media ecology, in the cultural and socio-economic organisation of media production, distribution and consumption, and in the status and role of the individual that, together, transformed every aspect of media experience and use.

Third, if media studies is a product and reflection of the broadcast era then a digital, post-broadcast era demands a digital, post-broadcast media studies. This requires a systematic upgrading of the discipline and its organisation, themes, concepts and concerns and a refocusing of the subject around digital media and their history, forms, and contemporary uses: a media 2.0 requires a media studies 2.0. This requires rethinking 'media literacy' and the way in which we teach people to 'read' and 'write' media. In the broadcast era these existed in a competitive relationship, with media practice teaching students to produce for and serve the mass media industries and theoretical modules teaching students how to understand and defend themselves against broadcast products. Now, however, the digital post-broadcast era allows for the unification of reading and writing skills. Whereas the broadcast era was marked by a minority having the ability to produce and the majority being limited to consumption, today everyone is a producer and media studies needs to reorientate itself around this, exploring and teaching the reading and writing skills required by this digital user.

If we want to train students for employment within production then we need to change our emphasis. Teaching students how to use digital equipment has a limited value and most of our future students will – like my son – come to us already experienced in creation. Instead we need to teach how to produce digitally. If digital media are the result of the meeting and merger of computing and mass media then we need to teach our students computing to enable them to produce software and products for themselves. One thing at least is certain: filling students' time by teaching them how to use a video camera or making them pretend to be a newsreader in a fake studio is a waste of their fees and an inadequate training for the 21st century.

But the aim of the discipline isn't limited to employability. More importantly these coding and computational production skills are part of the key practical skills the digital user needs. In order to be able to write media today our students need to know how to produce software, how to employ or create digital tools and platforms, and how to navigate and use the digital ecology. 'Media practice', therefore, needs to be reorientated towards training students in computing and the digital ecology. Today's user needs up-to-date, practical knowledge of how to best take advantage of digital technologies and, like the hacker, how to secure their communications, anonymise or hide their activities and delete and control their digital footprint. These may well be the most important 'practice' skills of the 21st century.

Similarly, the reading skills needed by the digital user have also changed. Consumption skills about how to understand audiences and content are less important than understanding digital technologies and issues around privacy, surveillance, law, copyright, freedom of speech, censorship, etc. The entire theoretical framework of the discipline needs to privilege digital understanding above broadcast content. When your media use could get you arrested, like Liam Stacey, or impact upon your future life, career and freedom, then 'narrative', 'genre', and 'semiology' mean very little. To continue to emphasise these is to fail our students, as is to continue the vanity publishing of our own research interests in our favourite films, genres and directors and the latest television drama. Today it is a political necessity to train our students for their own digital defence, not to train them in our personal interests. It is a necessity to understand the real issues our students face, not the false problems the discipline has identified. A media studies that thinks that 'technological determinism' is a greater threat than government and corporate surveillance and control is intellectually bankrupt.

Fourth, media studies needs to embrace openness. It needs to avoid over-specialisation, remaining open to broader ecological relationships, aiming to understand the entire, interconnected system and its processes; it needs to be open for its students, laying out its assumptions, biases and source code for their exploration and improvement; it needs to be open to the real world of media, rather than following the interests of the discipline and the publications of colleagues; and it needs to be open to the public, not just in terms of their access to its ideas but in going out into their debates, in offering faster responses, in engaging in real time with media developments, and in developing a radical presentology that attempts to divine today and capture and critique the media world as it forms around and with us. What we need is a media studies that is *in* the media world it wants to explain and that is helping make and direct it.

Fifth, therefore, we need a relevant media studies. Media studies isn't an entirely secure discipline. Though it has expanded significantly over the last few decades its institutional position isn't always strong. Whilst many universities value its recruitment and the success of staff research others only moved into the discipline to exploit its rise in popularity and use it to shore up other aspects of provision. Many departments are under-resourced, under-staffed and, being relatively new, have fewer roots within universities and are prey to management intervention and interference in ways other disciplines wouldn't be. As the anonymous author of 'The new assault on media studies' argues in the November 2011 MECCSA 'Three-D' newsletter, media expertise is often denigrated and management exploitation of the discipline is common.

That this is institutionally acceptable owes much to the broader reputation of the discipline, with media studies being regularly criticised in the press or by political commentators as a 'soft' subject or as having little value. The discipline, however, is increasingly tackling these criticisms. James Curran's 2013 MECCSA keynote address, 'Mickey Mouse Squeaks Back', for example, defends the academic integrity of media degrees and the employability of their graduates and correctly identifies the origin of much criticism in the hostility of journalism to public scrutiny and the journalists' fear of a discipline helping produce their more clued-up replacements. These arguments shouldn't have to be made. If basic literacy in one medium is considered essential for all children, then training in the ecology of media forms from which they derive all their knowledge of the world beyond their immediate experience must be just as fundamental and central to any democracy. The explosion of media means the case should be even easier to make. Again, compare my childhood with my son's: there simply wasn't *as much media* in the past – there were fewer channels, limitations on access, fewer devices, less storage, higher costs and often more effort required. My son, however, swims in information, filling his day with media, moving from one device to another, carrying it with him everywhere he goes.

But media studies isn't helping itself here. The discussion of digital media is happening everywhere today – among the public, commentators, the media, the government and within nearly every other academic discipline. Everywhere, that is, except in media studies where it remains an optional interest and where the broadcast mindset and conceptual categories prevail. But the broadcast model and its audiences are the past of the discipline and so too are many of its major approaches. US-style empirical communications research is too specialised, is dull, is unable to follow the ecological complexity and speed of digital transformations and remains uncritical and administrative in orientation. The UK Culturalist tradition that, as James Curran observes, became globally famous has become obsolete. Reduced to a caricature of its once-political self, committed to the performance of its own privileged methodologies and viewing reception through the anachronistic prism of the 'audience', its simplistic humanism uncritically valorises all individual behaviour, refusing to think the user in any more complex way. And meanwhile television and film studies continue apace, with the continual discovery and discussion of new programmes, films, directors, genres and national cinemas, like an academic perpetual motion machine, with no necessary reference to the changing media realities outside.

The discipline, therefore, faces a choice. It has the potential to be one of the most important subject areas going into the 21st century, at the forefront of debates around digital technologies and their remaking of the world. But equally it has the possibility of being left behind, its focus on reception and content and broadcast forms and concepts condemning it to an increasing irrelevance for everyone but itself. Media studies has no necessary right to lead debates on media: it has to fight to prove it understands it better and has the most effective critical tools to train and guide its students and the public in the future. What we need is a discipline able to teach the practical and theoretical skills for digital survival and success; a discipline that would, in the case of Liam Stacey have prompted the immediate public response, 'why didn't he do a useful degree such as media instead of choosing a science?' We won't arrive at that until we realise the limits of the existing discipline – until we realise that, as McLuhan says, 'most of our assumptions have outlived their uselessness' – and until we realise that this uselessness is an opportunity to build what we really need, for as McLuhan also suggests: 'Obsolescence never meant the end of anything, it's just the beginning.'

Bibliography

In order to make the book as readable as possible I've avoided using footnotes or references in the text. As befits a book discussing the digital age I'm assuming that if the reader wants to trace anything mentioned in the text or find out more about any author, idea or book discussed they can do so using Google, Wikipedia, Amazon and Google Books, etc. It isn't worth listing here the details of every text mentioned when the reader can quickly find out online its current availability or even find the book itself. The aim of this bibliography, therefore, is not to provide an exact reflection of the text but rather to indicate the most important sources I've used and act as a guide for further reading on selected topics.

First, students would benefit from a detailed knowledge of the history of mass media, computing and networking, as covered in Chapters 1 and 2. For the discussion of the development of mass media I've drawn from a number of good overviews, including Briggs and Burke (2005), Curran and Seaton (2010), Crisell (1997), Gorman and McLean (2003), McDonnell (1991), Wheen (1985) and Williams (1998). Information on writing and the alphabet can be found in Jean (1992); printing is discussed by Eisenstein (1983), Febvre and Martin (1997) and Man (2002), whilst Wilson (2005), Conboy (2004) and Williams (2009) offer histories of journalism and the newspaper. Altick (1978) offers an astonishing survey of the range of entertainments and media available in the 18–19th century, whilst the visual media of the era are well covered by Crompton, Franklin and Herbert (1997), Greenacre (1999), Heard (2006), Mannoni (2000), Merrin (2005), Stafford and Terpak (2002) and Weynants (2008). Bajac (2002) provides an introduction to photography, Wichard and Wichard (1999) cover Victorian cartes-de-visite, whilst the development of cinema is covered by Nasaw (1993), Chanan (1995), Gunning (1990), Robinson (1996) and Toulet (1995). Developments in electricity through this era are covered by Fara (2002), Bodanis (2005) and Rhys Morus (2004), whilst Standage (1998) offers a superb account of the electrical telegraph. Information on the development of sound-recording and the music industry can be found in Welch and Stenzel Burt (2006), Gronow and Saunio (1999), Millard (1995) and Steffen (2005).

Introductory surveys of the history of computing can be found in Agar (2001), Barrett (2006), Campbell-Kelly and Aspray (2004), Ceruzzi (2000), Frauenfelder (2005) and Hally (2005), whilst Campbell-Kelly (2003) provides a history of software. More specifically, Swade (2000) discusses the life of Babbage and Conway and Siegelman (2005) provide a good account of the life of Norbert Wiener. The history of networked computing is covered in Hafner and Lyon (1996) and Naughton (2000). Banks (2008) gives a good history of the early years of the web whilst Ryan (2010) also covers the main points of the invention of the internet. Knowledge of the technical principles of digital media would also be useful for media students and Challoner (2002) and Lax (2009) are useful introductory texts whilst Manovich's two books (2001, 2008) are also important.

The third chapter discusses the idea of media ecology and students would benefit from understanding key theoretical approaches and sources such as Shannon (in Shannon and Weaver, 1963), Hall (2006), McLuhan (1994), Bolter and Grusin (1999), Strate (2004), Channell (1991), Wiener (1948; Conway and Siegelman, 2005) and Shamberg (see Shamberg and the Raindance Corporation, 1971 and Merrin, 2012).The best way to understand the actual digital ecology isn't from a book but from the digital world itself. I'd recommend students spend time following and researching news about digital developments, new technologies, digital companies and issues relating to digital media. The best way to do this is to follow a selection of news pages, newspaper sites and technology news sites and to tag stories you're interested in on sites such as Diigo so you can easily find them again for your essays or research.

Chapter 4's discussion of the move to a post-broadcast era draws upon an emerging academic and popular literature exploring the digital changes that students should be following. I'd recommend especially Benkler's discussion of non-market peer-production (2006); Bruns on user generated content (2008); Gillmor on citizen journalism (2006), Shirky (2008, 2010) and Leadbetter (2008) on the empowered individual; Anderson on the 'long tail' (2006); and Howe on crowdsourcing (2008). Though they say little explicitly on media, Johnson on 'emergence' (2002) and Surowiecki on 'the wisdom of crowds' (2005) are important for understanding the idea of 'collective intelligence'. O'Reilly's essay on 'Web 2.0' is rather business-oriented but it has proven an important text in understanding a new era of web experience (2005) and Jenkins (2006, 2013) provides a good discussion of its user practices but its Culturalism needs supplementing with a material analysis of technology of the kind offered by Manovich (2001), Lessig (1997, 1998) and Zittrain (2008). Other commentators concerned with emerging controls or threats to the internet include Goldsmith and Wu (2006), Wu (2011) and MacKinnon (2012). Keen (2007, 2012), Siegel (2008), Lanier (2011, 2013) and Morozov (2010, 2013) all offer polemical critiques of contemporary digital culture that, though simplistic in places, are worth reading. Anyone wanting to read more about the historical background to the concept of me-dia covered in Chapter 5 is directed to Tarnas (1996) and Collinson (2005) who, respectively, discuss the philosophical and historical aspects of the Protestant revolution. Pariser's concept of the 'filter bubble' is an important idea and fits well with the literature discussed above (2011).

Students also need a detailed knowledge of the academic, theoretical and institutional history of media studies covered in Chapter 6. The best discussions of the discipline itself are found in Hardt (1992), Park and Pooley (2008) and Glander (2000), whilst Berelson (1958), Gitlin (1978) and Gerbner and Siefert (1983) are important additional readings. Craig (1999), Donsbach (2006) and Nordenstreng (2004, 2007) offer useful contemporary reflections on communication studies. A range of student textbooks provide an overview of 'media theory' – such as Czitrom (1982), Mattelart and Mattelart (1998), Stevenson (2002), Katz et al (2003), Williams (2003), Laughey (2007) and Scannell (2007) – though they focus on broadcast-era thinkers, say little about the institutional discipline, begin from different points and display little agreement as to what authors or movements to include. The limitations of this broadcast-era approach are pointed up by the range of thinkers covered by Durham Peters (1999). Specific authors and texts mentioned in this chapter could be explored further by interested readers. More information about them and their availability can be found online.

The following chapters discuss the limitations of media studies and the new approaches and subjects it should follow. It's difficult to recommend readings to cover everything the discipline has overlooked or marginalised but students would benefit from a better understanding of the question of technology and for this I'd recommend Taylor's discussion of its role in the evolution of humanity (2010), Channell's remarkable historical survey of the ways in which we've conceived it (1991) and introductory surveys of the philosophy of technology such as Scharrff and Dusek (2003) and Dusek (2006). My discussion of the treatment of pre-broadcast media draws on Freedberg (1989), whose book should also be read by everyone interested in media, whilst Barasch (1992) supplements its discussion of images well. Other important areas for students to consider include the need for computer education, as discussed by Naughton (2011) and Rushkoff (2010), and the roots of the concept of 'the user' discussed in Chapter 9, which are found in a range of computing texts including Bush (1945), Wiener (1948), Licklider (1960), Licklider and Taylor (1968), Engelbart (1962, 1968) and Kay (1972, 1977, 1989).

The final chapter includes a discussion of the role of digital technologies in contemporary education. Further information about these debates can be found in Facer (2011), Selwyn (2011), Thomas and Seely Brown (2011). McLuhan's ideas are used and quoted throughout this book and *Understanding Media* remains an essential book for any media student to deal with (1994; originally 1964). Other good sources for McLuhan's work include McLuhan and Zingrone (1995), Benedetti and Dehart (1997) and McLuhan and Carson (2003) and a range of interview clips easily available on YouTube.

The idea of media studies 2.0 has attracted a lot of debate. Those interested in this can look up David Gauntlett's original essay (2007) and later Kindle book (2011) and my own article (2008; 2009). Taylor (Taylor, P., 2009) and Berger and McDougall (2012) contain important edited collections discussing the concept. Finally, my son's video, discussed in the introduction, is unfortunately still available on YouTube (Merrin, H., 2011).

Agar, J. (2001) *Turing and the Universal Machine*, Cambridge: Icon Books.

Adorno, T. W. and Horkheimer, M. (1997) *Dialectic of Enlightenment*, London: Verso.

Altick, R. (1978) *The Shows of London*, London: Harvard University Press.

Anderson, C. (2006) *The Long Tail*, London: Random House Business Books.

Anonymous (2011) 'The New Assault on Media Studies', in *Three-D*, Meccsa Newsletter, 1st November, http://www.meccsa.org.uk/news/three-d-issue-17-the-new-assault-on-media-studies/

Arthur, C. (2012) *Digital Wars: Apple, Google Microsoft & The Battle For the Internet*, London: Kogan Page.

Bajac, Q. (2002) *The Invention of Photography*, London: Thames and Hudson.

Banks, M. A. (2008) *On the Way to the Web*, Berkeley, CA: Apress.

Barasch, M. (1992) *Icon: Studies in the History of an Idea*, London: New York University Press.

Barrett, N. (2006) *The Binary Revolution*, London: Weidenfeld and Nicolson.

Benedetti, P. and Dehart, N. (eds.) (1997) *Forward Through the Rear-View Mirror: Reflections On and By Marshall McLuhan*, London: MIT Press.

Benkler, Y. (2006) *The Wealth of Networks*, London: Yale University Press.

Berelson, B. (1958) 'The State of Communication Research', *Public Opinion Quarterly*, Vol. 22, No. 3, pp. 1–6.

Berger, R. and McDougall, J. (eds.) (2012) *MERJ – Media Education Research Journal*, Vol. 2, No. 2. Themed Issue – Media Studies 2.0: A Retrospective, Leighton Buzzard: Auteur Publishing.

Bodanis, D. (2005) *Electric Universe*, London: Abacus.

Bolter, J. D. and Grusin, R. (1999) *Remediation: Understanding New Media*, London: MIT Press.

Briggs, A and Burke, P. (2005) *A Social History of the Media*, Cambridge: Polity.

Bruns, A. (2008) *Blogs, Wikipedia, Second Life and Beyond. From Production to Produsage*, New York: Peter Lang Publishing.

Bush, V. (1945) 'As We May Think', in *The Atlantic*, 1 July, available at: http://www.theatlantic.com/magazine/archive/1945/07/as-we-may-think/303881/

Campbell-Kelly, M. and Aspray, W. (2004) *Computer. A History of the Information Machine*, Oxford: Westview Press.

Campbell-Kelly, M. (2003) *From Airline Reservations to Sonic the Hedgehog: A History of the Software Industry*, London: MIT.

Castells, M. (2009) *Communication Power*, Oxford: Oxford University Press.

Ceruzzi, P. E. (2000) *A History of Modern Computing*, London: MIT Press.

Chanan, M. (1995) *Repeated Takes*, London: Verso.

Challoner, J. (2002) *The Digital Revolution*, London: Dorling Kindersley.

Channell, D. F. (1991) *The Vital Machine*, Oxford: Oxford University Press.

Clark, C. (2007) *Iron Kingdom: The Rise and Downfall of Prussia, 1600–1947*, London: Penguin, p. 333.

Collinson, P. (2005) *The Reformation*, London: Phoenix.

Conboy, M. (2004) *Journalism: A Critical History*, London: Sage.

Conway, F. and Siegelman, J. (2005) *Dark Hero of the Information Age. In Search of Norbert Wiener*, Cambridge, MA: Basic Books.

Craig, R. T. (1999) 'Communication Theory as a Field', *Communication Theory*, Vol. 9., No. 2, pp. 119–60.

Crisell, A. (1997) *An Introductory History of British Broadcasting*, London: Routledge.

Crompton, D., Franklin, R. and Herbert, S. (eds.) (1997) *Servants of Light: The Book of the Lantern*, London: E. G. Bond Ltd.

Cubitt, S. (2005) 'Distribution and Media Flows', in *Cultural Politics*, Vol. 1, No. 2, July, pp. 193–214.

Curran, J. (2013) 'Mickey Mouse Squeaks Back: Defending Media Studies', in *Three-D*, Issue 20, April, MeCCSA Newsletter, pp. 20-22, available at: http://www.meccsa.org.uk/news/mickey-mouse-squeaks-back-defending-media-studies/.

Curran, J. and Seaton, J. (2010) *Power Without Responisbility: Press, Broadcasting and the Internet in Britain*, London: Routledge.

Czitrom, D. J. (1982) *Media and the American Mind*, Chapel Hill: University of North Carolina Press.

Dayan, D. and Katz, E. (1992) *Media Events*, Cambridge, MA: Harvard University Press.

Donsbach, W. (2006) 'The Identity of Communication Research', *Journal of Communication*, 56, pp. 437–48.

Durham Peters, J. (1999) *Speaking Into the Air: A History of the Idea of Communication*, London: University of Chicago Press.

Dusek, V. (2006) *Philosophy of Technology–An Introduction*, Oxford: Blackwell.

Edgerton, D. (2006) *The Shock of the Old*, London: Profile Books.

Eisenstein, E. L. (1983) *The Printing Revolution in Early Modern Europe*, Cambridge: Cambridge University Press.

Engelbart, D. (1962) 'Augmenting Human Intellect: A Conceptual Framework', Stanford Research Institute Summary Report, available at: http://www.invisiblerevolution.net/engelbart/full_62_paper_augm_hum_int.html

——(1968) 'The Demo', presentation given at The Fall Joint Computer Conference, the Convention Centre, San Francisco, 9th December, available at: http://sloan.stanford.edu/mousesite/1968Demo.html

Facer, K. (2011) *Learning Futures*, Abingdon, Oxon: Routledge.

Fara, P. (2002) *An Entertainment for Angels*, Cambridge: Icon Books.

Febvre, L. and Martin, H. J. (1997) *The Coming of the Book*, London: Verso [1958].

Ferry, G. (2003) *A Computer Called LEO*, London: Fourth Estate.

Frauenfelder, M. (2005) *The Computer: An Illustrated History*, London: Sevenoaks.

Freedberg, D. (1989) *The Power of Images*, London: University of Chicago Press.

Fuller, M. (2005) *Media Ecologies*, London: MIT Press.

Gauntlett, D. (2007) 'Media Studies 2.0', February, available at: http://www.theory.org.uk/mediastudies2.htm

——(2011) *Media Studies 2.0 and Other Battles Around the Future of Media Research*, 22nd July, Kindle e-book.

Gerbner, G. and Siefert, M. (eds.) (1983) 'Ferment in the Field [Special Issue]', *Journal of Communication*, Vol. 33, No. 3.

Gillespie, M. (ed.) (2005) *Media Audiences*, Maidenhead, Berks: Open University Press.

Gillmor, D. (2006) *We the Media*, Sebastopol, CA: O'Reilly Media Inc.

Gitlin, T. (1978) 'Media Sociology: The Dominant Paradigm', *Theory and Society*, Vol. 6., No. 2, September, pp. 205–53. Also available at: http://www.julietdavis.com/COM443/articles/Media%20Sociology%20-%20Todd%20Gitlin.pdf.

Gladwell, M. (2000) *The Tipping Point*, New York: Little Brown.

Glander, T. (2000) *Origins of Mass Communication Research During the American Cold War*, London: Lawrence Erlbaum Associates, Publishers.

Gorman, L. and McLean, D. (2003), *Media and Society in the Twentieth Century*, Oxford: Blackwell.

Goldsmith, J. and Wu, T. (2006) *Who Controls the Internet?* Oxford: Oxford University Press.

Greenacre, D. (1999) *Magic Lanterns*, Bucks: Shire Publications.

Gronow, P. and Saunio, I. (1999) *An International History of the Recording Industry*, London: Cassell.

Guattari, F. (2008) *Three Ecologies*, London: Continuum.

Gunning, T. (1990) 'The Cinema of Attractions: Early Film, Its Spectator and the Avant-Garde', in Elsaesser. T. (ed.) *Early Cinema: Space, Frame, Narrative*, London: British Film Institute, pp. 56–62.

Hally, M. (2005) *Electronic Brains. Stories From the Dawn of the Computer Age*, London: Granta Books.

Hafner, K. and Lyon, M. (1996) *Where Wizards Stay Up Late. The Origins of the Internet*, New York: Touchstone.

Hall, S. (2006) 'Encoding/Decoding', in Durham, M. G. and Kellner, D. M. (eds.) *Media and Cultural Studies: Key Works*, Oxford: Blackwell, pp. 163-173.

Hardt, H. (1992) *Critical Communication Studies: Communication, History and Theory in America*, London: Routledge.

Heard, M. (2006) *Phantasmagoria – The Secret History of the Magic Lantern*, London: The Projection Box.

Illich, I. (1995) *Deschooling Society*, London: Marion Boyars.

Isaacson, W. (2012) *Steve Jobs: The Exclusive Biography*, London: Little, Brown.

Howe, J. (2008) *Crowdsourcing*, New York: Random House.

Jean, G. (1992) *Writing: The Story of Alphabets and Scripts*, London: Thames and Hudson.

Jenkins, H. (2006) *Convergence Culture*, London: New York University Press.

——(2013) *Spreadable Media*, New York: New York University Press.

Johnson, S. (2002) *Emergence*, London: Penguin Books.

Katz, E., Durham Peters, J., Liebes, T., and Orloff, A. (eds.) (2003) *Canonic Texts in Media Research*, Cambridge: Polity.

Kay, A. (1972) 'A Personal Computer For Children of All Ages', in *Proceedings of the ACM National Conference*, Boston, August, available at: http://www.mprove.de/diplom/gui/kay72.html

——(1977) 'Personal Dynamic Media', in Wardip-Fruin, N. and Montfort, N. (eds.) *The New Media Reader*, Cambridge, Mass: MIT Press, pp. 393–404, available at: http://www.newmediareader.com/book_samples/nmr-26-kay.pdf

——(1989) 'User Interface: A Personal View', available at: http://meidosem.com/work/articles/kay1990.pdf

Keen, A. (2007) *The Cult of the Amateur*, London: Nicholas Brealey.

——(2012) *Digital Vertigo*, London: Constable.

Kelly, K. (2005) 'We Are the Web', in *Wired*, 13.08. August, at: http://www.wired.com/wired/archive/13.08/tech.html

Kierkegaard, S. (1977) *The Present Age*, New York: Harper and Row.

Kuhn, T. (1962) 'Chapter IX: The Nature and Necessity of Scientific Revolutions', in *The Structure of Scientific Revolutions*, available at: http://www.marxists.org/reference/subject/philosophy/works/us/kuhn.htm

Lanier, J. (2011) *You Are Not a Gadget: A Manifesto*, London: Penguin.

——(2013) *Who Owns the Future?* London: Allen Lane.

Lasswell, H. D. (1927) *Propaganda Technique in the World War*, Cambridge, MA: MIT Press

——(1948) 'The Structure and Function of Communication in Society', in Bryson, L. (ed.) *Communication of Ideas*, New York: Harper and Row, pp. 37-51, available at: http://www.dhpescu.org/media/elip/The%20structure%20and%20function%20of.pdf

Laughey, D. (2007) *Key Themes in Media Theory*, Maidenhead: Open University Press.

Lax, S. (2009) *Media and Communication Technologies: A Critical Introduction*, Houndmills, Basingstoke: Palgrave Macmillan.

Leadbetter, C. (2008) *We-Think: The Power of Mass Creativity*, London: Profile Books.

Lessig, L. (1997) *Code. And Other Laws of Cyberspace*, New York: Basic Books.

——(1998) 'The Laws of Cyberspace', available at: http://lessig.org/content/articles/works/laws_cyberspace.pdf

Levy, S. (2011) 'Exclusive: Inside Facebook's Desire to Reinvent Music, News and Everything', *Wired*, September 22nd, available at: http://www.wired.com/epicenter/2011/09/facebook-new-profile-apps/all/1

Licklider, J. C. R. (1960) 'Man–Computer Symbiosis', in *IRE Transactions on Human Factors in Electronics*, Vol. HFE-1, pp. 4–11, March, available at: http://groups.csail.mit.edu/medg/people/psz/Licklider.html

——(1967) 'Televistas: Looking Ahead Through Side Windows', available at: http://web.mit.edu/~schultze/www/Licklider-Televistas-Carnegie-1967.pdf

Licklider, J. C. R. and Taylor, R. (1968) 'The Computer as Communication Device', *Science and Technology*, April, available at: http://www.comunicazione.uniroma1.it/materiali/20.20.03_licklider-taylor.pdf

Luther, M. (1998) 'On the Freedom of a Christian', available at: http://www.fordham.edu/halsall/mod/luther-freedomchristian.asp

MacKinnon, R. (2012) *Consent of the Networked*, Philadelphia, PA: Basic Books.

Man, J. (2002) *The Gutenberg Revolution*, London: Review.

Mannoni, L. (2000) *The Great Art of Light and Shadow: Archaeology of the Cinema*, Exeter: University of Exeter Press.

Manovich, L. (2001) *The Language of New Media*, London: MIT Press.

——(2002) 'The Anti-Sublime Ideal in Data Art', available at: http://imi.myblog-staging. arts.ac.uk/files/2012/05/TheAnti-SublimeIdealinDataArt1818.pdf

——(2013) *Software Takes Command*, London: Bloomsbury Academic. Also also available at: http://www.manovich.net/softbook/.

——(2010) 'What is Visualization?', available at: http://www.datavisualisation.org/2010/ 11/lev-manovich-what-is-visualization/

Mattelart, A. and Mattelart, M. (1998) *Theories of Communication: A Short Introduction*, London: Sage Publications.

Mayer-Schonberger, V. (2009) *Delete: The Virtue of Forgetting in the Digital Age*, Princeton, NJ: Princeton University Press.

McDonnell, J. (1991) *Public Service Broadcasting: A Reader*, London: Routledge.

McLuhan, M. (1969) 'The Playboy Interview', *Playboy* Magazine, March, in McLuhan, E. and Zingrone, F. (1995) *Essential McLuhan*, New York: Basic Books, pp. 233-69, Also available: http://www.nextnature.net/2009/12/the-playboy-interview-marshall-mcluhan/

——(1971) 'Convocation Address, the University of Alberta', 20 November, in *McLuhan Studies*, issue 5, available at: http://projects.chass.utoronto.ca/mcluhan-studies/v1_iss5/ 1_5art3.htm

——(1994) *Understanding Media*, London: MIT Press.

McLuhan, E. and Gordon, W. T. (eds.) (2005) *McLuhan Unbound. Volume 1*, Berkeley, CA: Ginko Press.

McLuhan, E. and Zingrone, F. (1995) *Essential McLuhan*, New York: Basic Books.

McLuhan, M. and Carson, D. (2003) *The Book of Probes*, Corte Madera, CA: Gingko Press.

Merrin, H. (2011) 'Love Gone Wrong', *Youtube*, 24th September, available at: http:// www.youtube.com/watch?v=hHYwx5Wxh_0

Merrin, W. (2005) 'Skylights Onto Infinity: The World in a Stereoscope' in Toulmin, V. and Popple, S. (eds.) *Visual Delights Two: Exhibition and Reception*, Eastleigh: John Libbey Publishing, pp. 161–74.

——(2008) 'Media Studies 2.0–My Thoughts', 4th January, available at: http://two pointzeroforum.blogspot.com/

——(2009) 'Media Studies 2.0: Upgrading and Open-Sourcing the Discipline', in *Interactions: Studies in Communication and Culture*, Vol. 1, No. 1, pp. 17–34.

——(2012) 'Still Fighting "The Beast": *Guerrilla Television* and the Limits of Youtube', in *Cultural Politics*, Vol. 8, No. 1, pp. 97–119.

Millard, A. (1995) *America on Record*, Cambridge: Cambridge University Press.

Mitchell, D. and Webb, R. (2009) 'That Mitchell and Webb Look – Send Us Your Reckons', in *Youtube*, 7th June, available at: http://www.youtube.com/watch? v=OQnd5ilKx2Y

Morozov, E. (2010) *The Net Delusion*, London: Allen Lane.

——(2013) *To Save Everything, Click Here*, London: Allen Lane.

Nasaw, D. (1993) *Going Out: The Rise and Fall of Public Amusements*, London: Harvard University Press.

Naughton, J. (2000) *A Brief History of the Future: The Origins of the Internet*, London: Phoenix Books.

——(2011) 'Kids today need a licence to tinker', in *The Observer*, 28th August, available at: http://www.guardian.co.uk/technology/2011/aug/28/ict-changes-needed-national-curriculum

——(2012) *From Gutenberg to Zuckerberg*, London: Quercus.

Negroponte, N. (1995) *Being Digital*, New York: Vintage Books.

Nelson, T. (1974) *Computer Lib/Dream Machines*, self-published. Later republished (1987) by Tempus Books of Microsoft Press.

Nordenstreng, K. (2004) 'Ferment in the Field: Notes on the Evolution of Communication Studies and Its Interdisciplinary Nature', *The Public*, Vol. 11, No. 3, pp. 5–18.

——(2007) 'Discipline or Field? Soul-Searching in Communication Research', *Nordicom Review*, Jubilee Issue, pp. 211–22.

Oetterman, S. (1997) *The Panorama: History of a Mass Medium*, New York: Zone Books.

O'Reilly, T. (2005) 'What is Web 2.0?', available at: http://www.oreillynet.com/pub/a/oreilly/tim/news/2005/09/30/what-is-web-20.html

Papert, S. (1984) 'Trying to Predict the Future?', in *Popular Computing*, Vol. 3, No. 13, pp. 30–44.

Park, D. and Pooley, J. (2008) *The History of Media and Communication Research: Contested Memories*, New York: Peter Lang.

Pariser, E. (2011) *The Filter Bubble*, London: Viking.

Pooley, J. (2008) 'The New History of Communications Research', in Park, D. and Pooley, J. (eds) *The History of Media and Communication Research: Contested Memories*, New York: Peter Lang, pp. 43–69.

Postman, N. (1979) *Teaching as a Conserving Activity*, New York: Delacorte Press.

Rhys Morus, I. (2004) *Michael Faraday and the Electrical Century*, Cambridge: Icon Books.

Robinson, D. (1996) *From Peepshow to Palace: The Birth of American Film*, New York: Columbia University Press.

Ronnell, A. (1989) *The Telephone Book*, Lincoln: University of Nebraska Press.

Rushkoff, D. (2010) *Program or Be Programmed*, New York: OR Books.

Ryan, J. (2010) *A History of the Internet and the Digital Future*, London: Reaktion Books.

Scannell, P. (2006) 'An Interview with Professor Paddy Scannell, Oxford, July 2006' (with Tarik Sabry), *Westminster Papers in Communication and Culture*, Vol. 4, No. 2, available at: http://www.westminster.ac.uk/__data/assets/pdf_file/0015/20085/002WPCC-VolFour-NoTwo-Tarik_Sabry_Paddy_Scannell.pdf

——(2007) *Media and Communication*, London: Sage.

Scharff, R. and Dusek, V. (eds) (2003) *Philosophy of Technology*, Oxford: Blackwell.

Schivelbusch, W. (1992) *The Railway Journey*, Berkeley, CA: The University of California Press.

Scramm, W. (ed.) (1948) *Communications in Modern Society*, Urbana: University of Illinois Press.

——(ed.) (1949) *Mass Communications*, Urbana: University of Illinois Press.

——(ed.) (1953) *The Process and Effects of Mass Communication*, Urbana: University of Illinois Press.

Selwyn, N. (2011) *Education and Technology*, London: Continuum.

Shamberg, M. & The Raindance Corporation (1971) *Guerrilla Television*, New York: Holt, Rinehart and Winston.

Shannon, C. E. and Weaver, W. (1963) *The Mathematical Theory of Communication*, Illinois: The University of Illinois Press.

Siegel, L. (2008) *Against the Machine*, London: Profile Books.

Shirky, C. (2008) *Here Comes Everybody*, London: Allen Lane.

——(2010) *Cognitive Surplus*, London: Penguin.

Stafford, B. M. and Terpak, F. (2002) *Devices of Wonder: From the World in a Box to Images on a Screen*, Los Angeles: Getty Publications.

Standage, T. (1998) *The Victorian Internet*, London: Weidenfeld and Nicolson.

Steffen, D. J. (2005) *From Edison to Marconi: The First Thirty Years of Recorded Music*, London: McFarland and Co.

Stein, J. (2007) 'Dear Reader, Please Don't Email Me', in *The Guardian*, 8 January, available at: http://www.guardian.co.uk/media/2007/jan/08/mondaymediasection13

Stevenson, N. (2002) *Understanding Media Cultures*, London: Sage.

Strate, L. (2004) 'A Media Ecology Review', in *Communication Research Review*, Vol. 23, No. 2, pp. 3–48, available at: http://cscc.scu.edu/trends/v23/v23_2.pdf

Surowiecki, J. (2005) *The Wisdom of Crowds*, New York: Anchor Books.

Swade, D. (2000) *The Cogwheel Brain*, London: Little, Brown and Company.

Tapscott, D. and Williams, A. (2007) *Wikinomics. How Mass Collaboration Changes Everything*, London: Atlantic Books.

Tarnas, R. (1996) *The Passion of the Western Mind*, London: Pimlico.

Taussig, M. (1993) *Mimesis and Alterity*, London: Routledge.

Taylor, P. (ed.) (2009) *Interactions: Studies in Communication and Culture*, Vol. 1, No. 1. Themed issue on Media Studies 2.0, Bristol: Intellect.

Taylor, T. (2010) *The Artificial Ape*, London: Palgrave.

The Magic Lantern Society (2008) http://www.magiclantern.org.uk/.

Thomas, D. and Seeley Brown, J. (2011) *A New Culture of Learning*, Seattle: Createspace Publishing.

Thompson, J. B. (1995) *The Media and Modernity*, Cambridge: Polity Press.

Toffler, A. (1981) *The Third Wave*, London: Pan Books Ltd.

Toulet, E. (1995) *Cinema is 100 Years Old*, London: Thames and Hudson.

Turing, A. (1937) 'On Computable Numbers, With an Application to the Entscheidungsproblem' from *Proceedings of the London Mathematical Society* (Ser. 2, Vol. 42, 1937), available at: http://classes.soe.ucsc.edu/cmps210/Winter11/Papers/turing-1936.pdf.

Van Loon, J. (2008) *Media Technology*, Maidenhead: Open University Press.

Wiener, N. (1948) *Cybernetics*, Cambridge, Mass: MIT Press.

Welch, W. L. and Stenzel Burt, L. B. (2006) *From Tinfoil to Stereo*, Florida: University Press of Florida [1959].

Weynants, T. (2008) 'Early Visual Media', at http://www.visual-media.be/

Wheen, F. (1985) *Television: A History*, London: Century Publishing.

Wichard, R. and Wichard, C. (1999) *Victorian Cartes de Visite*, Bucks: Shire Publications.

Williams, K. (1998) *Get Me a Murder a Day! A History of Mass Communication in Britain*, London: Arnold.

——(2003) *Understanding Media Theory*, London: Arnold.

——(2009) *Read All About It: A History of the British Newspaper*, London: Routledge.

Williams, R. (1992) *Television: Technology and Cultural Form*, London: Wesleyan University Press.

Wilson, B. (2005) *The Laughter of Triumph*, London: Faber and Faber.

Witte, J. Jr. (2005) 'The Freedom of a Christian: Martin Luther's Reformation of Law & Liberty', March, available at: http://cslr.law.emory.edu/fileadmin/media/PDFs/Lectures/Witte_Freedom_Christian.pdf.

Wu, T. (2011) *The Master Switch*, New York: Vintage Books.

Zittrain, J. (2008) *The Future of the Internet*, London: Penguin.

Index

Lightning Source UK Ltd.
Milton Keynes UK
UKOW07n1100220115

244904UK00008B/191/P